Economic Growth
and
Employment
in
China

A World Bank Research Publication

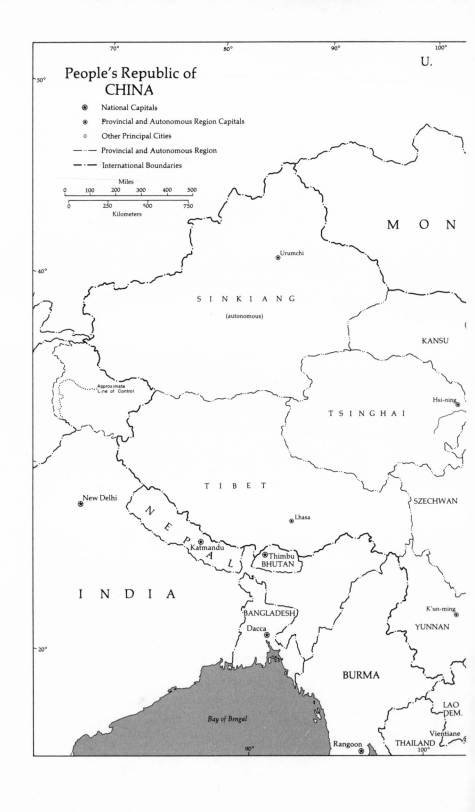

70°   80°   90°   100°

U.

People's Republic of
CHINA

⊛   National Capitals
◉   Provincial and Autonomous Region Capitals
○   Other Principal Cities
—·—   Provincial and Autonomous Region
—··—   International Boundaries

Miles
0   100   200   300   400   500
0   250   500   750
Kilometers

50°

M O N

Urumchi
◉

40°

S I N K I A N G

(autonomous)

KANSU

Approximate
Line of Control

T S I N G H A I

Hsi-ning
◉

TIBET

New Delhi
⊛

N
E
P
A
L

SZECHWAN

Lhasa
◉

Katmandu
⊛

⊛Thimbu
BHUTAN

I N D I A

BANGLADESH

Dacca
⊛

BURMA

K'un-ming
◉

YUNNAN

20°

LAO
DEM.

Bay of Bengal

Vientiane

Rangoon
⊛

THAILAND
100°

90°

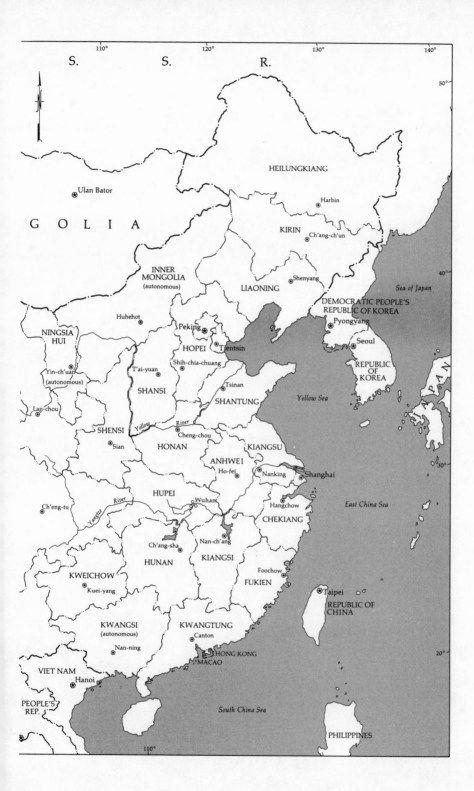

Economic Growth
and
Employment
in
China

Thomas G. Rawski

Published for the World Bank
Oxford University Press

Oxford University Press

NEW YORK OXFORD LONDON GLASGOW
TORONTO MELBOURNE WELLINGTON HONG KONG
TOKYO KUALA LUMPUR SINGAPORE JAKARTA
DELHI BOMBAY CALCUTTA MADRAS KARACHI
NAIROBI DAR ES SALAAM CAPE TOWN

© 1979 by the International Bank
for Reconstruction and Development / The World Bank
1818 H Street, N.W., Washington, D.C. 20433 U.S.A.

Library of Congress Cataloging in Publication Data

Rawski, Thomas G 1943–
    Economic growth and employment in China.
    Bibliography: p. 177
    Includes index.
    1. Labor supply—China. 2. Employment forecasting—
China. 3. Unemployed—China. 4. China—Economic conditions—1949–
1976. I. Title.
HD5830.A6R38   331.1'0951   79-19550
ISBN 0-19-520151-5
ISBN 0-19-520152-3 pbk.

Table of Contents

List of Tables

Foreword

THE PRESENT DECADE has seen much soul-searching about employment policies in developing countries. The volume of literature on the subject is large. Several particular aspects have been the subject of intensive debate: appropriate technology, small-scale enterprise, rural industries, farm mechanization, and the employment and distributive aspects of small-scale farming and agrarian reform. In some instances the debate is of long standing, but it continues with as much intensity as before. Whatever the benefits of industrial exports for growth and employment may be in general, in the more populous developing countries the main market for industry is the domestic one, and it is likely to remain so for some time. Since, in addition, the labor force is preponderantly rural, agricultural development strategy has a critical bearing on the pattern, location, and pace of industrial development.

In writings on these matters, it is common to find some reference to China's experience. Nevertheless, despite the rapid growth of the literature, there are few studies that have attempted to map out China's policies on employment and, in particular, to make a quantitative assessment of what most observers agree to have been considerable achievements during the past two decades. The World Bank asked that such a study be undertaken; this book was commissioned to help the Bank in its understanding of urban and rural development, rural enterprise and nonfarm employment, and the development of small enterprise.

The emphasis placed by China on labor-intensive methods of raising agricultural output, supported by its rural industries' program, and the resulting effects on the regional dispersion of industry provide valuable insight, both for countries that have not opted for this as one of the elements of an employment and growth policy and for others that have or are in the throes of doing so. As the author concludes, even if China's political, social, and economic system is radically different, there are many examples of how knowledge of its experience can enrich the understanding of those concerned with employment policy elsewhere.

BENJAMIN B. KING
Director
Development Economics Department

Preface

THIS BOOK is a revise and updated version of a report prepared for the World Bank in 1977. In writing the original report and the present manuscript, I have benefited from the assistance of a number of individuals and organizations.

My primary obligation is to Alice S. Y. Chan, whose diligent efforts unearthed much of the detailed information presented in the following pages. Evelyn Rawski read and discussed countless drafts.

The following individuals and organizations generously supplied me with bibliographic assistance, unpublished research results, and good advice: John Aird, Dennis Anderson, David M. Brown, Kang Chao, the Committe on Scholarly Communication with the People's Republic of China, Robert Dernberger, John Philip Emerson, Robert Michael Field, Thomas Gottschang, Shigeru Ishikawa, Ramon Myers, Dwight Perkins, Peter Schran, Benedict Stavis, Anthony Tang, Joseph Whitney, Peter Wiles, Bobby Williams, Florence Yuan, and several anonymous critics. Portions of the study were discussed in seminars at the World Bank, the Midwest Seminar of the Association for Asian Studies, and the Universities of Pittsburgh and Toronto. Financial support came from the World Bank, the University of Toronto–York University Joint Centre on Modern East Asia, and the University of Toronto.

Marilyn French typed the manuscript with speed and efficiency. The final manuscript was edited by Goddard Winterbottom and Christine Houle; the index was prepared by Nancy E. MacClintock; the maps were drawn by Larry A. Bowring; Richard Stoddard designed the cover and dustjacket; and Brian J. Svikhart su-

pervised production. Although many people have contributed to
this study, its shortcomings must still be blamed on the author.

THOMAS G. RAWSKI

Economic Growth
and
Employment
in
China

Chapter One

Introduction and Summary

THE LEVEL OF EMPLOYMENT IS A CRITICAL INDICATOR of economic performance in developing countries, a fact that economists have come to recognize only during the past decade. The principal conclusion of this study of the relation between economic growth and employment in the People's Republic of China is that China has succeeded in providing greater employment opportunities for a large and rapidly growing labor force, with much of this absorption of labor occurring in agriculture.

Economic Growth in China

China's economy has grown rapidly, though at times erratically, since the creation of the People's Republic in 1949.[1] In addition to the expansion of production both in aggregate and in per capita values, this growth process has brought with it important changes in economic structure, in technology, and in the level of economic welfare enjoyed by the Chinese people. Quantitative indicators of China's recent progress along the path of modern economic growth are compiled in Table 1-1.

1. For detailed accounts of China's recent economic development and its historical antecedents, consult Alexander Eckstein, *China's Economic Revolution* (Cambridge, England: Cambridge University Press, 1977); Christopher Howe, *China's Economy: A Basic Guide* (New York: Basic Books, 1978) and *China's Modern Economy in Historical Perspective*, ed. Dwight H. Perkins (Stanford, Calif.: Stanford University Press, 1975).

3

TABLE 1-1. INDICATORS OF CHINESE ECONOMIC DEVELOPMENT, SELECTED YEARS, 1952–78

Indicator	1952	1957	1965	1974	1978	Average annual growth rate, 1952–78 (percent)
1. Gross domestic product (billions of 1957 yuan)	70.41	104.68	150.64	266.24	338.62	6.2
Components[a]						
Agriculture	32.15	44.72	49.10	67.09	n.a.	3.4[b]
	(45.7)	(42.7)	(32.6)	(25.2)		
Industry and transport	19.31	34.16	64.60	138.84	n.a.	9.4[b]
	(27.4)	(32.6)	(42.9)	(52.1)		
Construction	1.48	4.00	8.00	13.96	n.a.	10.7[b]
	(2.1)	(3.8)	(5.3)	(5.2)		
Services	17.47	21.80	28.94	46.35	n.a.	4.5[b]
	(24.8)	(20.8)	(19.2)	(17.4)		
2. Population, January 1 (millions)	564	633	745	915	994	2.2
3. Output per capita (yuan)	130	163	202	291	341	3.8
4. Gross fixed capital formation (billions of 1957 yuan)	7.70	19.52	35.46	68.01[c]	n.a.	10.9[c]
5. Capital formation proportion (percent)	10.9	18.6	23.5	26.5[c]	n.a.	—
6. Urban retail price index	100	109	n.a.	124	n.a.	1.0[b]
7. Commodity output						
Grain (millions of tons)	161	191	194	275	305	2.5
Cotton (millions of tons)	1.3	1.6	1.6	2.5	2.2	2.0
Coal (millions of tons)	66	131	232[d]	411[d]	618	9.0
Crude oil (millions of tons)	0.4	2	11	66	104	23.8
Electricity (billions of kilowatt hours)	7	19	42[d]	108[d]	256	14.8
Crude steel (millions of tons)	1	5	12	21	32	14.3
Cotton cloth (billions of meters)	4	5	6	8	11	4.0
8. Foreign trade turnover (billions of 1963 U.S. dollars)						
Exports	0.8	1.3[e]	2.2[f]	2.8	n.a.	6.0[b]
Imports	1.0	1.7[e]	1.9[f]	3.2	n.a.	5.4[b]

n.a. Not available. — Not applicable.

a. Percentage share of each component is shown in parentheses.

b. Growth rate is for 1952–74.

c. Estimated capital formation is for 1973; growth rate is for 1952–73.

d. Figure is probably an underestimate of actual output.

TABLE 1-1 *(continued)*

  e. 1955 data.
  f. 1966 data.

  Sources: *Line 1* Dwight H. Perkins, "Estimating China's Gross Domestic Product," *Current Scene* 15.3 (1976), p. 16, extended from 1974 to 1978 and, for calculating the figures in Line 5, to 1973 using an index calculated from U.S. National Foreign Assessment Center, *China: Economic Indicators* (Washington, D.C.: Central Intelligence Agency, 1978), p. 1. *Line 2* Aird's estimates shown in Table 2-1. *Line 4* Robert M. Field, "Real Capital Formation in the People's Republic of China, 1952–1973," in *Quantitative Measures of China's Economic Output*, ed. Alexander Eckstein (Ann Arbor: University of Michigan Press, forthcoming), Table 19. *Line 6* Dwight H. Perkins, "Growth and Changing Structure of China's Twentieth-Century Economy," in *China's Modern Economy in Historical Perspective*, ed. Dwight H. Perkins (Stanford: Stanford University Press, 1975), p. 153; and Christopher Howe, *China's Economy: A Basic Guide* (New York: Basic Books, 1978), p. 176. *Line 7* data for 1978 from "Communiqué on Fulfillment of China's 1978 National Economic Plan," *Beijing Review*, no. 27 (1979), pp. 37–38; other data, U.S. National Foreign Assessment Center, *China: Economic Indicators*, p. 1, except for the estimate of 1974 cotton cloth output, which is from Robert M. Field, "Civilian Industrial Production in the People's Republic of China: 1949–74," in U.S. Congress, Joint Economic Committee, *China: A Reassessment of the Economy* (Washington, D.C.: U.S. Government Printing Office, 1975), p. 167. *Line 8* Alexander Eckstein, *China's Economic Revolution* (Cambridge, England: Cambridge University Press, 1977), p. 246.

In quantitative terms, these data show that aggregate and per capita output have grown at rates that, although not exceptional, exceed average performance among countries of the Third World by a considerable margin.[2] Extensive changes in the structure of the economy—formerly dominated by agriculture and handicrafts, with industry contributing only a small and isolated segment of total output—have pushed industry ahead of agriculture as the largest contributor to China's gross domestic product. Rising domestic saving and production of capital goods have lifted the share of output devoted to investment from the 5 percent level recorded before World War II to approximately 25 percent in the mid-1970s. Massive growth of output in energy, metallurgy, engineering, and other basic industries has enabled China to supply itself with most of the commodities needed to support its economic expansion. The level of foreign trade, although small in proportion to overall output, has kept pace with the growth of the domestic economy, allowing imported goods and the exports that finance import purchases to make a continuing contribution to the expansion of China's economy.

2. David Morawetz, *Twenty-five Years of Economic Development, 1950 to 1975* (Baltimore and London: Johns Hopkins University Press, 1977), p. 19.

Qualitative changes are less easily documented, but they have been of equal significance. China has made great strides in providing adequate food, shelter, health care, and other basic necessities to its entire population, including the lowest income groups. Mastery of modern technology has spread rapidly over a broad range of manufacturing industries and scientific disciplines. A nation that until 1957 could not manufacture tractors, power plants, or wristwatches now produces computers, earth satellites, oral contraceptives, and nuclear weapons. The technical skills required for industrial development are no longer confined within a few isolated urban enclaves. The spread of rural electrification, local industry, technical training, and publishing has brought modern science and technology to the doorstep of most of China's 200-odd million households. Nearly universal participation by Chinese youth in primary education and the rapid expansion of secondary education ensure that the dissemination of knowledge will continue to broaden and deepen.

Employment Problems and Goals during the 1950s

In the experience of many developing countries economic growth and industrial expansion have often failed to provide adequate employment opportunities for broad segments of the labor force. With its huge and thickly clustered population, China has had a long history of urban unemployment and rural underemployment. In the early years of the People's Republic, in the early 1950s, a concentration of resources on a small number of large-scale, capital-intensive industrial projects that formed the core of China's First Five-Year Plan (1953–57) produced what is a classic pattern: a rapid growth in output alongside open unemployment in the cities and seasonal idleness in the countryside.

Chinese and foreign accounts agree that urban unemployment was both severe and persistent during the 1950s. The rapid growth of urban and industrial job opportunities could not keep pace with the sheer number of job seekers, which was swollen by masses of peasants flocking to the towns to escape the consequences of local food shortages or of the land reform and collectivization that followed the establishment of the People's Republic. Chinese reports of this period regularly mention urban unemployment figures running into the millions.

An excessive supply of labor in the countryside led to widespread seasonal idleness both before and after 1949. Peter Schran has estimated that the average peasant worked only 119 days each year during the early 1950s. The formation of farming cooperatives during 1955–56 and the collectivization of farming in 1958 enabled the Chinese government and the Communist Party to mobilize labor for more intensive cultivation, rural construction projects, and production of nonagricultural commodities, but this increase in peasant effort left the average number of labor-days far below the full-employment norm of 250 used by Chinese economic planners during the 1950s.[3]

Despite these problems of urban and rural underemployment, China's leaders mapped out ambitious plans for attaining full employment. Urban unemployment would be curbed despite rapidly rising productivity by accelerating the rate of industrial growth, by transferring idle urban dwellers to rural units, and by strictly limiting peasant migration to the cities. At the same time, the newly formed collectives, which had the potential to undertake projects whose scale would be beyond the reach of smaller organizations, were also expected to implement changes in methods of agricultural production that would expand employment opportunities in the countryside. Here, targets were spelled out in detail: "In the seven years starting from 1956, every able-bodied man in the countryside should be able to work at least about 250 working days a year. . . . [E]very able-bodied woman in the countryside should, apart from time spent on household work, be able to give no less than 80 to 180 days a year, to agriculture or sideline occupations."[4]

3. Peter Schran, *The Development of Chinese Agriculture, 1950–1959* (Urbana: University of Illinois Press, 1969), chap. 3.

4. From *The National Program for Agricultural Development, 1956–67*, as reproduced in Leslie T. C. Kuo, *Agriculture in the People's Republic of China* (New York: Praeger, 1976), p. 276.

Critical Factors in Raising
the Level of Employment

The principal conclusion of this study is that, as of the mid-1970s, China had succeeded in reaching these ambitious goals. Unemployment certainly exists in the cities, but despite recent Chinese statements emphasizing the growing seriousness of this problem, urban unemployment appears less prevalent in China than in most developing countries. In the countryside seasonal idleness has been greatly reduced, and the average number of annual labor-days contributed by farm workers—of whom nearly 45 percent are women—has risen to approximately 250.

China's success in providing employment for a labor force that increased by roughly 150 million men and women between 1957 and 1975 was primarily the result of the ability of the agricultural sector to absorb two-thirds of those new workers. As will be shown in Chapter Four, these large increases in demand for labor in the farm sector were facilitated by two principal changes: by the collectivization of farming, which occurred during 1956–58, and by the rapid growth in the supply of manufactured farm inputs, which began in the early 1960s.

Collectivization of farming meant that China's millions of peasant households were compelled to surrender their lands and their animals to collective units, the People's Communes, which compensate their members only in proportion to the labor services that they render to the collective economy. Disorganization, poor management, and an erosion of economic incentive caused serious problems in the early years of the communes, and these difficulties contributed heavily to the disastrous harvests of 1959–61. Thereafter, an increase in managerial experience and the return of control over production and income-sharing decisions to small groups comprising no more than a few dozen households allowed the commune system to undertake and direct agricultural reforms that have subsequently raised the demand for labor and output of the farms as well. These measures have included increased preparation and application of organic manures, the supply of which has risen as a result of collective animal raising and animal protection schemes; intensification of cultivation techniques by increasing the labor inputs for planting, weeding, pruning, irrigation, plant protection, and other farming tasks; diversification of the farm economy in directions that enhance the relative importance of labor-intensive activities; and annual campaigns to mobilize seasonally idle labor for construction projects designed to stimulate agricultural output by leveling and terracing hilly lands, expanding water supplies, providing better protection against flood and drought, and improving the rural transport network.

For these new patterns of farm activity to be undertaken, a kind and level of industrial support that was not available during the 1950s had to come into being. In the wake of the economic readjustments made necessary by the agricultural collapse that occurred in China in 1959–61, growing quantities of industrial supplies began to flow into the farm sector. These commodities, many of them produced by small and medium-size rural enterprises, came to play an important role in promoting labor-absorbing agricultural policies. Cement, steel, and explosives for water conservancy and land improvement projects, pumps and piping to move water from newly built reservoirs to the fields, electricity to operate irrigation equipment, chemical fertilizers to combine with increased water supplies to raise crop yields, power tillers to haul earth, stone, building materials, and organic fertilizers, machine tools to stock the thousands of repair shops that now dot China's countryside—all were essential ingredients in the process of raising the demand for labor sufficiently to absorb nearly 100 million new workers into the farm sector while simultaneously raising the number of days worked each year throughout rural China.

Evidence of High Employment Levels in the 1970s

After 1961, as the pace of winter construction campaigns and inflows of manufactured farm inputs quickened and agricultural output returned to normal levels, the demand for labor in rural areas began to rise much as had been anticipated in the plan documents of the mid-1950s. Beginning in the late 1960s and continuing to the present, a variety of evidence of high employment levels and sharply reduced involuntary idleness is found in both urban and rural regions of China.

Recent accounts by foreign visitors are filled with observations of high levels of employment. Visitors find that urban enterprises now experience difficulty in obtaining permission to recruit new workers. Daytime gatherings of idle young men on city streets, a common phenomenon in the cities of both developed and developing countries, are not encountered. Together with statistical information reported for some cities, as is discussed in Chapter Two, this visual evidence points to high levels of urban employment during the 1970s. The exception to this favorable view comes from reports, considered in Chapter Five, that as many as several million youths assigned to rural areas may have illegally returned to their urban homes in search of employment.

In the countryside visitors are surprised to hear of a shortage of labor rather than of a surplus. Officials of communes emphasize the need for increased mechanization of farm work to overcome seasonal shortages of labor and to intensify even further the cropping system. An American Wheat Studies Delegation found in 1976 that "all officials insisted that there was no labor surplus" at the units visited; "instead they expressed concern about labor shortage, at least during the transplanting and harvesting seasons."[5]

Visitor accounts, even those of specialists whose knowledge of Chinese allows them to converse with persons other than official spokesmen, leave much to be desired. Visitors are taken to outstanding rather than typical units. The same Wheat Studies Delegation, for example, toured ten units at which the smallest wheat yield for 1975 was almost two-thirds greater than the national average figure for 1972; the average wheat yield at the ten units was 230 percent above the national figure for 1972.[6] Furthermore, visits to China are brief and often rushed. Foreign guests receive tightly scheduled itineraries that allow scant opportunity for detailed inquiry into the affairs of individual units.

Evidence of high employment levels in the 1970s, however, comes from Chinese as well as foreign accounts. Chinese publications reveal an enthusiasm for mechanization throughout the

5. Peter Schran, "Farm Labor and Living in China" (Champaign: University of Illinois, 1976; processed), p. 11.

6. Virgil A. Johnson and Halsey L. Beemer, Jr., *Wheat in the People's Republic of China* (Washington, D.C.: National Academy of Sciences, 1977), pp. 91 and 166.

economy that would hardly be consistent with widespread unemployment or underemployment. The following examples typify thousands of positive reports about the effect of mechanization in industry, agriculture, and services:[7]

> Shih-chia-chuang [Hopei] Rolling Stock Works made 12 pieces of pneumatic equipment to mechanize the main work line. Personnel dropped by one-third and productivity doubled.

> Local industry in Fukien's Yung-ch'un County is developing rapidly. About 90 percent of the county's farm and subsidiary products are now processed by machine, saving 1.1 million man-days.

> Agricultural mechanization is no doubt the center of agrotechnical reform. It signifies the level of agricultural productivity, and abundant forces must be made available to carry it out actively. But it should also be perceived that the most prominent role of agricultural mechanization is to save labor power.

> The Haining postal machinery works has successfully trial-produced several high-speed letter stampers which perform well. The stamper can stamp 36,000 letters an hour, thereby raising work efficiency by more than ten times.

Chinese writers are well aware of the direct effect of mechanization on labor requirements. As these statements show, they welcome the saving of labor inherent in machinery. Their reports rarely contain persuasive arguments directed at opponents of new equipment, because they evidently expect readers to share these views.[8] The rapid rise in stocks of rural machinery (see Table 4-3),

---

7. *Ching-chi tao-pao* [The Economic Reporter], no. 1,228 (1971), p. 20, and no. 1,177 (1970), p. 23; ECMM, no. 409 (1964), p. 37; and BBC, no. W954 (1977), pp. A13–14.

8. Evidence of resistance to farm mechanization may be found in Huang Ching, "On Agricultural Mechanization in China," *Chi-hsieh kung-yeh* [Machinery Industry], no. 21 (1957), translated in ECMM, no. 120 (1958), pp. 36–37, and Benedict Stavis, *The Politics of Agricultural Mechanization in China* (Ithaca, N.Y.: Cornell University Press, 1978), pp. 106, 157, 181, and 205–10. Ironically, the strongest resis-

most of which are purchased by communes and production brigades out of collective funds, also points to the popularity of mechanization, as does information showing that machinery is used more intensively in China than in other countries.[9]

China has already attained a modest degree of farm mechanization: data presented in Chapter Four indicate that supplies of machinery are now approaching Japanese levels of the early 1960s. Recent experience with farm machinery has convinced China's leaders that accelerated mechanization holds the key to raising the growth rate of farm output. The Third National Conference on Agricultural Mechanization, held in January 1978, adopted a target of achieving basic agricultural mechanization by 1980. More specifically, current plans anticipate the following:

> [B]y 1980, 70 percent of the major agricultural, forestry, animal husbandry, sideline production and fishery operations should be mechanized; large and medium-size tractors increased by 70 percent over the present figure; machine-drawn farm implements by 110 percent; hand-guided tractors by 36 percent; drainage and irrigation machines by 32 percent. . . . The meeting also decided that there should be fairly large increases in production of machines for farmland capital construction, plant protection, transportation, harvesting, and agricultural and sideline processing, as well as increases in the output of agricultural chemicals, dynamite, plastic sheet, forestry, animal husbandry, and fishery machines, and small rural power stations and semimechanized farm implements.[10]

This across-the-board drive toward mechanization would make no sense in the presence of widespread rural underemployment.

China's unique program of conscripting urban school graduates to migrate to the countryside provides additional evidence that the demand for rural labor cannot fall far short of available

---

tance to mechanization seems to have come from officials in Shantung Province, which is now hailed as a national leader in farm mechanization.

9. Dwight Perkins and others, *Rural Small-Scale Industry in the People's Republic of China* (Berkeley: University of California Press, 1977), pp. 150–51.

10. FBIS, January 31, 1978, p. E7.

supplies. Peasants sometimes oppose settlement of urban youths in their local units, but rural hostility to newcomers arises not because there is no work to be done, but because urban youths tend to be weak, unskilled, and often unwilling to take on the grueling physical labor required of China's farmers.

Reports of difficulties encountered by the program to "rusticate" urban youth reveal that employment standards of the 1970s are much higher than those of the late 1950s:

> After . . . study, the educated youths sent to Chi County, Hopei, made encouraging progress. In 1972 each person worked an average of 269 days, 64 days more than in 1971.

> Under the tutelage of the party, the work attendance of the educated youths in this commune [Huai-te County, Kirin] increases each year; the boys and girls on the average each reported for work 225 days in 1970, 245 days in 1971, and 267 days in 1972.

> The youths in the countryside say, "Ch'ien-ying [Feng-jung County, Hopei] is our home, and the poor and lower-middle peasants are thus our family." In the past eight years, they have spent every Spring Festival with the . . . peasants of Ch'ien-ying. In 1972 every person participated in 300 days of labor on the average.[11]

At the national level, a regulation in 1974 required "communes to guarantee urban youths a minimum annual wage of 200 yuan, provided they work . . . for at least 250 days per year."[12] Finally, demands that commune and brigade leaders should participate in manual labor for from 200 to 300 days a year provide further evidence that the typical work-year in China's countryside now includes far more than the 190 labor days estimated for 1959 by Schran.[13]

It is not easy to define with any degree of precision what "full

11. Peter J. Seybolt, ed., *The Rustication of Urban Youth in China* (White Plains, N.Y.: M. E. Sharpe, 1975), pp. 24, 38, and 54–55.

12. Thomas P. Bernstein, *Up to the Mountains and Down to the Villages* (New Haven: Yale University Press), p. 153.

13. Ibid., pp. 325–26; and Schran, *Chinese Agriculture*, p. 75.

employment" means as it relates to agricultural workers. A rough approximation is possible if it is assumed that the age and sex distribution of China's present farming population resembles available estimates of national figures. If the prime labor force members, men aged from 15 to 54 and single women aged from 15 to 24 are assumed to work 330 days each year (allowing ten days of leisure at New Year and the Spring Festival and an extremely low total of fifteen additional holidays for rest or illness) and the secondary labor force, of housewives aged from 25 to 54 and men aged from 55 to 64 is assumed to work from 80 to 180 days a year, the range mentioned in the plan document cited above, then the average work schedule for all workers may be calculated at between 246 and 279 days each year.[14] These rough calculations show that an average work year of 275 days represents an extremely high utilization of rural labor; this will be taken as the definition of "full employment" for agricultural workers.

Methodological Problems

Before beginning a detailed investigation of the relation between economic growth and employment in China, two issues require brief discussion. They concern the reliability of Chinese economic statistics and the influence of political events on China's economy.

China's government stopped publishing regular statistical reports on economic performance during the late 1950s; even during the earlier period of relatively liberal publication, many types of information that are readily and routinely made available for noncommunist nations were not released. As a result, studies of China's economy are of necessity based on quantitative estimates painstakingly compiled by foreign specialists from whatever sources can be found. Most of this work consists of piecing together information from Chinese sources—newspapers, journals, radio broadcasts, and the like—but other sources, including Chi-

14. These calculations are based on a breakdown of the July 1977 population by age and sex as estimated in U.S. National Foreign Assessment Center, *China: Economic Indicators* (Washington, D.C.: Central Intelligence Agency, 1977), p. 7.

nese emigrés, foreign press reports, and returned visitors, are also used.

An empirical study such as the present book is limited by the quantity and quality of available data. Since a large proportion of the data used in this study is compiled in this unorthodox fashion, it is natural for readers to question its value and authenticity. Three questions must be asked. First, is China's statistical reporting system good enough to permit the government to collect reasonably accurate data on output, employment, and other quantities with which this study is concerned? Second, does the published information that serves as the principal source material for this study coincide with the internal figures used by Chinese planners and policymakers? Third, do the Chinese publish enough information to permit an outsider to approximate unpublished magnitudes with a reasonable degree of accuracy?

These issues are discussed in Appendix A, in which it is argued that the answer to each of the three questions is a qualified yes. China's system of state-dominated central planning requires vast amounts of statistical information to function with a reasonable degree of efficiency. There is voluminous evidence showing that China's factories, communes, and government agencies can and do compile detailed and accurate data on a wide range of topics. China's statistical reporting system is set up in such a way that it is difficult to measure some economic variables, of which population is the most familiar example. Nevertheless, there is good evidence that the range and quality of statistical information available to economic policymakers are significantly greater in China than in most countries in which average annual incomes fall below US$1,000 per capita.

Although China's government publishes only a fraction of the economic data it collects, there are no valid grounds for suspecting that Peking issues data that are known to be false. Since most data available to foreigners are either taken from, or repeated in, domestic Chinese media, the principal effect of such deception would be to undermine the government's credibility with its own citizens. Having experienced the corrosive effect of false reporting during the Great Leap Forward of 1958–60, when the collapse of accurate statistical reporting led Peking to issue exaggerated claims of bumper harvests and soaring production that were later retracted at considerable political cost, the Chinese scrupulously avoid publishing false claims. This is not to say that Chinese economic reporting is well balanced or that individual Chinese units do not attempt to embellish their reputations by reporting false achievements to their superiors. Both problems certainly exist. The outside observer, however, must pay careful attention only to the danger of taking the (published) part for the (unavailable) whole. The problem of false reporting can be left to the present Chinese administration under Deputy Premier Teng Hsiao-p'ing, whose motto, "Seek Truth from Facts," indicates the prevalent attitude toward statistical deception.

The question concerning the accuracy with which outsiders can estimate actual economic magnitudes from the partial information available from Chinese and other sources will be fully answered only when the Chinese government chooses to release a substantial flow of economic data. In the meantime, however, both the history of the research project of which this book is the result and, more generally, the history of foreign studies of China's economic development show that careful sifting of available information has made it possible to establish a sound empirical foundation for investigating quantitative as well as qualitative aspects of China's economy. This can be seen in the growing international consensus among specialists concerning the basic quantitative pattern of China's economic growth since 1949,[15] in the extent to which the enlarged flow of information resulting from scholarly exchanges with the People's Republic has reinforced rather than upset this consensus, and in the frequency with which Chinese statements confirm the inferences of empirical researchers.

In regard to the second methodological issue, readers of this book may be surprised at the extent to which political developments are neglected. This is not accidental, but reflects the author's belief that, contrary to the familiar slogan, politics is rarely "in command" of economic developments in China. Political activity dictates the course of economic events only during campaigns that take aspects of economic life as their central target. The

15. This consensus emerged at a conference in 1975 arranged by Alexander Eckstein. Its results will appear in *Quantitative Measures of China's Economic Output*, ed. Alexander Eckstein (Ann Arbor: University of Michigan Press, forthcoming).

land-reform campaign, the process of transferring ownership of large-scale industry and commerce to the state, and the collectivization of agriculture all represented notable political initiatives that were intended to bring about considerable and discontinuous economic changes—and did so.

All of these campaigns occurred before 1960. Since then only the decentralization of responsibility within the communes in the early 1960s stands out as an example of a political decision that caused a fundamental structural change in the economy. After 1960 both policy and performance display a high degree of continuity; in comparison with the 1950s, politically inspired change is conspicuous by its absence. Only the emergence of an outward-looking administration from the confusion surrounding the decline and death of Chou En-lai and Mao Tse-tung, an administration dedicated to economic and technical modernization, can perhaps be seen as another change that could influence economic life as profoundly as the earlier innovations of land reform, socialization and collectivization.

The absence of significant political initiatives directed at the economy does not mean that politics and economics move in isolated orbits. On the contrary, political activity directed toward the pursuit of power or any of a wide range of other objectives often includes economic components. But when the principal objective of political effort lies elsewhere, its effect on economic patterns depends upon the extent to which secondary or tangential political energies can displace the forces that normally compete for influence over economic life: the economic institutions of the state and the bureaucracies that run them; the regional and local aspirations of provinces, counties, and towns; the individual interests of workers, peasants, and their families; and the internal logic of a dynamic economy. The history of China's economy during the 1960s and 1970s shows that, when the central concern of political life remains outside the economy, economic forces tend to predominate on the inside. The period of the Cultural Revolution, 1966–68, illustrates this perfectly. There was no shortage of suggested economic reforms, and high officials were cashiered for allegedly placing "profit in command" and "taking the capitalist road." But with political energies expended outside the economic arena, resistance to reform was largely successful. Some proposed changes were never implemented, whereas others received initial but superficial acceptance and were later sloughed off. Liu Shao-ch'i, Teng Hsiao-p'ing, and many other leaders disappeared from view, but the policies for which they were castigated hardly weakened. A decade later, denigration of professional expertise, contempt for foreign technology, schools without examinations, and other "newborn things" prescribed for the economy during the Cultural Revolution are forgotten in China. They live on only in the nostalgic writings of foreign enthusiasts.

Organization of the Book

The following chapters present the results of a detailed study of economic growth and employment in China. Discussion in Chapter Two provides a quantitative picture of China's population, labor force, and patterns of sectoral employment in two benchmark years, 1957 and 1975. The results show that, despite rapid growth, the nonfarm sectors of China's economy could not absorb more than a fraction of new entrants into the labor force between 1957 and 1975. Chapter Three constitutes an investigation of the determinants of employment growth in industry, the largest and fastest-growing sector of China's economy. Chapter Four contains a detailed investigation of how China's agricultural sector, burdened with a fixed land base and an already unfavorable man-land ratio, succeeded in absorbing nearly 100 million new workers during 1957–75 while providing added employment opportunities for the existing labor force. The results show that this enormous task of labor absorption was accomplished only at the cost of substantial declines in both labor productivity and total factor productivity in agriculture. Chapter Five presents a summary of the findings of the study, considers the future balance between labor supply and demand in China's economy, and briefly discusses the transferability of Chinese economic patterns to other developing nations. Three appendices discuss the reliability of Chinese economic data and provide statistical background for Chapters Two and Three.

Chapter Two

Size and Sectoral Distribution of China's Labor Force in 1957 and 1975

ESTIMATES OF THE SIZE AND SECTORAL ATTACHMENT of China's labor force in the benchmark years 1957 and 1975 are based on incomplete data and of necessity incorporate a variety of assumptions. The results nonetheless indicate the character of the general trends in both the size and the sectoral distribution of this labor force.

The Population of China

Demographers have argued for many years about the size of China's population. Before a direct examination of the labor force is possible, it is necessary to come to some general notion of the size of the population and to evaluate the various sets of conflicting statistics.

Recent reports of remarkably low birthrates and low rates of natural increase for individual urban neighborhoods, rural communes, major cities, and individual provinces have heightened the interest of foreign observers in obtaining accurate information about China's population.[1] The Chinese authorities, however,

1. Recent studies of China's population include John S. Aird, "Population Growth in the People's Republic of China," in U.S. Congress, Joint Economic Committee, *Chinese Economy Post-Mao* (Washington, D.C.: U.S. Government Printing Office, 1978), vol. 1, pp. 439–75; Leo A. Orleans, *Every Fifth Child: The Population*

have not issued systematic demographic information since the late 1950s, because either they prefer not to publicize population statistics or, as was stated in a remarkable interview by Deputy Premier Li Hsien-nien, Peking itself does not possess good estimates of China's total population.[2]

Available population data from Chinese sources are shown in Table 2-1. The figures for the 1950s are based on the census of 1953. Although some observers have questioned the validity of the 1953 figures, independent studies have invariably taken them as the starting point for estimating population figures for later years. The data for 1964 and 1972 were released without detailed descriptions of how they were derived; perhaps the figures for both years are estimates of the 1964 population. The figure for 1976 is the sum of recently published population figures for China's provinces and major municipalities.

These data are generally plausible, but John Aird's detailed critique leads him to conclude that the recent totals, along with the data relating to 1964 and 1972, understate the actual population by a substantial margin. Szechwan, China's most populous province, offers the clearest example of implausibly low figures. Szechwan is not cited as a leader in efforts at birth control and has not experienced large outmigrations, but the recently reported total of 90 million inhabitants suggests the unbelievably low rate of natural increase of only 1.17 percent a year between 1957 and 1977.[3]

---

of China (Stanford, Calif.: Stanford University Press, 1972); H. Yuan Tien, China's Population Struggle (Columbus: Ohio State University Press, 1973); and Judith Banister, "China's Demographic Transition in the Asian Context," in "The Current Vital Rates and Population Size of the People's Republic of China and Its Provinces" (Ph.D. dissertation, Food Research Institute, Stanford University, 1977).

2. The following statements are reproduced from Li's 1971 interview with an Arab newsman in A. Doak Barnett, Uncertain Passage (Washington, D.C.: Brookings Institution, 1974), p. 166: "Some people estimate the population of China at 800 million and some at 750 million. Unfortunately, there are no accurate statistics in this connection. Nevertheless, the officials at the supply and grain department are saying confidently, 'The number is 800 million people.' Officials outside the grain department say the population is '750 million only,' while the Ministry of Commerce insists on the bigger number in order to be able to provide goods in large quantities. The planning men reduce the figure in order to strike a balance in the plans of the various state departments."

3. John S. Aird, "Recent Provincial Population Figures," China Quarterly, no. 73 (1978), pp. 1–44; the Szechwan figure is from p. 24.

TABLE 2-1. ESTIMATED POPULATION OF THE PEOPLE'S REPUBLIC OF CHINA,
SELECTED YEARS, 1952–78
(millions of persons as of January 1)

Year	Estimates from Chinese sources	Independent estimates		
		Aird	Banister	Orleans
1952	563	564	n.a.	n.a.
1953	575	576	n.a.	n.a.
1954	588	589	n.a.	588
1955	602	603	n.a.	600
1956	615	618	n.a.	613
1957	628	633	n.a.	626
1960	n.a.	677	n.a.	663
1964	680–713[a]	729	n.a.	710
1965	n.a.	745	n.a.	723
1970	n.a.	837	n.a.	788
1972	686–691[b]	877	858	813
1974	880	915	890	838
1975	898	934	905	850
1976	916	952	920	863
1977	934	971	933	875
1978	953	994	947	887

n.a. Not available.

a. These data are rumors concerning the possible outcome of a population investigation in 1964.

b. These data are from *Shih-chieh ti-t'u ts'e* [World Atlas] (Peking: Ti-t'u ch'u-pan she, February and December 1972). See John S. Aird, "Recent Provincial Population Figures," *China Quarterly*, no. 73 (1978), p. 16.

Sources: Chinese reports for 1952–57, Nai-ruenn Chen, *Chinese Economic Statistics* (Chicago: Aldine, 1967), p. 124; *for 1964 and 1974*, John S. Aird, *Population Estimates for the Provinces of the People's Republic of China: 1953 to 1974* (Washington, D.C.: U.S. Department of Commerce, 1974), p. 6, and "Recent Provincial Population Figures," *China Quarterly*, no. 73 (1978); pp. 15–16; *for 1974–78*, figures are the sum of reported provincial population totals as adjusted to midyear 1976 by Aird, "Recent Provincial Population Figures," p. 27, and projected forward and backward at an annual rate of 2 percent, "the figure cited repeatedly by Chinese authorities as the average annual growth rate of the population" (Aird, ibid., p. 27). *Aird estimates for 1952*, U.S. National Foreign Assessment Center, *China: Economic Indicators* (Washington, D.C.: Central Intelligence Agency, 1978), p. 6; *remaining figures*, John S. Aird, "Population Growth in the People's Republic of China," in U.S. Congress, Joint Economic Committee, *Chinese Economy Post-Mao* (Washington, D.C.: U.S. Government Printing Office, 1978), p. 465. Aird's intermediate model is used here. *Banister estimates*, Judith Banister, "China's Demographic Transition in the Asian Context," in "The Current Vital Rates and Population Size of the People's Republic of China and Its Provinces" (Ph.D. dissertation, Food Research Institute, Stanford University, 1977). *Orleans estimates*, Leo A. Orleans, "China's Population: Can the Contradictions be Resolved?" in U.S. Congress, Joint Economic Committee, *China: A Reassessment of the Economy* (Washington, D.C.: U.S. Government Printing Office, 1975), p. 77.

Aird has long argued that the census of 1953 resulted in an undercount and that subsequent Chinese statements have continued to understate actual population size by a considerable margin. Building on an exhaustive review of available demographic information, Aird has attempted to estimate the size and structure of China's population by means of three statistical models incorporating assumptions that imply high, intermediate, and low rates of population growth.[4] The results generated by the intermediate model fit well with recent Chinese statements concerning size of population. The population figures predicted by Aird's intermediate model are shown in Table 2-1, together with series compiled by other outside observers who regard Aird's population estimates as too high.

Recent Chinese statements provide an opportunity to test these competing estimates for consistency with other types of data. Leading officials often refer to population totals in round numbers. For years the figure 800 million appeared in Chinese media reports and interviews with visitors. But in 1978, Chinese officials began to mention a total of 900 million, and then, in a November 1 conversation between Deputy Premier Teng Hsiao-p'ing and Italian Foreign Trade Minister Renaldo Ossala, referred to a round figure of "1 billion Chinese." These developments support Aird's estimates; they are not consistent with the competing series, especially the low figures advanced by Leo Orleans, Colin Clark, and several U.S. and U.N. agencies.[5]

Age distribution is another area in which limited verification of the total population figure is now possible. In 1977, China's primary schools were reported to have enrolled 146,164,200 pupils, or 95.5 percent of the school-age population.[6] The implied figure of 153 million boys and girls in the primary school age group of from 7 to 12 years fits well with Aird's intermediate and high popu-

4. The methodology and assumptions underlying these models are discussed in Aird, "Population Growth in the People's Republic of China," pp. 457–65.

5. Recent Chinese statements are from John Aird, personal communication, and from his "Population Growth in the People's Republic of China," pp. 455–57. The low population estimates, which appear to have little foundation beyond the intuition of their authors, are listed in Aird, "Recent Provincial Population Figures," pp. 36–38.

6. *Peking Review*, no. 36 (1978), p. 15.

lation models, which yield figures of 148 and 156 million children in the relevant age group for 1977.[7] Although Aird's is the only available estimate of age distribution, the lower population estimates shown in other sources appear inconsistent with recent Chinese statements about school attendance.

Foodgrain supply is another area in relation to which the plausibility of competing population estimates can be assessed. Hu Ch'iao-mu, the president of China's newly established Academy of Social Sciences, reports that "[i]n 1977, the average amount of grain per capita in the nation was the same as the 1955 level; in other words the growth of grain production was only about equal to the population growth plus the increase in grain requirements for industrial and other uses."[8] Although information is lacking about the "industrial and other uses" of grain, a category that presumably includes such items as fodder and losses in flour milling, widespread agreement that China's grain harvest remained stagnant at approximately 285 million tons during 1975–77 allows comparison of the grain-supply implications of alternative population estimates with Hu's assertion that per capita output and availability of foodgrains did not change between 1955 and 1977.

This is done in Table 2-2, in which the calculations show that Hu's observations fit best with the higher population figures. Aird's population series produces changes of only 2 percent in per capita grain production and supply between 1955 and 1977. Lower population figures produce larger deviations from constant per capita production and supply. The inconsistency with Hu's observations increases as the assumed figures for the 1977 population decline. Orleans' figures, for example, imply increases of 9 percent and 14 percent, respectively, in per capita production and availability of foodgrains between 1955 and 1977.

None of these comparisons is conclusive, but together they consistently support Aird's view that China's actual population must

7. John Aird, personal communication. China has begun to shift from a six-year program of primary education for children aged 7 to 12 inclusive to a five-year program for children aged 6 to 10. To the extent that the new system was already in place during 1977, the 153 million figure refers to a narrower age cohort and thus implies a population larger than Aird's estimate.

8. Hu Ch'iao-mu, "Observe Economic Laws, Speed Up the Four Modernizations," *Peking Review*, no. 47 (1978), p. 18.

TABLE 2-2. GRAIN PRODUCTION AND SUPPLY PER CAPITA, 1955 AND 1977

| | | | Grain availability per capita | | | |
| | | Year-end population | Production | | Supply | |
Authority	Year	(millions)	Kilograms	Index	Kilograms	Index
Chinese						
sources	1955	615	293	100	288	100
	1977	934	305	104	312	108
Aird	1955	618	292	100	286	100
	1977	994	287	98	293	102
Banister	1955	n.a.	n.a.	n.a.	n.a.	n.a.
	1977	947	301	n.a.	307	n.a.
Orleans	1955	613	294	100	289	100
	1977	887	321	109	328	114

n.a. Not available.

Sources: Population, Table 2-1. Grain production, Robert M. Field and James A. Kilpatrick, "Chinese Grain Production: An Interpretation of the Data," China Quarterly, no. 74 (1978), p. 380, estimate grain output at 180 million tons for 1955 and 285 million tons for 1977. Grain supply, sum of grain production and net imports. In 1955, China had an export balance of 3 million tons of grain (average of figures for 1954/55 and 1955/56 shown in Nai-ruenn Chen, Chinese Economic Statistics, p. 408). In 1977 net grain imports were 6 million tons (average of figures for 1976/77 and 1977/78 shown in China Business Review, vol. 5, no. 5 [1978], p. 54).

substantially exceed the sum of recently published provincial totals, which amount to approximately 900 million persons as of early 1975 (Table 2-1). In comparison with alternative reconstructions, Aird's intermediate model represents the most plausible picture of China's population size and structure. This model provides the starting point from which estimates of China's labor force are made below. Alternative estimates are derived from the 1975 population figures presented in Chinese sources and summarized in Table 2-1. Fortunately, it will be possible to show that the principal conclusions concerning the growth of China's labor force, the distribution of new entrants into the labor force between farm and nonfarm occupations, and the balance between labor supply and demand are not crucially dependent upon the choice of population data.

Urban Population

In view of the emphasis placed on rural development in Chinese policy statements, it is important to obtain a rough quantitative indication of recent trends in urbanization. Chinese literature of the 1950s provides the following definitions of urban areas.[9]

All urban agglomerations with 100,000 or more inhabitants are municipalities or cities. Smaller cities may also be placed in this category if they are industrial or mining centers, seats of important administrative or transport activities, or key nodes within border regions. Towns are smaller urban agglomerations with 2,000 or more inhabitants, of whom at least half are engaged in nonagricultural pursuits. Places with populations of as small as 1,000 persons may also become towns if 75 percent of the populace is nonagricultural and if they are centers of nonfarm economic activity. Urban places are therefore agglomerations with populations of over 2,000 (and in some cases, 1,000), of whom the majority are engaged in nonfarm pursuits.

In 1953 the total population of China's 164 municipalities was 52.4 million, of which 83 percent was urban and 17 percent rural (that is, the farming population of city suburbs). The total urban population was 77.7 million. By 1958 the number of municipalities had increased to 185, and their combined population had surpassed 70 million.[10] Total urban population reached 92 million by the end of 1957 and undoubtedly surpassed 100 million during 1958.[11]

Policy statements emphasizing the primacy of rural development and the well-publicized program of compulsory migration to the countryside for urban school graduates have created the im-

---

9. This and the following paragraph are based on Morris B. Ullman, *Cities of Mainland China: 1953 and 1958,* International Population Reports Series P-95, no. 59, (Washington, D.C.: U.S. Department of Commerce, 1961), chap. 2.

10. Ullman's figures (*Cities of Mainland China,* pp. 35–36) imply a minimum of 69.5 million. Since this calculation makes use of earlier data when the 1958 figures are not available, the correct figure must be higher.

11. The 1957 total is from Ullman, *Cities of Mainland China,* p. 7. Orleans, *Every Fifth Child,* p. 65, states that "it was commonly reported (and usually accepted) that the urban population of China increased by some twenty million persons during the Great Leap, over a 1957 figure of almost ninety million. Some estimates of urban population in 1959 ran as high as 130 million." One source gives a 1957 figure of 99.5 million; see John S. Aird, "Population Growth and Distribution in Mainland China," in U.S. Congress, Joint Economic Committee, *An Economic Profile of Mainland China* (Washington, D.C.: U.S. Government Printing Office, 1967), vol. 2, p. 381.

pression that China's urban population may have stopped growing during the 1960s and 1970s.[12] This is not the case. Data for
fifty-five cities that accounted for nearly three-fourths of the total
population of China's municipalities in 1953 indicate an expansion of from 44 to 68 percent between 1958 and the mid-1970s;
these figures are compiled in Table 2-3. In addition, statements
such as the following indicate that smaller urban areas have also
expanded, perhaps more rapidly than the larger cities for which
data are most readily available: "China has built up many small
cities and towns in outlying and sparsely populated places, in the
interior and in border and minority nationality areas which now
have their own industry. The capitals of many provinces and autonomous regions and many county seats have become industrial
cities of varying sizes. . . . New China puts stress on building
small and medium cities."[13] Furthermore, new cities have appeared: only thirteen of twenty-nine cities described in a 1974
pamphlet entitled "Newly Brilliant Cities of the Fatherland" were
listed as municipalities in 1958.[14]

The conclusion of this survey is that China's urban population
has increased substantially since 1958. The data for fifty-five cities,
most of them large, indicate overall growth of from 44 to 68 percent
between 1958 and 1975; since smaller cities may have grown more
rapidly than larger urban areas, national urban population growth
is probably near or even above the upper end of this range. Given
the near certainty that China's urban population surpassed 100
million during 1958 and grew by at least two-thirds between 1958
and 1975, an assumption of an urban population of some 175 million persons for 1975 is not unrealistic. This figure implies that the
proportion of urban dwellers to total national population has risen
from 13 percent in 1953 and 14 percent in 1957 to slightly under 19
percent in 1975.

---

12. Pi-chao Chen, "Overurbanization, Rustication of Urban-Educated Youths,
and Politics of Rural Transformation," *Comparative Politics* (April 1972), pp. 373–74,
cites statements indicating that Chinese officials may have hoped to stabilize the
urban population at 110 million during the mid-1960s.

13. BBC, no. W899 (1976), p. A1.

14. *Tsu-kuo hsin-kuang ch'eng-shih* [Newly Brilliant Cities of The Fatherland]
(Shanghai: Jen-min ch'u-pan she, 1974).

TABLE 2-3. POPULATION OF CHINESE CITIES, 1953, 1957, AND MID-1970s
(thousands of persons)

Province and city	1953	1957	Mid-1970s Low estimate	Mid-1970s High estimate
Anhwei				
Hofei	184	304	400	500
Pangfou	253	330	400	400
Wuhu	242	240	400	400
Chekiang				
Hangchou	697	794	700	700
Shaohsing	131	160	300	300
Wenchou	202	210	300	300
Ch'inghai				
Hsining	94	150	500	500
Fukien				
Amoy	224	308	300	300
Heilungkiang				
Chichihaerh	345	704	1,000	1,000
Harbin	1,163	1,595	2,000	2,000
Honan				
Anyang	125	153	500	500
Chengchou	595	785	700	1,600
Hsinhsiang	170	203	420	420
K'aifeng	299	318	500	1,000
Loyang	171	500	500	500
Hopei				
Shihchiachuang	373	623	500	500
T'angshan	693	812	1,000	1,000
Hunan				
Ch'angsha	651	709	800	800
Chuchou	127	190	200	200
Hengyang	235	240	400	400
Hsiangt'an	184	247	400	400
Hupei				
Wuhan	1,427	2,226	3,000	3,500
Inner Mongolia				
Huhehot	148	320	400	400
Paot'ou	149	490	800	800
Kansu				
Lanchou	397	732	1,200	2,000
Kiangsi				
Chingtechen	92	266	460	460
Nanch'ang	398	520	600	600
Kiangsu				
Ch'angchou	296	300	290	400
Nanking	1,092	1,455	1,300	2,400
Soochow	474	651	540	540
Wuhsi	582	616	650	650

(Table continued on the following page)

TABLE 2-3 *(continued)*

| | | | Mid-1970s | |
| | | | Low | High |
Province and city	1953	1957	estimate	estimate
Kirin				
Ch'angch'un	855	988	1,300	1,300
Ssup'ing	126	130	200	200
Kwangsi				
Kueilin	145	170	210	210
Nanning	195	260	400	400
Kwangtung				
Canton	1,599	1,867	2,000	2,000
Foshan	122	120	200	200
Kweichow				
Ts'unyi	98	200	300	300
Liaoning				
Lüta	892	1,590	4,000	4,000
Shenyang	2,300	2,423	2,000	4,400
Peking	2,768	4,148	8,000	8,000
Shanghai	6,204	6,977	5,700	10,000
Shansi				
T'aiyuan	721	1,053	1,000	1,000
Yangch'uan	177	200	400	400
Shantung				
Chinan	680	882	1,100	1,100
Ch'ingtao	917	1,144	1,000	1,000
Weifang	149	190	240	240
Shensi				
Sian	787	1,368	2,000	2,500
Sinkiang				
Ining	108	85	100	100
Urumchi	141	320	800	1,000
Szechwan				
Ch'engtu	857	1,135	3,600	3,600
Chungking	1,772	2,165	6,000	6,000
Tientsin	2,694	3,278	7,000	7,000
Yunnan				
Kochiu	160	180	240	240
K'unming	699	900	1,500	1,500
Total, fifty-five cities	37,379	48,924	70,750	82,160
Index	76.4	100.0	144.6	168.0

Sources: For 1953 and 1957; Morris B. Ullman, *Cities of Mainland China: 1953 and 1958* (Washington, D.C.: U.S. Department of Commerce, 1961), pp. 35–36, and Nai-ruenn Chen, *Chinese Economic Statistics,* pp. 129–30. *For the mid-1970s;* based on a variety of published sources and travelers' reports. The figures are not all for the same year; data closest to 1975 were used when several figures were found. When there are two figures for a single city, the lower figure often refers to the urban area only, whereas the higher figure includes suburban and rural areas administered by city governments.

Participation Rates in the Labor Force—Urban

Available information on employment rates among urban residents is compiled in Table 2-4. The population-weighted average of employment rates for four major urban areas during the 1950s is calculated at 33.3 percent, which is nearly identical with the figure of 32.6 percent compiled from a national sample survey conducted in 1956. It can therefore be assumed with reasonable confidence that approximately 33 percent of urban residents were employed in 1957. Since unemployment is estimated below at roughly 8.5 percent of the urban population, urban labor force participation for 1957 amounted to approximately 41.5 percent of the urban population.

Repeated campaigns to resettle idle town dwellers in the countryside and the emergence of new employment opportunities for urban housewives in neighborhood industries lead to the expectation that both employment rates and participation rates should be higher in urban areas for the 1970s than for the 1950s.[15] This expectation is confirmed by the data in Table 2-4, which show that employment rates in Nanking and Shanghai jumped from about 33 percent to more than 50 percent between the late 1950s and the mid-1970s.[16] Survey results summarized in Table 2-4 show that urban employment rates of 50 percent or higher are common except in mining centers, where women find only limited

15. Christopher Howe, *Employment and Economic Growth in Urban China, 1949–1957* (Cambridge, England: Cambridge University Press, 1971), p. 39, estimates open unemployment in 1957 at 670,000 for Shanghai alone. Chinese observers measured what they called the "temporary and floating" populations of the cities in the millions; see SCMP, no. 1,764 (1958), p. 39. A typical report on neighborhood industries states that "women dependents of workers and staff of plants, mines and other enterprises in Sining Municipality had set up 93 factories by the end of 1975 with over 9,200 women dependents working in them" (BBC, no. W878 [1976], p. A6). For further discussion, see James B. Stepanek, "Planning of Urban Small-Scale Industry in China" (paper presented at a conference on "Regionalism and Economic Development in China: Historical and South Asian Comparative Perspectives," Philadelphia, January 20-21, 1978).

16. David M. Brown of the University of Toronto has obtained time series data for employees as a percentage of Nanking's nonagricultural population. The percentage rises from 25.7 percent in 1953 to 36.2 percent in 1964 and 50.6 percent in 1974.

TABLE 2-4. EMPLOYED POPULATION AS A PERCENTAGE OF URBAN
POPULATION, THE 1950s AND 1974 AND 1975

City	Percentage employed	Population, 1958 (thousands)
Data for the 1950s		
Canton	25.0	1,867
Lushun-Talien	32.5	1,590
Nanking-Wuhsi	33.2	2,071
Shanghai	35.8	6,977
Weighted average of above cities[a]	33.3	—
National urban sample survey, 1956	32.6	—
Data for 1974 and 1975		
Nanking[b]	50.6	1,296
Shanghai[c]	52.6	5,700
Survey of 150 cities[d]		
Comprehensive centers	50–55	n.a.
County towns	50–60	n.a.
Industrial centers	50	n.a.
Mining centers	35–45	n.a.
Regional transport and communication centers	50–55	n.a.
Special function cities	40	n.a.

n.a. Not available.

a. Weighted average using population figures for 1958 as weights.

b. Data refer to the nonagricultural population of Nanking.

c. Data appear to exclude Shanghai's farm population.

d. These data come from a survey in 1975 of 150 cities in eastern China from Heilungkiang to Fukien; 85 cities were taken as representative for purposes of compiling these figures.

Sources: Data for the 1950s, Christopher Howe, *Employment and Economic Growth in Urban China* (Cambridge, England: Cambridge University Press, 1971), p. 44. *Data for 1974 and 1975,* for Shanghai, BBC, no. W792 (1974), A4; remaining data were supplied by David M. Brown, University of Toronto, from lecture notes taken at the Department of Geography, University of Nanking, May 24, 1978.

employment opportunities, and in cities performing unspecified "special functions." On the basis of these data, an employment rate of 50 percent can be assumed for urban residents in 1975. Since unemployment in 1975 appears limited to less than 1 percent of the urban population (Table 2-7, below), this figure also provides an estimate of participation in the urban labor force in 1975.

Participation Rates in the Labor Force—Rural

Open unemployment does not appear as part of the Chinese rural scene either before or after 1949. Underutilization of labor does exist, however, mainly in the form of seasonal idleness. Under these circumstances, participation and employment rates are indistinguishable, and the number of workdays per man-year becomes the most useful indicator of the balance between the supply and demand for labor.

Participation rates in the rural labor force are difficult to measure. Chinese communes do not appear to use a clear and consistent definition of "labor force." When questioned by visitors, commune representatives cannot explain the precise meaning of statements such as "this commune has a population of 55,000 and a labor force (*lao-tung-li*) of 22,000."[17] Although some communes include part-time workers as fractional members of their labor force, it appears that the term "labor force" usually refers to the number of commune members who regularly earn work points (used to compute year-end shares of collective income) in collective activities; and that occasional participants such as housewives, old people, and students who work only during intervals of peak labor demand are typically excluded from enumeration as part of the rural labor force. As will be seen, however, employed persons can work more or fewer days each year, a fact that creates further problems of measurement.

Despite these uncertainties, available data on labor force as a percentage of rural population fall consistently in the neighborhood of 45 percent. Peter Schran's review of rural surveys showed that the share of employed persons in China's peasant population was approximately 46 to 48 percent during both the 1930s and the 1950s.[18] Extreme labor mobilization associated with the Great Leap Forward (1958–60) undoubtedly increased these rates, but only temporarily.

S.J. Burki's survey of thirteen communes in 1965 found that 40.2 percent of the 287,111 inhabitants were classified as "able-bodied workers." In addition, at least one unit had released workers to

17. This was the impression of the American Rural Small-Scale Industry Delegation sponsored by the Committee on Scholarly Communication with the People's Republic of China, National Academy of Sciences, of which the author was a member. This group visited China during June and July 1975.

18. Peter Schran, *The Development of Chinese Agriculture, 1950–1959* (Urbana: University of Illinois Press, 1969), p. 53.

TABLE 2-5. POPULATION, LABOR FORCE, AND LABOR FORCE PARTICIPATION
IN SELECTED RURAL AREAS, 1975

Locality	Population	Labor force	Participation rate (percent)
County and province			
Hsiyang (Shansi)	200,000	78,000	39.0
Wuhsi (Kiangsu)	900,000	350,000	38.9
Total for county data	1,100,000	428,000	38.9
Commune or brigade (county and province)			
Anp'ing commune (Hsiyang)	10,000	3,800	38.0
Ch'iliying commune (Hsinhsiang, Honan)	55,000	30,000	54.5
Holei commune (Wuhsi)	15,002	7,000	46.7
Kaochuang commune (Hui, Honan)	42,000	13,000	20.9
Malu commune (Chiating, Shanghai)	28,000	18,000	64.3
Meits'un commune (Wuhsi)	38,817	10,200	33.1
Shihp'in brigade (Hsiyang)	1,970	640	32.5
Yangshih commune (Wuhsi)	22,000	10,500	47.7
Total for commune and brigades	204,789	93,140	45.5
Combined total[a]	1,225,000	489,000	39.9

a. Commune and brigade units located in Hsiyang and Wuhsi counties are excluded from these totals to avoid double counting.

Source: Author's trip notes as a member of the Rural Small-Scale Industry Delegation, June–July 1975.

urban employers. These were excluded from enumeration among the commune's labor force but apparently were included in the population total, thus imparting a downward bias to the 40.2 percent overall participation rate.[19]

Data collected by the Rural Small-Scale Industries Delegation in 1975 appear in Table 2-5. Participation rates for several communes and brigades average out to 45.5 percent; figures for two counties give rates slightly below 40 percent. These data, like Burki's, may contain a downward bias because of the temporary migration of commune members to nearby cities. This is especially likely in the suburban communes located near industrial centers such as Shanghai and Wusih. Labor force data for eight units observed by a Wheat Studies group that visited China in 1976 show an average

19. Shahid Javed Burki, *A Study of Chinese Communes, 1965* (Cambridge, Mass.: East Asian Research Center, Harvard University, 1969), pp. 50–97.

TABLE 2-6. RURAL POPULATION AND EMPLOYMENT, BY SEX, 1957 AND 1975
(millions of persons)

Category	1957			1975		
	Total	Male	Female	Total	Male	Female
1. National population	632.7	319.4	313.3	933.7	469.7	464.0
2. Rural population						
A. Total	540.7	273.0	267.7	758.7	381.6	377.1
B. Working age	263.1	137.9	125.2	368.7	193.2	175.5
3. Rural employment						
A. Total	243.3	137.9	105.4	341.4	193.2	148.2
B. Sex composition						
(percent)	100.0	56.7	43.3	100.0	56.6	43.4
4. Working-age population						
A. Percent employed	92.5	100.0	84.2	92.6	100.0	84.4
B. Percent not employed	7.5	0	15.8	7.4	0	15.6
5. Rural births per nonworking						
female of working age	0.97			0.83		

Sources: *Line 1*, unpublished worksheet provided by John S. Aird, intermediate model, January 1. *Line 2A*, derived by subtracting estimated urban population (92 million in 1957, 175 million in 1975) from the total and applying the national sex ratio to the rural populace. *Line 2B*, derived by assuming that rural age structure is identical with the national figures shown in Aird's worksheet. In this analysis Aird defines the working-age population to include males aged 16 to 55 years and females aged 16 to 50 years. *Line 3A*, rural labor force is assumed to be 45 percent of rural population (see text). All working age males are assumed to be employed. Female employment is derived as a residual. *Line 4A*, quotient of lines 3A and 2B expressed in percentages. *Line 5*, total births are calculated from the estimated number of births per thousand persons shown in John S. Aird, "Population Growth in the People's Republic of China," p. 467, and the population totals in line 1. The share of rural areas in total births is assumed to equal their share in total population.

participation rate of 42.8 percent for a population of just under 150,000 persons.[20]

These fragmentary data give the impression that rural participation rates in the mid-1970s are not significantly different from those of the 1950s and suggest a rural participation rate of 45 percent for both 1957 and 1975. In view of the widespread impression that collectivization has raised female participation rates in the countryside, this may be seen as a surprising conclusion. Table 2-6

20. Calculated from Virgil A. Johnson and Halsey L. Beemer, Jr., eds., *Wheat in the People's Republic of China* (Washington, D.C.: National Academy of Sciences, 1977), p. 157.

explores the implications of this result for the sex composition of the rural labor force in 1957 and 1975. With use of Aird's estimates of age and sex structure, employment figures for rural females are calculated as residuals on the basis of a 45 percent overall partici-pation rate by assuming that all males of working age (16 to 55 years) are employed. Although this assumption overstates the pro-portion of male employment, the resulting employment figures for females are high. For both 1957 and 1975, a 45 percent overall par-ticipation rate implies that no fewer than 84 percent of rural fe-males aged from 16 to 50 years were regularly employed.[21] Since the number of nonworking females of working age corresponds closely with the number of rural births in both years, it is evident that female participation rates were already near their natural limit during the 1950s. A rural participation rate of 45 percent for both 1957 and 1975 carries no unacceptable implications with regard to the sex composition of the rural work force. This 45 percent rate is therefore applied both to 1957 and 1975 rural population totals.

The Total Labor Force

The foregoing discussion makes it possible to construct estimates of China's urban, rural, and overall labor force in the benchmark years 1957 and 1975. The results appear in Table 2-7. These calcu-lations use the figures for national and urban population and for urban and rural participation rates obtained in the manner de-scribed above; rural population is derived as a residual by sub-tracting the urban from the national population totals.

Although open unemployment does not appear as a significant phenomenon in rural China, urban unemployment does exist. In the absence of comprehensive data, assumptions regarding its magnitude are needed to complete the task of estimating the size of the labor force. The discussion in Chapters One and Five sug-gests that open urban unemployment amounted to no more than 1 million persons during 1975. If one works backwards from 1975 by

21. Marina Thorborg, "Chinese Employment Policy in 1949-78 with Special Emphasis on Women in Rural Production," in U.S. Congress, Joint Economic Committee, *Chinese Economy Post-Mao*, vol. 1, cites reports indicating that from 65 to 80 percent of working age rural women were employed in agriculture during 1956 and 1957 (pp. 572–73) and guesses at a comparable figure of 70 percent in 1974 (p. 584).

TABLE 2-7. ESTIMATES OF CHINA'S LABOR FORCE, 1957 AND 1975
(millions of persons)

	Version A		Version B	
Category	1957	1975	1957	1975
Total population	628	898	633	934
Urban sector				
Population	92	175	92	175
Percent employed	33	50	33	50
Rural sector				
Population	536	723	541	759
Percent employed	45	45	45	45
Labor force				
Urban employed	30.4	87.5	30.4	87.5
Rural employed	241.2	325.4	243.4	341.6
Urban unemployed	7.8	1.0	7.8	1.0
Total labor force	279.4	413.9	281.6	430.1
Increase in labor force, 1957–75				
Urban		50.3		50.3
Percent share in increase		37.4		33.9
Rural		84.2		98.2
Percent share in increase		62.6		66.1
Total		134.5		148.5
Average annual labor force increase,				
1957–75 (percent)				
Urban		4.8		4.8
Rural		1.7		1.9
Total		2.2		2.4

Sources: Tables 2-1 and 2-6 and discussion in the text.

assuming that half of the increase in urban employment rates between 1957 and 1975 was the result of reduced levels of involuntary unemployment, urban unemployment during 1957 may
be calculated as 8.5 percent of the urban population. This is an
arbitrary assumption, and the resulting figure represents no more
than a guess that is intended to give some idea of the order of
magnitude of urban unemployment during 1957.

With these assumptions, two sets of labor force estimates can
be obtained from the alternative population series shown in Table
2-1. Version A, based on population figures given in Chinese
sources, shows that the labor force rose by 134.5 million, or 48
percent, between 1957 and 1975, with 63 percent of the increment
occurring in rural areas. Version B, based on Aird's population
estimates—which, it will be recalled, are thought to give a more

realistic picture of actual demographic conditions—shows a labor force increment of 148.5 million, or 52 percent, between 1957 and 1975, with 66 percent of the increment occurring in rural areas.

Although the results shown in Table 2-7 incorporate a variety of assumptions, some of which undoubtedly contain significant errors, several conclusions can be drawn from the data that do not appear sensitive either to possible errors in assumptions or to variations between the underlying population figures. The broad accuracy of the labor force estimates for 1957 is confirmed by an article in which a vice chairman of the State Planning Commission says that the number of labor force units in 1957 was approximately 260 million, or within 10 percent of either of the estimates shown in Table 2-7.[22]

These results show that between 1957 and 1975, China's labor force rose at a rate equal to, or perhaps slightly greater than, the rate of population growth. This rise produced a large increase in the supply of labor, most of which occurred in the countryside. Given the absence of large-scale open unemployment in either urban or rural areas during the 1970s, there can be no doubt that employment opportunities have also risen substantially between 1957 and the mid-1970s, and that the increase in demand for labor has also included a large rural component. The data in Table 2-7 point strongly to the conclusion that China's farm sector absorbed very large numbers of new workers between 1957 and 1975. This implication is confirmed by estimates of the level and growth of nonagricultural employment.

Nonagricultural Employment

Estimates of nonagricultural employment in 1957 and 1975 are shown in Table 2-8. The derivation of these figures, which exclude part-time employees and workers in farmland capital construction (such as land leveling, reclamation, and terracing) and water conservancy projects, is explained in Appendix B. Although these results incorporate a variety of assumptions, they appear to provide

22. Wang Kuang-wei, "How to Organize Agricultural Labor Power," *Chi-hua ching-chi* [Planned Economy], no. 8 (1957), translated in ECMM, no. 100 (1958), p. 12.

reasonable approximations to the actual numbers of workers in the nonagricultural branches of China's economy. A 1978 report indicating that the number of "workers and employees"—a category that includes "personnel of enterprises owned by the whole people [that is, state enterprises] . . . as well as those who draw wages from the government"—was approximately 90 million checks closely with the 1975 figure of eighty-eight and eight-tenths million workers and employees derived in Table B-1.[23] Another

TABLE 2-8. NONAGRICULTURAL RURAL EMPLOYMENT, 1957 AND 1975
(millions of persons)

Sector	1957	1975
Industry		
State sector, including utilities	8.0	25.0
Collective	0	14.3
Handicrafts	6.6	0.3
Construction[a]	1.9	6.5
Transport, posts, and communication	4.4	8.9
Trade, food and drink, finance, banking, and insurance	8.4	18.0
Personal services	0.5	1.1
Health	1.9	6.6
Education and culture	2.7	7.6
Government administration and mass organizations	2.9	6.2
Salt	0.5	1.1
Fishing	1.5	1.2
Civilian nonagricultural employment	39.3	96.8
Military personnel	3.0	3.5
Total nonagricultural employment	42.3	100.3

a. Excludes employment in farmland improvement and water conservancy.

Sources: For 1957, John P. Emerson, Nonagricultural Employment in Mainland China, 1949–1958 (Washington, D.C.: U.S. Government Printing Office, 1965), p. 128; and Ta-chung Liu and Kung-chia Yeh, The Economy of the Chinese Mainland (Princeton, N.J.: Princeton University Press, 1965), p. 209. For 1975, Appendix B.

23. The 1978 figure is from a statement by Teng Ying-ch'ao (the wife of the late premier, Chou En-lai), who reported that the number of female workers and employees had increased fifty times from the 1949 level of 600,000 and now accounted for one-third of the national total, which would therefore be 0.6 · 50 · 3, or 90 million (FBIS, October 24, 1978, p. E2). The definition of workers and employees is from Ch'en Chih-ho, "The Question of Groups Included in Labor Force Statistics," Chihua yü t'ung-chi [Planning and Statistics], no. 11 (1959), translated in John P. Emerson, Nonagricultural Employment in Mainland China, 1949–1958 (Washington, D.C.: U.S. Government Printing Office, 1965), pp. 195–96. The estimated number of workers and employees for 1975 is shown in Table B-1.

1978 report states that "in all, 17 million commune members work in commune- and brigade-run enterprises." Since output of these enterprises rose by 22 percent during 1975–76 and by 49.6 percent during the first half of 1977, the figure of 17 million workers in rural collective industry seems consistent with the present estimate of 14.2 million workers in all collective industries for 1975.[24]

The Agricultural Labor Force and Employment

The estimates shown in Tables 2-7 and 2-8 permit derivation of estimates of China's agricultural labor force in 1957 and 1975 by subtracting nonagricultural employment and urban unemployment from the overall labor force totals. Since open unemployment appears to be a purely urban phenomenon, the categories "agricultural labor force" and "agricultural employment" are identical. This assumption, however, conceals possible changes in the annual number of days worked by agricultural laborers. This subject is taken up in Chapter Four, in which it is shown that the average number of days worked is substantially higher, and the extent of seasonal idleness correspondingly smaller, in 1975 than in 1957.

The figures for China's agricultural labor force presented in Table 2-9 amply confirm the expectation of large increases in farm employment between 1957 and 1975. Because the calculations in version B seem more realistic than those in version A and because of possible overestimation of nonagricultural employment in 1957 (see Appendix B), it is entirely plausible to conclude that agriculture and subsidiary farming activities, farmland construction, and water conservancy have among them absorbed nearly 100 million new workers between 1957 and 1975, representing an increase of 42 percent in the agricultural work force (version B). The general validity of these results, which indicate an agricultural work force of from 313 to 329 million men and women in 1975, is confirmed by recent Chinese statements that "some 300 million able-bodied

24. The 1978 report of employment and of output growth for 1975/76 (fifteen provinces only) and for 1976/77 is in FBIS, January 6, 1978, p. E17.

TABLE 2-9. THE AGRICULTURAL LABOR FORCE, 1957 AND 1975
(millions of persons)

Category	Version A 1957	Version A 1975	Version B 1957	Version B 1975
1. *Total labor force*	279.4	413.9	281.6	430.1
2. *Less* Nonagricultural employment *and*	42.3	100.3	42.3	100.3
Urban unemployment	7.8	1.0	7.8	1.0
3. *Equals* Agricultural labor force	229.3	312.6	231.5	328.8
Increase, 1957–75	83.3		97.3	
Average annual growth rate, 1957–75 (percent)	1.7		2.0	

Sources: Tables 2-7 and 2-8.

people take part in agricultural production" and that "our country has an agricultural labor force of 300 million people."[25]

The annual growth rate of either 1.7 or 2.0 percent implied in these figures is high by recent international standards. Regional data for developing countries covering the period 1950-70 show that only eastern Africa experienced so rapid an expansion of its agricultural labor force. In South Asia, where man-land ratios more closely resemble those in China, the agricultural work force grew at estimated yearly rates of 0.81 percent during 1950-60 and 1.16 percent during 1960-70.[26] This comparison shows that the challenge of agricultural labor absorption in China was large in relative as well as absolute terms.

How has China's agricultural sector managed to absorb nearly 100 million new workers within a period of less than two decades? This question provides the focus for Chapter Four. Before probing into that question, however, the subject of industrial employment deserves attention, since industry is the sector responsible for the

25. FBIS, October 4, 1978, p. E18, and August 15, 1978, p. E21.
26. World Bank, *Development Issues in Rural Non-farm Employment* (Washington, 1977), Table A-2. Note that the absence of major shifts in the sex composition of

largest single increment in nonagricultural employment in the years after 1957.

China's rural labor force (Table 2-6) and the age structure of the entire population (John S. Aird, "Population Growth in the People's Republic of China," pp. 468–73) indicates that conversion of the present labor force figures to man-equivalents would not substantially alter the conclusions reached in the text.

Chapter Three

Determinants of Industrial Employment

RAPID EXPANSION OF THE SIZE and technological sophistication of the industrial sector has been an outstanding feature of China's economic growth since 1949. Industrial production has risen at an average annual rate of approximately 10 percent for three decades, and the share of industry in total national output, which stood at 15 to 20 percent in the early 1950s, had risen to more than 40 percent in the early 1970s. Important changes have occurred in the structure as well as the size of the industrial sector. Engineering and petroleum have replaced textiles and food processing as the largest contributors to value of output. Metallurgy and chemicals have also enlarged their share of total output at the expense of older industries based on an earlier generation of raw materials.[1] Considerable insight into the effect of industrial growth on

1. The growth of industrial output is calculated from the estimates of the gross value of industrial output shown in Table 3-1. Output shares are taken from estimates of gross domestic product compiled in Dwight H. Perkins, "Issues in the Estimation of China's National Product," in *Quantitative Measures of China's Economic Output*, ed. Alexander Eckstein (Ann Arbor: University of Michigan Press, forthcoming), Table 7. Gross output, which is called "global output" in some studies of the Soviet bloc countries, includes the value of intermediate goods consumed in the production process and can therefore lead to highly misleading measures of growth of industrial output. In the Soviet case, officially compiled gross- or global-value data typically grow more rapidly than industrial value added. Chinese gross-value figures, however, appear free of upward bias, and can therefore be used as indicators of the growth of value added in industry. For further discussion, see Thomas G. Rawski, "Chinese Industrial Production, 1952–1971," *Review of Economics and Statistics*, vol. 55, no. 2 (1973), pp. 169–81, and "China's Industrial Performance, 1949–1973," in *Quantitative Measures of China's Economic Output*.

the size of China's industrial labor force can be gained, after a brief quantitative overview, by examining the political, technological, and institutional determinants of industrial employment.

Patterns of Industrial Employment, 1957–75

The estimates compiled in Table 2-8 indicate that industrial employment nearly tripled between 1957 and 1975, with the number of workers in manufacturing, mining, and utilities rising from less than 15 million to nearly 40 million in less than two decades. In view of industry's great overall contribution to China's recent economic growth, it is not surprising to find that it accounts for a large share of incremental nonagricultural employment. Data compiled in Appendix B and summarized in Table 2-8 show that the state sector of industry alone absorbed 29 percent of new nonagricultural employees during 1957–75. Employment in handicrafts and in collective enterprises operated by rural communes and production brigades and by urban neighborhood groups absorbed another 14 percent of new nonagricultural employees, bringing the combined share of state and collective industry in incremental nonagricultural employment to 43 percent during 1957–75.

If, however, industrial job creation is related to the estimated labor force increment of 148.5 million persons (Table 2-7), its effect appears much smaller. New industrial employment absorbed only 11 to 17 percent of estimated labor force growth during 1957–75, with the exact percentage depending on the definition of industry. If these figures are compared with industry's much larger share in incremental product, which amounted to approximately 59 percent for 1957–71, it becomes evident that in China, as in many other developing nations, the effect of industrial expansion on employment has been modest.[2]

2. Industry's share in incremental product is calculated from Dwight H. Perkins, "Growth and Changing Structure of China's Twentieth-Century Economy," in *China's Modern Economy in Historical Perspective*, ed. Dwight H. Perkins (Stanford, Calif.: Stanford University Press, 1975), p. 161.

TABLE 3-1. NATIONAL AND SELECTED REGIONAL LABOR PRODUCTIVITY
IN INDUSTRY, 1952–75

Category	Value of gross output (billions of yuan)	Industrial employment (millions)	Gross output per worker (yuan)
	National totals		
1952	34.330[a]	12.7[a]	2,703
1957	78.390[a]	14.6[a]	5,369
1975	378.480	39.6	9,558
State sector	325.493[b]	25.0	13,020
Collective sector	52.987[b]	14.6[a]	3,629
"Five small industries"	25.909[c]	4.5	5,758
	Provincial figures		
Liaoning			
1955	7.929[a, d]	0.996[a]	7,961
1975	44.202	2.0	22,101
Peking			
1955	1.291[a]	0.129[a]	10,008
1975	19.607	1.0	19,607
Shanghai			
1955	9.047[a, d]	0.599[a]	15,104
1975	55.707	2.3	24,220
Tientsin			
1955	2.853[a, d]	0.157[a]	18,172
1975	18.748	1.0	18,748

Note: Figures for 1952–57 are in 1952 prices; those for 1975 are in 1957 prices except for estimated output of the "Five Small Industries," which is based on 1952 prices. Comparison between data in 1957 prices and earlier figures in 1952 prices understates actual growth of output value or productivity.

a. These measures of output or employment specifically include a handicraft component.

b. Chang Ch'un-ch'iao, "On Exercising All-Round Dictatorship over the Bourgeoisie," *Peking Review*, vol. 14 (1975), p. 6, states that the output shares of state and collective industry for 1973 were 86 and 14 percent of the industrial total. The same proportions are used to decompose output for 1975.

c. Obtained by applying the 30.4 percent rise in producer industry output estimated for 1972–75 in U.S. National Foreign Assessment Center, *China: Economic Indicators* (Washington, D.C.: Central Intelligence Agency, 1977), p. 15, to the estimate for 1972 shown in Table 3-7. The term "five small industries" refers to the small-plant component of the following industries: building materials, chemical fertilizer, energy (coal mining and hydropower), iron and steel, and machinery.

d. Derived from data on the gross value of factory output, which excludes handicrafts, by assuming that the ratio of total industrial output to factory output alone was the same for 1955 as for 1956 or 1957.

Sources: *Value of gross output*, Robert M. Field, Nicholas R. Lardy, and John P. Emerson, *A Reconstruction of the Gross Value of Industrial Output by Province in the People's Republic of China: 1949–73* (Washington, D.C.: U.S. Department of Commerce, 1975), pp. 6, 17, and 20–21; and *Provincial Industrial Output in the People's Republic of China: 1949–75* (Washington, D.C.: U.S. Department of Commerce, 1976), pp. 11, 17, and 20. *Employment*, national total for 1952 is from John P. Emerson, *Nonagricultural Employment in Mainland China: 1949–1958* (Washington, D.C.:

TABLE 3-1 *(continued)*

U.S. Department of Commerce, 1965), p. 128; for 1957 and 1975, see Tables 2-8 and C-1. *Provincial data for Liaoning and Shanghai* are from Tables B-3 and B-4; *for Peking and Tientsin,* see Nai-ruenn Chen, *Chinese Economic Statistics* (Chicago: Aldine, 1967), p. 483; and *Chung-kung yen-chiu* [Studies on Chinese Communism], September 1976, p. 20.

Another aspect of the process of industrial job creation emerges from Table 3-1, which presents available national and regional data for industrial output, employment, and labor productivity. These figures reveal a strong upward trend in labor productivity. The most plausible explanation of this trend lies in the gradual process of industrial capital deepening that began with the influx of Soviet equipment and technology during the 1950s.

Although existing data relating to capital stock and investment are sparse, the rough estimates presented in Table 3-2 for the growth of output, employment, and fixed assets in the producer-goods industries indicate a rapid increase in fixed assets per worker and after 1957 a parallel rise in the ratio of capital to gross output for the dominant sector of industry.[3]

The degree of labor intensity in Chinese industry remains much higher than in U.S., European, or Japanese industry, but the direction of change is consistently toward substitution of capital for labor. This is evident even in rural industry, whose origins are linked with the capital-saving policies associated with the Great Leap Forward of 1958–60. After investigating approximately fifty plants during the summer of 1975, an American Small-Scale Industry Delegation noted that "[t]ime and again we were told by factory representatives of the efforts they were making to eliminate manual, highly labor-intensive methods and to substitute mechanized methods. To some degree these modern methods seem to be desired for their own sake, but often the firm appeared to be under pressure to expand output without any major increases in employment. China's rural small-scale industries remain highly labor intensive when compared to urban enterprises in China, and the contrast is even greater with similar industries in the United

3. The share of China's producer industries in the value of gross industrial output has risen from about one-third in 1952 and one-half in 1957 to more than three-quarters in the mid-1970s. See Rawski, "Industrial Performance," in *Quantitative Measures,* Table H-12.

TABLE 3-2. AVERAGE ANNUAL PERCENTAGE GROWTH OF OUTPUT, EMPLOYMENT, AND FIXED CAPITAL IN PRODUCER-GOODS INDUSTRIES, 1952–65 AND 1957–65

Period	Value of gross output[a]	Employment	Fixed capital
1952–65	17.5–20.1	3.6–8.3	14.2–18.9
1957–65	12.4–16.5	0.0–7.4	19.5–27.5

a. Excludes handicrafts.

Source: Thomas G. Rawski, "The Growth of Producer Industries, 1900–1971," in China's Modern Economy in Historical Perspective, ed. Dwight H. Perkins (Stanford, Calif.: Stanford University Press, 1975), pp. 222–23.

States. But most Chinese efforts at the moment appear to be directed not at exploiting the employment potential of labor-intensive techniques, but toward modernizing those techniques in a capital-intensive direction."[4]

What factors are responsible for the steady increase in capital intensity that is characteristic of Chinese industry in all periods save that of the Great Leap? Why have investment policies not placed greater emphasis on labor-using, employment-creating production methods?

Economic Objectives and Industrial Structure

China's economic ambitions were well summarized in an address in 1975 by Premier Chou En-lai, who called on his fellow citizens to build plans "to accomplish the comprehensive modernization of agriculture, industry, national defense, and science and technology before the end of the century, so that our national economy will be advancing in the front ranks of the world."[5]

In a large economy that must inevitably supply most of its own intermediate and capital goods, it is the industrial sector—and especially engineering, chemicals, metallurgy, mining, and other branches of the producer sector—whose output is essential to the transformation of society's production possibilities. As one Chi-

4. Dwight Perkins and others, Rural Small-Scale Industry in the People's Republic of China (Berkeley: University of California Press, 1977), p. 8.

5. Peking Review, no. 4 (1975), p. 23.

nese writer observed, it is these branches of industry which use "modern technology to equip agriculture, industry, the military, and science for achieving the modernization of all these sectors."[6]

To the natural propensity of a continental nation to rely primarily on domestic sources of supply, there must be added the experience of China's present leaders in their guerrilla days before 1949 and, more recently, in the years following the abrupt withdrawal of Soviet technicians in 1960. Chinese economists fully understand that there are economic gains to be derived from domestic and international specialization and division of labor. The history of these two periods shows, however, that isolation and autarky can provide sufficient incentive to seek solutions to problems that would never be confronted if outside supplies could be obtained. This view, which is supported by the experiences of the advanced industrial nations during World War II, has led Chinese planners to limit dependence on external supplies—from domestic as well as foreign sources—to situations in which local products cannot meet the quality, cost, or time requirements of current demand. Showing an awareness of the costs of excessive specialization and of the potential benefits of isolation, as well as of the traditional benefits of interregional and international division of labor, the Chinese policy of economic self-reliance has brought about an investment program that seeks to develop a broad range of industries at the regional as well as the national level.

This decision—to limit dependence on external supplies of industrial commodities by pursuing a broad-ranging program of import substitution—obliged China to commit a large share of its investment resources to the development of steel, fuel, engineering, and other basic industries having a myriad of interindustrial links to other sectors of the economy. Available production technologies in most of these industries have relatively high degrees of capital intensity. This emerges clearly from Table 3-3, which provides separate rankings for various industries relative to their fixed assets per worker and output growth. The correlation between capital intensity and rapidity of growth is striking: with the exception of paper, a capital-intensive but slowly growing indus-

6. Wang Hu-sheng, "Several Problems of Classifying Heavy and Light Industry," *Ching-chi yen-chiu* [Economic Research], no. 4 (1963), p. 18.

TABLE 3-3. CAPITAL INTENSITY AND OUTPUT GROWTH,
BY INDUSTRIAL SECTOR, 1952–1972

Sectors ranked in order of decreasing capital-labor ratio, 1952–53	Productive fixed assets per production worker (yuan)	Sectors ranked in order of output growth, 1952–72	Gross output, 1972 (1952 = 1)
1. Electric power	51,197	1. Petroleum	76.4
2. Petroleum	24,945[a]	2. Machinery	61.8
3. Paper	9,528	3. Chemicals	35.4
4. Ferrous metallurgy	9,251	4. Ferrous metallurgy	16.0
5. Chemicals	8,120	5. Electric power	15.2
Average for all industry	5,656	Average for all industry	11.6
6. Coal	5,029	6. Building materials	10.4
7. Textiles	4,806	7. Paper	6.3
8. Machinery	4,750[b]	8. Coal	5.8
9. Food processing	3,373	9. Food processing	2.9
10. Building materials	2,431	10. Textiles	2.8
11. Timber	1,210	11. Timber	1.5

Note: Assets per worker are 1952–53 figures for state and joint state-private enterprises, categories that include large factories and exclude small handicraft workshops. Output figures are for the gross value of factory output (excluding handicrafts) based on 1952 prices.

a. Crude oil extraction.

b. Data refer to metal processing, which includes manufacture of metal products and repair work as well as manufacture of machinery.

Source: Thomas G. Rawski, China's Transition to Industrialism: Producer Goods and Economic Development in the Twentieth Century (Ann Arbor: University of Michigan Press, forthcoming), Table 4.9.

try, and machinery, a relatively labor-intensive industry with a high growth rate, all industries with above average capital intensity grow at above average rates, whereas sectors with relatively low capital intensity experience below average growth. As a result, structural change alone can be identified as an important cause of capital deepening within the industrial sector.

Within individual enterprises, the gradual adoption of mechanization has tended to raise capital per worker and probably the ratio of capital to output as well. Reasons for mechanization, which include worker pressure for relief from physically onerous duties and the widespread availability of machine shops, are discussed below. The results of mechanization are visible throughout industry: in fertilizer and cement plants that plan to install automatic bagging devices to limit the workers' exposure to dust and fumes; in textile enterprises that provide mobile seats so that individual workers can tend more machines; and in machinery plants in which overhead cranes, conveyer belts, and pneumatic tools are used to reduce manual labor in assembly and intraplant transport.

Several aspects of China's industrial strategy have, however, partially offset the trend toward capital deepening. Rural industrialization, for example, which gained national prominence from the campaign to produce steel in "backyard furnaces" during the Great Leap Forward, was carried on in part because of its promise of low capital requirements, a promise that the experience of two decades has only partially fulfilled. As the output of rural industry has grown, tiny units with low capital-labor ratios have been abandoned in favor of substantial plants employing hundreds of workers, large complements of machinery and equipment, and technical processes that on the whole offer few surprises to Western engineers. Although capital per worker is less in small-scale rural plants than in large-scale urban units, the more successful rural plants often have capital-labor ratios that exceed the relevant sectoral averages for the 1950s. Furthermore, Jon Sigurdson has found that investment costs per ton of capacity are often larger in relatively small plants.[7] All of this leads to the conclusion that, in assessing the contribution of rural industry to China's economic development, the capital-saving contribution of small plants is of relatively little significance.

A second area of industrial policy that may have helped to slow the growth of capital intensity involves efforts to separate, or decompose, advanced technologies so that some operations can be carried out with labor-intensive techniques without affecting product quality. Reports by visitors who discover "an incredible mixture of ancient and modern" production techniques, with some operations "done in a very elementary way while others were tooled with highly sophisticated machinery" indicate the degree to which Chinese manufacturers of engineering and electronics products have succeeded in grafting labor-intensive ancillary operations onto a technological core of more advanced and capital-intensive processes.[8] It appears, however, that opportunities for

7. Jon Sigurdson, *Rural Industrialization in China* (Cambridge, Mass.: Harvard University Press, 1977), chap. 4.

8. Quotations from "Report of SMMT [Society of Motor Manufacturers and Traders] Trade Mission to the People's Republic of China, 2–17 November 1973" (Lon-

such technological decomposition exist only in certain industries. Industries with continuous processes, such as petrochemicals and cement, and those with major scale economies, such as ferrous metallurgy and electric power, seemingly offer little scope for cost reduction through partial substitution of labor for capital in peripheral activities. Furthermore, a recent flood of complaints about product quality and overall efficiency in the farm machinery sector, which is among the leading practitioners of technological decomposition, suggests that reductions in capital-intensity may carry a significant cost.[9]

Additional policies that have acted to reduce capital requirements in industry are those designed to increase the overall level of resource utilization. These programs include transfer of secondhand machinery to small enterprises; setting industrial prices high enough so that even the most backward producers can aspire to break even; exploitation of resource deposits that are too small to permit the use of mechanized techniques; and recruitment of urban housewives to staff enterprises that use waste and scrap from larger factories. Each of these policies has other objectives and effects, but each has encouraged activities that tend to reduce the average capital requirement per worker and per unit of industrial output.

Despite the presence of factors tending to move industry in the direction of more capital-extensive production techniques, the trend over the past twenty-five years has been one of increasing capital intensity. This is evident both from limited statistical data and from the observations of visitors familiar with Chinese factories. Recent discussions by Chinese economists and officials make it clear that this trend will continue. Growing imports of complete plants and industrial equipment from Europe, North America, and Japan will contribute to increased capital intensity both directly and, if imports serve as models for domestic producers to imitate, indirectly as well.

don, 1974; processed), p. 32; and David Scott, "China Opens Doors for Rare View of Auto Production," *Automotive Engineering*, vol. 82, no. 8 (1974), p. 30.

9. Vice Premier Yü Ch'iu-li's "Summation Report on Agricultural Mechanization" in January 1978, translated in FBIS, January 31, 1978, pp. E6–25, is representative of recent critical comment about the state of China's farm machinery industry.

Reform plans for industries supplied by domestic producers also appear directed toward increased capital intensity. In the farm machinery sector Vice Premier Yü Ch'iu-li has called for "extensive utilization of highly effective and specialized equipment, the organization of assemblyline methods and automation in production, and the improvement of enterprise management and technology," which he expects will "greatly enhance the quality and quantity of farm machinery, considerably reduce the consumption of manpower and materials, and significantly lower production costs."[10] In the lagging coal industry Vice Premier Teng Hsiao-p'ing has called for a "great mining campaign" to construct new mines, develop capable leadership, and "aggressively develop advanced and large mining equipment, transportation equipment, and other mining machines"—a capital-intensive prescription that specifically rejects the alternative of large increases in employment.[11] Plans for accelerated development of consumer industries with relatively low capital coefficients will slow, but cannot reverse, the trend toward capital deepening.[12]

Technology and Employment in Three Types of Industrial Units

Given the general pattern of industrial investment, growth, and mix of output, what determines the level of employment at the

10. Ibid., p. E13.

11. "Some Problems in Speeding Up Industrial Development," translated in *Issues and Studies*, vol. 13, no. 7 (1977), pp. 103–04. Hsiao Han, the minister of coal industry, states that "the key to speedy development of the coal industry lies in mechanization" ("Developing Coal Industry at High Speed," *Peking Review*, no. 8 [1978], p. 7), while an editorial in *People's Daily* observed that "we should not resort to great increases in manpower to quicken the development of the coal industry" (FBIS [December 13, 1977], p. E15).

12. Chinese sources indicate that output of light industry, including textiles, processed foods, and other consumer manufactures, is expected to grow at an annual rate of 12 percent during 1976–85. Although this exceeds the 10 percent annual growth rate projected for the entire industrial sector, much of the added output is to come "from fuller utilization of capacity and more efficient use of inputs" rather than from new plants. See U.S. National Foreign Assessment Center, *China: In Pursuit of Economic Modernization* (Washington, D.C.: Central Intelligence Agency, 1978), pp. 8 and 14.

enterprise level? Insight into Chinese industrial technology can be gained by considering the character and contribution of three types of industrial units that have figured prominently in China's industrial achievements during successive periods: the large Soviet-aid projects that dominated the investment program under the First Five-Year Plan (FFYP; 1953–57); smaller units (most inherited from the Republican era of 1911–49) that attained technical leadership in some industrial sectors during the 1960s by substituting experience and entrepreneurship for capital equipment; and the revived and expanded rural industries that since the mid-1960s have begun to forge increasingly close ties between industry and agriculture.

Soviet-assisted projects of the First Five-Year Plan

China's First Five-Year Plan sought to implement a strategy of balanced growth by developing a group of large, modern producer-goods enterprises that would cater primarily to demand generated within the emerging heavy industry complex. The core of the plan consisted of about 150 Soviet-aided investment projects for which the Soviets provided designs, equipment, engineers, and repayable loans.[13]

These plants were large, integrated, and capital intensive. As can be seen from the data in Table 3-4, each of 154 projects was expected to absorb an average of more than 70 million yuan during 1953–57 alone (many were not completed until later). Together with 143 ancillary projects, these undertakings absorbed more than half of all industrial investment undertaken during the FFYP years. These projects included a major expansion of the Japanese-built steel complex at Anshan in the northeast, construction of new steelworks at Wuhan in central China and at Paot'ou in Inner Mongolia, development of a number of giant machinery plants in Shenyang, Harbin, and other cities in the northeast, and development of a new industrial complex adjoining the north China city of Loyang. Several projects were enormous, with budgets for invest-

13. *1967 Fei-ch'ing nien-pao* [1967 Yearbook of Chinese Communism] (Taipei: Fei-ch'ing yen-chiu tsa-chih-she, 1967), pp. 850–54, gives a list of projects that received foreign technical assistance during the FFYP period.

TABLE 3-4. NATIONAL AND REGIONAL INVESTMENT OUTLAY
AND PROJECT SIZE, 1953–57
(millions of current yuan)

Region	Percentage share in industrial gross output, 1957	Investment outlay, 1953–57		Average industrial project size
		Overall	Industry only	
National data				
Total	100.0	55,000[a]	25,030[a]	n.a.
Soviet-aided projects[b]	n.a.	n.a.	11,000	70.512
Support projects[b]	n.a.	n.a.	1,800	12.587
Provincial data				
Shanghai	19.5	1,371	500+[c]	0.200[c]
Liaoning	17.2	7,770	n.a.	n.a.
Shantung	5.1	n.a.	450+[d]	0.960[d]
Kwangtung	4.0	1,438	550[e]	0.835[f]
Kirin	3.3	2,150	1,716[g]	n.a.
Chekiang	3.0	n.a.	276[h]	n.a.
Hupei	2.5	2,210	802[i]	n.a.
Hunan	2.1	1,217	350+[j]	n.a.
Honan	1.9	2,590	654[k]	n.a.

n.a. Not available.

a. *Ten Great Years* (Peking: Foreign Language Press, 1960; reprint edition, Bellingham: Western Washington State College, 1974), p. 44.

b. Planned outlays shown in *First Five-Year Plan for Development of the National Economy of the People's Republic of China in 1953–1957* (Peking: Foreign Language Press, 1956), p. 39.

c. *Kuang-ming jih-pao* [Kuang-ming Daily], September 24, 1957. Average project outlay is for 600–700 projects undertaken in 1956.

d. *Ta-chung jih-pao* [Mass Daily], September 30, 1957; data refer to 1952–56.

e. *Wen-hui pao* [Wen-hui News], October 14, 1957.

f. *Ta-kung pao* [Impartial Daily], July 9, 1957, reported that 177 million yuan was to be spent on 212 major units during 1957.

g. Derived by applying the 79.8 percent share of industry in total investment for 1953–56 reported in *Chi-lin jih-pao* [Kirin Daily], August 9, 1957.

h. Data for 1949–57 in *Wen-hui pao* [Wen-hui News], September 19, 1957.

i. *Hu-pei jih-pao* [Hupei Daily], December 31, 1957, reported that 36.3 percent of the province's investments had gone to industry during 1953–57.

j. *Hsin Hu-nan pao* [New Hunan News], September 30, 1957.

k. Figure for 1953–56 only was reported in JMJP, March 31, 1957.

Source: Except as noted, data are from Nicholas R. Lardy, "Centralization and Decentralization in China's Fiscal Management," *China Quarterly*, 61 (1975), pp. 31 and 40. The gross output total for industry in 1957 (excluding handicrafts) amounted to 65.02 billion 1952 yuan.

ment exceeding aggregate industrial investment for whole provinces (see Table 3-5).

The figures in Table 3-5 also illustrate the capital intensity of the new plants. Comparison of data on employment and construction cost for individual new plants with sectoral and national data on fixed assets per production worker (Table 3-3) shows that capital

TABLE 3-5. FACTOR PROPORTIONS AND LABOR PRODUCTIVITY, SELECTED
SECTORS IN THE 1950s AND MAJOR FIRMS IN 1965
(yuan)

	Sectoral data, 1950s			Major firms, 1965		
	Fixed assets per worker[a]		Gross output per worker, 1956[a]	Number of workers	Construction cost per worker	Gross output per worker
Category	1952	1955				
All industry	5,656	6,835	12,172	—	—	—
Metal processing	4,750	6,035	12,569	—	—	—
Loyang Tractor	—	—	—	20,500[b]	19,512[c]	15,244[b]
T'aiyuan Heavy Machinery	—	—	—	7,200[d]	27,778[e]	n.a.
Wuhan Heavy Machinery	—	—	—	7,000[b]	18,571[f]	32,500[b]
Iron and steel	9,251	13,302	19,625	—	—	—
Wuhan Steel	—	—	—	35,000[b]	54,285[c]	28,571[b]

n.a. Not available. — Not applicable.
Note: Data for the 1950s are for state and joint state-private enterprises; small handicraft
workshops are excluded. Several of the items for 1965 are the midpoints between alternative
figures.
  a. Production workers only.
  b. Barry M. Richman, *Industrial Society in Communist China* (New York: Random House,
1969), pp. 154 and 827–33.
  c. *Chūgoku shiryō geppō* [China Materials Monthly], no. 95 (1956), pp. 17 and 21. Entry under
Wuhan Steel is the cost of constructing an unspecified steel facility with annual capacity of 1.5
million tons.
  d. *Chūgoku kagaku gijutsu no genjō bunseki* [Analysis of the Current State of China's Science
and Technology] (Tokyo: Shokoku kagaku gijutsu kenkyūkai, 1965), vol. 1, pp. 64–65.
  e. *1967 Fei-ch'ing nien-pao* [1967 Yearbook of Chinese Communism] (Taipei: Fei-ch'ing yen-
chiu tsa-chih she, 1967), p. 928.
  f. Furui Yoshimi and others, *Hōchū shoken* [A Visit to China] (Tokyo: n.p., 1959), p. 26.
  Source: Except as noted, data are from Nai-ruenn Chen, *Chinese Economic Statistics,* (Chicago:
Aldine, 1967), pp. 260 and 485–86.

per worker at the Soviet-aided plants was several times the national average in both machinery and ferrous metallurgy.

These plants have achieved a mixed record. On the positive
side, gradual completion of the Soviet-aided projects during the
mid- and late 1950s led to a major expansion of import substitution
and output volume in a wide range of industries. Much of the
growth in industrial output volume during 1957–65 is attributable
to these plants.[14] On the qualitative side, these new enterprises

14. Time series estimates of physical output for a number of industrial products
are available in Robert M. Field, "Civilian Industrial Production in the People's
Republic of China: 1949–71," in U.S. Congress, Joint Economic Committee, *China:*

manufactured many import substitutes, often at a much lower cost than the foreign products that they replaced. References to the opposite tendency are rare.

Nevertheless, construction and manufacturing operations at these plants encountered difficulties that led Chinese economists to question the value of large, capital-intensive facilities several years before the abrupt withdrawal of Soviet technical assistance in 1960 forced China to abandon the investment policy of the preceding decade. The weakness of the economic analysis underlying the FFYP investment program led to many problems. Wuhan's Heavy Machinery Plant was designed in the mid-1950s on the basis of demand expected in 1967 and therefore faced marketing problems.[15] Investment in nitrogenous fertilizers was four to five times that in phosphate fertilizers, but this proportion was fixed without any systematic effort to ascertain a desirable ratio between output of various types of fertilizers.[16] In automobiles and tractors, although demand was "large in varieties but small in quantity, we planned for the future and built big integrated plants with many specialized machine tools."[17] These blunders necessitated expensive model changes at some plants and conversion to entirely different product lines at others.

Many of the new plants embodied standards of mechanization that, as Chinese writers soon recognized, were not appropriate for China. The automated casting shop at Shenyang's #1 Machine Tool Plant, for example, was attacked as being pleasant (for the workers) but a costly and irrational frill. A reply to the critics actually supported their position. Mechanized casting admittedly failed to improve upon technical performance or quality indicators at other plants. And despite reductions in unit labor and materials

---

A Reassessment of the Economy (Washington, D.C.: U.S. Government Printing Office, 1975), pp. 165–67; and Christopher Howe, China's Economy: A Basic Guide (New York: Basic Books, 1978), chap. 4.

15. Hsiang Lin, "How to Implement the Principle of Frugal National Construction," Chi-hsieh kung-yeh [Machinery Industry], no. 11 (1957), p. 18.

16. P'an Kuang-chi, "Opinions' on the Development of Basic Chemical Industries," Hua-hsüeh kung-yeh [Chemical Industry], no. 8 (1957), p. 34.

17. Pai Ou, "Brief Discussion of the Direction and Tasks of the Machinery Industry," Chi-hsieh kung-yeh [Machinery Industry], no. 12 (1957), p. 2.

costs, higher depreciation charges and operating expenses at the mechanized plant gave more primitive facilities a substantial cost advantage even with interest charges on fixed capital omitted from the calculation.[18] Numerous other reports document the inclusion in major projects of expensive items of equipment that added little to the performance of the enterprise.

As in any investment program, errors in planning were compounded by problems arising during implementation. Delays, discovery of incorrect drawings and technical specifications, cost overruns (expansion of Shenyang's #1 Machine Tool Plant cost five times the planned amount), and unexpected bottlenecks in supply (managers at the new Loyang Bearing Works found that designated suppliers had no plans to produce the required inputs) added to the difficulties encountered by the new plants.[19]

On balance, these plants have certainly made great contributions to China's industrialization. Their output forms the quantitative backbone of a vastly enlarged industrial sector. Problems of technology, product assortment, and management have been gradually ameliorated, in many cases under conditions of great difficulty created by the unexpected withdrawal of Soviet technical assistance in 1960. One feature of these plants which has not changed, however, is their high degree of capital intensity as measured by the complement of capital per worker. This can be seen from the data in Table 3-6, which indicate that employment has expanded quite slowly at major plants, including enterprises that did and did not receive Soviet aid during the 1950s. Slow growth of employment is particularly noteworthy when it is considered that many of these units were still under construction or at the stage of trial output during 1957–60 and that their output has subsequently risen steeply.

Enterprises inherited from the Republican era

A different type of industrial unit has become prominent in

18. Meng Chih-chien, "On Mechanization of Casting Shops," *Chi-hsieh kung-yeh* [Machinery Industry], no. 13 (1957), pp. 5–8.

19. Pai Ou, "Brief Discussion," p. 5; and Wang Te-yüan, "Perceive the Conditions of Steel Supply, Dig Up Latent Sources of Domestic Supply," *Chi-hsieh kung-yeh* [Machinery Industry], no. 9 (1957), p. 29.

TABLE 3-6. EMPLOYMENT CHANGES AT MAJOR ENTERPRISES
SINCE THE 1950s

Plant	Year	Number of workers
Plants built with Soviet assistance		
Loyang Tractor Plant	1959	20,000[a]
	1973	23,000[b]
Shenyang #1 Machine Tool Plant	1960	6,000[c]
	1964	4,800[d]
	1971	5,000[e]
Wuhan Heavy Machinery Plant	1959	7,000[a]
	1966	7,000[f]
	1975	9,000[g]
Wuhan Steel Works[h]	1959	40,000[a]
	1966	35,000[f]
Other major plants		
Peking #1 Machine Tool Plant	1959	6,000[a]
	1966	4,000[f]
Shanghai Boiler Plant	1957	3,300[i]
	1973	7,000[j]
Shanghai Machine Tool Plant	1957	4,500[k]
	1964	5,200[d]
	1975	6,000[l]
Shanghai Steam Turbine Plant	1959	6,700[a]
	1973	8,000[j]
T'aiyuan Heavy Machinery Plant	1957	5,000[k]
	1964	7,200[m]

a. Furui Yoshimi and others, *Hōchū shoken* [A Visit to China] (Tokyo: n.p., 1959), pp. 12–26.

b. Dr. Doris Dohrenwend, personal communication.

c. Ōzaki Shotarō, "Visit to Mukden No. 1 Machine Tool Plant," *Ajia keizai jumpō* [Asian Economic Weekly], no. 475 (1960), p. 10.

d. *Far Eastern Economic Review*, June 18 and June 30, 1964.

e. *Chūgoku kōgyō tsūshin* [China Industrial Bulletin], no. 2 (1971), p. 10.

f. Barry M. Richman, *Industrial Society in Communist China* (New York: Random House, 1969), p. 754.

g. Ross Terrill, *Flowers on an Iron Tree* (Boston: Atlantic–Little, Brown, 1975), p. 289.

h. Excludes miners.

i. *Chieh-fang jih-pao* [Liberation Daily], September 30, 1957.

j. *Report of the Canadian Electrical Power Mission to the People's Republic of China, August 29 to September 18, 1973* (Ottawa: Ministry of Industry, Trade and Commerce, 1973).

k. *Shin Chūgoku no kikai kōgyō* [New China's Machinery Industry] (Tokyo: Tōa keizai ken-kyūkai, 1960), pp. 136 and 145.

l. Dwight Perkins and others, *Rural Small-Scale Industry in the People's Republic of China* (Berkeley: University of California Press, 1977), p. 40.

m. *Chūgoku kagaku gijutsu no genjō bunseki* [Analysis of the Current State of China's Science and Technology] (Tokyo: Shokoku kagaku gijutsu kenkyūkai, 1965), vol. 1, pp. 64–65.

China since 1960. These are older, smaller enterprises, often part of the legacy of prewar industrial advance in the private sector; they have typically received only modest infusions of investment funds, imported equipment, and external technical aid. These firms deserve major credit for the flexibility, successful innovation, and responsiveness to demand that, in contrast to the 1950s, seem typical of industrial performance over the past fifteen years.

Shanghai's Ta-lung Machinery Works provides a well-documented example of this type of firm.[20] Ta-lung was established in 1902 as a ship repair works; it had eleven workers. In 1906, with a staff of fifty, the firm began to specialize in repairing machinery for Shanghai's growing textile industry. After 1911 the business gradually shifted toward manufacture, first of textile machine parts, later of individual machines, and by the 1930s of a full line of cotton spinning machinery that was installed in several profitable mills.

Following wartime efforts that included replacement of damaged equipment and munitions manufacture, Ta-lung resumed its pattern of manufacturing a variety of equipment. During 1949–52 its products included spindles, looms, machine tools, engines, and steel ingots. In 1953 machine tools and mining equipment were the major products. In 1955 the firm was assigned to specialize in producing formerly imported items of petroleum equipment. In 1958 chemical fertilizer equipment was added to Ta-lung's product list.

Since 1960, Ta-lung has produced equipment for the petroleum and fertilizer industries and for synthesizing diamonds, and it has experimented with advanced techniques for metallurgy and compressors. At the same time, the plant continues to function as a jobshop: "When a heavy chain on a 10,000 hp diesel manufactured by the Hutung Shipyard was found faulty and someone higher up insisted that it should be substituted by an imported chain, work-

20. Discussion of the Ta-lung Machinery Works is based on Thomas G. Rawski, "The Growth of Producer Industries, 1900–1971," in *China's Modern Economy in Historical Perspective*, ed. Dwight H. Perkins (Stanford: Stanford University Press, 1975), pp. 202–13 and 232; and "Choice of Technology and Technological Innovation in China's Economic Development," in *The Relevance of China's Experience for the Other Developing Countries*, ed. Robert F. Dernberger (forthcoming).

ers of the Ta-lung Machine Works overcame all difficulties and provided a high-quality chain to make sure that every part of the diesel was of Chinese origin."[21]

Features shared by most of these plants include moderate size, a lengthy and varied industrial history that often includes repair work as well as manufacturing, and a substantial proportion of equipment that is old, self-manufactured, or both. Despite their having low priority in China's investment policy and their consequent lack of advanced capital equipment, these plants, clustered in Shanghai, Tientsin, and other centers of prewar industrial development, form the cutting edge of Chinese technological advance. Their primary function is to respond to shifts in domestic demand by providing an appropriate mixture of embodied and disembodied (through training and consulting programs, conferences, and the like) technological change drawn from both foreign and domestic sources.

Chinese sources make it clear that Shanghai, whose industry is dominated by small and medium-size plants of the type described above, is the nation's technological leader. Manufacturers of steel, machine tools, cable, diesels, pumps, pneumatic tools, sewing machines, and many other commodities judge their products by comparing them with Shanghai's and to a lesser extent with Tientsin's.

The contribution of these older units to the development of new industries may be illustrated by reference to petroleum and chemical fertilizers, both of which were assigned secondary priority during the 1950s but emerged as vitally important after 1960. Output in both sectors has expanded rapidly with only limited reliance on imported equipment. The petroleum sector, in which output has risen from 1.5 to 104 million tons of crude oil since 1957 (Table 1-1), obtains much of its equipment from converted engineering works, including Ta-lung and other old plants.

The case of chemical fertilizers, in which output has risen from 0.6 to nearly 50 million tons since 1957 (Table 4-3)—again, with little reliance on foreign equipment—provides even clearer evidence of the role of older firms and especially of Shanghai's indus-

21. *Eastern Horizon*, vol. 15, no. 5 (1976), p. 40.

try as supplier of equipment.[22] Fertilizer equipment was produced in quantity beginning in 1962. Shanghai led the way, sup-
plying 25,000 tons of equipment to one major plant. In 1965,
Shanghai firms turned out China's first equipment for manufacture of urea. Small fertilizer plants, which have provided the bulk
of output growth since 1965, now obtain some machinery from
provincial and local sources. The core of the equipment industry
remains in Shanghai, however, where a group of more than 400
plants supplied 300 sets of equipment for synthetic ammonia
plants between 1970 and 1972.

The strength of older firms lies in their reservoirs of production
experience and their tradition of entrepreneurial behavior developed both before and after 1949. With their "skilled veteran workers and experienced technical persons" and superior development
of interenterprise cooperation, another legacy of the past, "old industrial bases and old enterprises . . . find it easier to tackle . . .
complicated technical problems than new enterprises and new industrial bases."[23]

With these advantages, it is the established centers that are best
able to copy and modify designs and samples of foreign equipment, to cull useful information from foreign technical literature,
and to apply it to domestic problems. More generally, experienced
firms act as technological intermediaries between the mass of Chinese producers, whose mission is to strive for "advanced national
levels" of quality, cost, and technique, and the outside world,
whose standards become the goal of Shanghai's technological aspirations.

Despite their major contribution to expanding the range and
technical sophistication of China's industries, these plants have
not provided employment opportunities for large numbers of new
workers. This limited growth in employment is the result of the
dependence of these enterprises on the skill and dedication of in-

22. Statements on sources of equipment for the fertilizer and petroleum sectors
and on Shanghai's overall technological leadership are based on Thomas G. Rawski, *China's Transition to Industrialism: Producer Goods and Economic Development in the
Twentieth Century* (Ann Arbor: University of Michigan Press, forthcoming), chap. 3.
    23. SCMP, no. 3,275 (1964), pp. 4–5.

dividual employees. Just as the functioning of the large Soviet-aided plants appears to require maintenance of a high degree of capital intensity, the operation of this second group of enterprises depends on maintaining a high degree of skill intensity, and this in turn limits the employment potential of these plants as a whole.

Small-scale industry

The general features of China's small industries are described in several sources and require little elaboration.[24] Small plants located in county seats and rural areas are relatively easy to equip and can make use of small local resource deposits. Rural industry can reduce rural claims on overburdened national transport facilities and cater to local requirements that are often overlooked by urban industry. If properly managed, small plants may have relatively low capital costs and short gestation periods. By meeting local demand, small industry can reduce the pressure on urban output, allowing advanced units to concentrate on innovation and quality control rather than on maximizing the volume of current product. Rural industry provides a constructive outlet for regional pride and allows localities to compensate for some of the errors and oversights of a centrally directed system of economic planning.

The initial impetus toward expansion of rural industry came at the end of the FFYP. Premature expansion of small plants during the Great Leap Forward led, however, to waste and confusion, and many units were closed during the retrenchment of 1960–62. Then, as agricultural conditions stabilized and the opportunity cost of rural industrial ventures declined, official policy began once again to encourage local industrial development.

The volume of resources devoted to small factories has expanded steadily since about 1963. Careful attention to pilot projects, cost reduction, and quality control has led to greatly improved results. In 1964, for instance, the Hsin-hui (Kwangtung) Farm Machinery Works turned out power tillers at only 55 percent

---

24. See, for example, Carl Riskin, "Small Industry and the Chinese Model of Development," *China Quarterly*, no. 46 (1971), pp. 245–73; Perkins and others, *Rural . . . Industry*; and Sigurdson, *Rural Industrialization*.

of the cost of useless models produced in 1960; by 1972 annual output had risen to 2,700 units.[25]

As a result of continued investment in rural industry, most of China's 2,000-odd counties are now active in one or more branches of the producer sector. In 1971 reports indicated that "more than half of the counties had established small machinery, chemical fertilizer, cement, and iron and steel plants and small coal pits." In 1972, 96 percent of all counties were reported to operate workshops for making and repairing farm machinery, and in 1974, 80 percent of counties possessed small cement plants. Recent years have seen a rapid expansion of industrial activity at the commune and brigade levels, which now operate more than 1 million "small factories and other enterprises."[26]

Small industry is not spread evenly over China's rural landscape. One Chinese account notes that "local industry has developed on a larger scale and at a faster speed in provinces that have a much better industrial foundation" and are therefore better equipped to aid new enterprises with equipment and technical advice.[27] Hilly districts with mineral deposits and hydropower potential, areas in which unusually high or rapidly rising grain yields make it easy to finance start-up costs, and counties close to the technical resources of urban industrial centers all seem to enjoy above average success in expanding the size and scope of local industry.

How large is the small-scale industry sector? Rural industrial activity can be divided into two segments: the collective and state-owned sectors. The collective sector consists mainly of enterprises owned, financed, and managed by agricultural communes and their constituent brigades and teams. Information on the scope of collective industry is limited, but it appears that processing of grains, cotton, and other plant products, handicrafts, repair of farm machinery, carpentry, and other sideline ventures predominate, although some communes also engage in coal mining,

25. *Nan-fang jih-pao* [Southern Daily], April 18, 1965, and BBC, no. W706 (1973), p. A12.

26. Statements in this paragraph are derived from SCMP, no. 4,992 (1971), p. 28; *Peking Review*, no. 48 (1972), p. 17, and no. 2 (1974), p. 23; and FBIS, January 6, 1978, p. E17.

27. *Peking Review*, no. 39 (1971), p. 9.

hydroelectric generation, and manufacture of machinery, cement, fertilizer, and other producer goods. In 1973 "industry under collective ownership accounted for 3 percent of the fixed assets, 36.2 percent of the industrial population, and 14 percent of the total output value" of all industry.[28]

The state sector of rural industry consists mainly of enterprises operated at the county level. These plants derive their fixed assets from the state budget and remit most of their profits to the state. They are typically located in or near the county seat, which is often a city of some size, and are much larger and better equipped than commune enterprises. The bulk of the producer-goods output of small industry, which is estimated for 1972 in Table 3-7, comes from these plants.

Estimates of the size, in output and employment, of the collective sector and of the "five small industries" are shown in Table 3-1. Calculations shown in this table draw on the more detailed estimates of small plant output and employment in Tables 3-7 and Appendix C. Although these figures are only approximations, there can be little doubt of the general validity of the conclusions drawn from the data in Table 3-1.

First, it is clear that, despite the crucial role of small industry products in the agricultural development process described in Chapter Four and the importance of the output of small plants in the growth of certain branches of industry (particularly building materials, chemical fertilizer, and farm machinery), small plants provide only a fraction of overall industrial output. The five sectors included in Table 3-7 account for 6.3 percent of estimated gross value of factory output in 1972; the addition of less developed small industry sectors for which data are not available might add one or two percentage points to this total, but no more. It is therefore evident that, despite the expansion of rural industry, large-scale urban industry has retained its position as the leading force in Chinese industrial expansion.

Second, the collective sector, which partially overlaps with the five small industries, also accounts for only a modest share of industrial output. Many of the collective enterprises included under

28. Chang Ch'un-ch'iao, "On Exercising All-Round Dictatorship over the Bourgeoisie," *Peking Review*, no. 14 (1975), p. 6.

TABLE 3-7. SHARE OF FIVE SMALL INDUSTRIES IN FACTORY OUTPUT, 1972

Product or sector	Small-scale share (percent)	Gross value of factory output (billions of 1952 yuan)	
		Total	Small-scale
Building materials	50[a]	6.480	3.240
Chemical fertilizer	60[b]	3.643	2.186
Energy			
Coal	28[c]	4.834	1.353
Electric power	6[d]	6.589	0.395
Farm machinery	67[e]	13.009[f]	8.716
Iron and steel	18[g]	22.108	3.979
Total for five small industries	35.1	56.663	19.869
Total for entire producer-goods sector	7.5	263.826	19.869
Gross value of factory output	6.3	312.991	19.869

a. Small plant share of 1974 cement output as estimated by Ian H. McFarlane, "Construction Trends in China, 1949–74," in U.S. Congress, Joint Economic Committee, *China: A Reassessment of the Economy* (Washington, D.C.: U.S. Government Printing Office, 1975), p. 315.

b. Calculated on the basis of tonnage estimates in Robert M. Field, "Civilian Industrial Production in the People's Republic of China: 1949–74," ibid., p. 166.

c. Figure for 1973 from BBC, no. W803 (1974), p. A15.

d. Small plants account for 20 percent of hydropower capacity (*Peking Review*, no. 21 [1975], p. 31), which in turn accounts for an estimated 28 percent of aggregate generating capacity (Thomas G. Rawski, "The Role of China in the World Energy Situation" [unpublished, 1973], p. 27). The output share of small plants may therefore be estimated at 20 · 0.28, or about 6 percent.

e. Figure for 1966 cited by Carl Riskin, "Small Industry and the Chinese Model of Development," *China Quarterly*, no. 46 (1971), p. 271.

f. Farm machinery accounted for from 6 to 7 percent of total machinery output in 1956 (Chao I-wen, *Hsin Chung-kuo ti kung-yeh* [Industry of New China] [Peking: T'ung-chi ch'u-pan she, 1957], p. 43). This share is assumed to have risen to 15 percent by 1972. Overall machinery output for 1972 is given in Appendix C.

g. In 1972 small plants accounted for 22 and 15 percent of China's output of pig iron and crude steel, respectively, (U.S. Central Intelligence Agency, *China: Role of Small Plants in Economic Development* [Washington, D.C., 1974], p. 15). The 18 percent small plant share is assumed on the basis of these estimates.

Source: Gross value data in the second column are from Thomas G. Rawski, "China's Industrial Performance, 1949–1973," in *Quantitative Measures of China's Economic Output*, ed. Alexander Eckstein (Ann Arbor: University of Michigan Press, forthcoming), Tables 21, 27, 34, and 37. Data in the third column are calculated from the figures in the first and second columns.

the rubric of "industry" engage in activities that might reasonably be classified as nonindustrial. Cotton ginning, flour milling, rice hulling, and other types of crop processing, as well as self-consumed handicraft production, included in agricultural output during 1953–57, are now assigned to industry. These activities now generate perhaps one-fourth of the output of collective industry.[29] Other semi-industrial activities apparently contained in the total for collective industry include carpentry shops, mat-weaving, basketry, and sewing and embroidery shops, as well as other types of traditional crafts.

These activities, which are not new to China's countryside, are increasingly mechanized and hence industrial in character. At the same time, part of the output of collective industry consists of modernized forms of traditional craft activities, and genuinely new activities, such as manufacture of cement, fertilizers, and machinery, contribute only a modest fraction to the total output of collective industry.

A third set of conclusions that become evident from the data in Table 3-1 concerns the effect of rural industrialization on patterns of employment. The data show that the direct employment effect of collective and small-scale industry is extremely small. The combined employment total in collective industry (including handicrafts) and in the five small industries for 1975 is 19.4 million workers. This figure is far higher than the actual level of industrial employment in rural areas for several reasons. First, employment in collective enterprises that produce commodities listed in Table 3-7 is counted twice. Second, most of the state-operated enterprises whose output and employment is estimated in Table 3-7 and Appendix C are located in county towns; their employment is part of urban rather than rural employment. Third, some collective enterprises are located in cities; their workers are also part of the urban labor force. Fourth, employment figures for collective enterprises in the countryside may include part-time workers. The 19.4 million figure includes state-sector small-scale plants in industries other than those shown in Table 3-7 (textiles, food processing, and so on), but such plants appear to be relatively few in number and also tend to have urban locations.

It can therefore be concluded that 15 million is a generous esti-

29. The activities transferred from agriculture to industry generated 15.4 percent of the 1955 gross value of agricultural output; see Robert M. Field, Nicholas R. Lardy, and John P. Emerson, *A Reconstruction of the Gross Value of Industrial Output by Province in the People's Republic of China: 1949–73* (Washington, D.C.: U.S. Department of Commerce, 1975), pp. 5 and 47. If this relation is assumed to have existed in 1975, the share of the transferred activities in the output of collective industry can be calculated from Tables 3-1, 4-8, and 4-12.

mate of full-time industrial employment in rural areas for 1975. Although rural industrial employment amounts to more than one-third of all employment in industry, the share of rural enterprises in national industrial output is limited to a portion of the overlapping totals for collective plants and for the five small industries shown in Table 3-1. This share is much smaller, perhaps from 10 to 15 percent. Furthermore, when employment in rural industry is compared with the agricultural rather than the industrial work force, its significance is much reduced. Rural industrial employment totaling 15 million persons represents less than 5 percent of the total rural labor force shown in Table 2-9 for 1975. This implies that the 5 percent limit on industrial employment reported in some rural areas applies in practice to China as a whole.[30]

The technological level of small-scale plants has been described in detail elsewhere. The basic conclusion of the Rural Small-Scale Industry Delegation was that the plants visited, most of which were identified by Chinese hosts or Chinese press reports as leading units in their field, are effective and productive enterprises that have succeeded in applying modern industrial technology and equipment to produce useful outputs. With some exceptions, notably the widespread production of ammonium bicarbonate, a fertilizer product that appears to be unique to China, the materials, equipment, processes, and products encountered in Chinese plants were not unfamiliar to American engineers and social scientists. Apprentice machinists were performing the same tasks assigned to apprentices at General Motors; fertilizer plants and tractor models resemble U.S. plants and tractors built during World War II; and a temporary disruption of operations at a Peking steel rolling plant reminded visitors of similar experiences at steel mills in Brazil and Canada.[31]

Small plants in any particular industry appear to include units of widely varying technical sophistication. Chinese publications

30. The five percent limit is reported in Jon Sigurdson, "Rural Industrialization in China," in U.S. Congress, Joint Economic Committee, *China: A Reassessment of the Economy* (Washington, D.C.: U.S. Government Printing Office, 1975), p. 412.

31. The statements in this paragraph are based on Perkins and others, *Rural . . . Industry*, chaps. 4–7, and on the author's observations as a member of the Rural Small-Scale Industry Delegation that prepared the report.

describe tiny plants rigged with primitive homemade equipment; these units are not shown to visitors and appear to contribute little to aggregate output. Their function is to develop rudimentary support facilities for agriculture in areas that are not able to obtain industrial farm inputs or capital equipment needed to produce the farm inputs, because of remote location, financial constraints, or the inadequacy of industrial output. Primitive plants also serve as training grounds to prepare the way for future expansion and upgrading of local industrial facilities.

The bulk of the output of small plants now comes from fairly large and sophisticated plants of the type shown to the Rural Small-Scale Industry Delegation. These plants are often neither small nor rural. County plants typically are located in or near the county seats, which may, as in the case of Hsinhsiang, Honan, have populations as large as 450,000 persons. As for size, the average employment level at 18 county plants toured by the group was 379 workers.[32]

These plants operate large quantities of machinery, sometimes including items obtained from leading national-level plants. At the same time, they invariably possess substantial machine shops that produce considerable quantities of equipment for their own use. Although small plants tend to use less capital per worker than larger units, workers at leading small enterprises nonetheless operate substantial quantities of equipment, frequently including automatic machine tools and other sophisticated items. Furthermore, falling machinery prices (both absolutely and relative to labor costs), growing skill of local engineering units, and a widespread desire to increase labor productivity have led to an increasing level of mechanization and hence capital intensity in plants visited by the Rural Small-Scale Industry Delegation.

The contribution of the output of small plants to China's economy has been assessed elsewhere by means of detailed cost comparisons for similar products of large and small enterprises.[33] The results of such studies indicate that small plants, although generally incapable of matching the current cost performance of large-scale enterprises, have succeeded in raising industrial capacity

32. Ibid., p. 68.
33. Ibid., chap. 4 and Appendix F; Sigurdson, *Rural Industrialization*, chap. 4; and Rawski, "Choice of Technology."

with minimal use of foreign exchange, interregional transport networks, and other resources of high opportunity cost, and without significant cost escalation from the standards established by larger enterprises during the 1950s. The substantial and positive benefits that local industrialization has provided to the agricultural sector, a topic to be discussed in the following chapter, add further substance to the conclusion that the expansion of small-scale industry has contributed significantly to the development of China's economy during the past two decades.

Institutional Determinants of Industrial Employment

Strong incentives to raise labor productivity and hence to limit labor requirements are implicit in China's industrial objectives, technological policy, and enterprise structure.

Chinese economic planners are highly conscious of a tradeoff between aggregate consumption and investment. Wages in the state industrial sector, including county-level plants, are much higher than incomes of agricultural workers.[34] This pay differential, inherited from the past, is now reinforced by an ideology that identifies industrial workers as the "vanguard of the proletariat," by the steadily widening gap in productivity between industrial and agricultural workers, and by the limited but very real political strength of urban workers. This large differential means that transfer of agricultural workers into the state industrial system raises aggregate disposable income and hence personal consumption. This process not only reduces the surplus available for investment but also necessitates reallocation of reduced investment outlays toward consumer products to avoid excess demand and consequent inflationary pressures. In addition, state-sector employees receive pensions, subsidized medical care, child-care facilities, and other fringe benefits not normally available to com-

34. Only a tiny minority of farm workers can hope to earn annual incomes equivalent to the wages of from 600 to 800 yuan that are common even among semiskilled industrial workers. A survey by Martin K. Whyte concludes that "the urban-rural incomes differential is something on the order of 2:1 (whether considered on a per capita or per labourer basis)." See "Inequality and Stratification in China," *China Quarterly*, no. 64 (1975), p. 687.

mune members. Urban housing, which is also heavily subsidized, adds substantially to the cost of higher employment in the state sector, so much so that government outlays for residential construction during 1953–57 exceeded state investment in water conservancy, nonrailway transport, and even agriculture.[35]

Planners' perceptions of costs attached to higher industrial employment relate primarily to the state sector. Commune members employed in collective enterprises at the commune or brigade level are paid in work points rather than in cash, live in privately financed housing, and enjoy only those fringe benefits which are extended to fellow members of their communes.

At the enterprise level, growth in employment is limited by the whole structure of Chinese economic planning, which encourages managers to make the most of existing resources. Expanding output by increasing labor productivity rather than the number of employees creates a gap between potential and planned output, at least in the short run, which increases an enterprise's ability to withstand unexpected breakdowns of equipment or supply lines without endangering plan fulfillment. Rising productivity also facilitates the attainment of goals for quality, cost, and profit, which in turn attracts favorable attention from superiors and increases the firm's prospects of obtaining investment funds.

In an economy in which real industrial wages did not rise perceptibly from 1957 until late 1977, when modest increases were given to about half of the industrial workers whose monthly wages were below ninety yuan, it is probable that worker morale responds favorably to innovations designed to reduce physically taxing, hazardous, and unpleasant tasks.[36] Such reforms demonstrate leaders' concern with workers' welfare, an important aspect of Chinese economic ideology, and are also likely to raise productivity. Sliding seats for machine tenders in textile plants, automatic bagging at fertilizer and cement plants, and ventilation and dust removal at textile and cement plants are examples of innovations that may be designed primarily to improve working conditions, but also have the effect of increasing capital intensity and labor productivity.

35. Nai-ruenn Chen, *Chinese Economic Statistics* (Chicago: Aldine, 1967), p. 165.
36. BBC, no. W957 (1977), p. A1.

Finally, growth in employment is limited by bureaucratic obstacles. To obtain new workers, factory managers are required to make formal application to labor bureaus, which allow additional hiring only after inquiries have shown that new workers are genuinely necessary.[37] A similar procedure is required to obtain allocations of state investment funds. But the latter, once obtained, are virtually a free good, for there appear to be no interest charges attached to capital grants. This certainly biases the choice of technology at the enterprise level toward capital-using alternatives.

In addition, and perhaps more important, is the ability of many firms to fulfill at least some of their equipment needs without entering into these application procedures. The high degree of vertical integration in Chinese industry is discussed in many sources.[38] China's relatively inflexible system of industrial resource allocation gives managers a strong incentive to develop captive ancillary facilities. Especially prized are repair shops that can alter or repair existing equipment, produce new and improved machines for self-use or barter, and in some sectors contribute to current output at critical times. The widespread existence of foundries and machine shops attached to factories in many sectors and the apparent ease with which they acquire raw materials create an additional bias toward expansion of output and quality of product along capital-intensive lines.

Conclusion

The growth of industrial employment, though impressive in absolute terms, is relatively modest in comparison with the extent of

37. Alexander Eckstein, *China's Economic Development* (Ann Arbor: University of Michigan Press, 1975), pp. 362–64. Reports of communes sending members to work in industrial and mining regions raise the possibility that factories may collude with rural units to circumvent these restrictions.

38. See, for example, Barry M. Richman, *Industrial Society in Communist China* (New York: Random House, 1969), p. 796, and Rawski, *China's Transition to Industrialism*, chap. 5. Vice Premier Yü Ch'iu-li's complaint that too many farm machinery plants "are either 'large and comprehensive' or 'small and comprehensive'; they manufacture everything from parts and accessories to entire machines" with deleterious effects on cost, quality, and customer service, illustrates Chinese views on this issue ("Summation Report," p. E12).

industrial expansion. The contrast between the dominant contribution of industry to China's incremental output and its limited
contribution to creating employment must be understood in the
context of China's industrial strategy, technological alternatives,
and institutional patterns. The prevalence of comparatively high
and rising capital-labor ratios and rising labor productivity in all
types of industrial enterprises means that the task of absorbing
large new cohorts of workers has fallen primarily to the agricultural sector. Absorption of labor in China's agricultural economy and
the contribution of industry to raising the demand for rural labor
are taken up in the following chapter.

Chapter Four

Labor Absorption in Agriculture from 1957 to 1975

CHINA'S LABOR FORCE INCREASED by an estimated 148.5 million persons between 1957 and 1975, as was demonstrated in Chapter Two. Of this number, 58 million entered industry and other non-agricultural pursuits (see Tables 2-7 and 2-8). If it is assumed that there is no open unemployment in the countryside, some 97.3 million workers are left to be absorbed into agriculture (Table 2-9), which is broadly defined to include water conservancy and land improvement as well as farming. In addition, the considerable growth of labor-augmenting mechanization has reduced several components of rural labor demand, thus enlarging the potential problem of labor absorption.

This chapter will show that these potential problems have not materialized. China's farm sector has succeeded in absorbing nearly 100 million new workers, amounting to an increase of more than 40 percent in the labor force, with no significant addition to cultivated acreage. Despite the resulting increase in the man-land ratio, which was high to begin with, both the number of work-days per laborer and the value of agricultural output per man-year increased between 1957 and 1975. At the same time, however, diminishing returns are discernible in the declining level of farm output per man-day and in falling total factor productivity in agriculture.

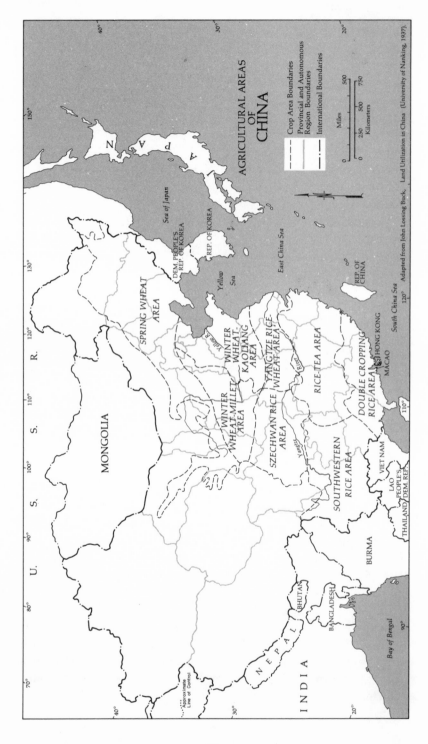

AGRICULTURAL AREAS OF CHINA

Crop Area Boundaries
Provincial and Autonomous
Region Boundaries
International Boundaries

Miles
0   250   500   750
0   500
Kilometers

Adapted from John Lossing Buck, Land Utilization in China (University of Nanking, 1937).

MONGOLIA

U. S. S. R.

SPRING WHEAT AREA

WINTER WHEAT-MILLET AREA

WINTER WHEAT-KAOLIANG AREA

YANGTZE RICE-WHEAT AREA

SZECHWAN RICE AREA

RICE-TEA AREA

DOUBLE CROPPING RICE AREA

SOUTHWESTERN RICE AREA

Yellow Sea

Sea of Japan

DEM. PEOPLE'S REP. OF KOREA

REP. OF KOREA

East China Sea

REP. OF CHINA

South China Sea

HONG KONG

MACAO

VIET NAM

LAO PEOPLE'S DEM. REP.

THAILAND

BURMA

NEPAL

BHUTAN

BANGLADESH

INDIA

Bay of Bengal

Approximate Line of Control

China's Agricultural System

Before discussing rural labor absorption during the past two decades, several important features of Chinese agriculture should be noted briefly. Varying conditions of temperature, rainfall, and population density divide China's landscape into several distinct farming regions that are shown on the accompanying map. China's southern and central regions, which enjoy relatively long growing seasons and abundant water supplies, cultivate irrigated rice as the staple crop, while farmers in the relatively dry northern provinces rely on wheat, maize, millet, and sorghum as their chief grain crops. The line separating the predominantly wheat-growing areas in the north from the rice-growing regions of the south runs slightly north of the Yangtze River, cutting through Kiangsu, Anhwei, Honan, and Shensi provinces.

In both the northern and southern regions, China's historic experience of rising population density and man-land ratios has stimulated the development of intensive methods of cultivation in which large inputs of labor, fertilizer, and, when available, water are applied to small plots of land. An early twentieth-century observer remarked that "[a]lmost every foot of land is made to contribute material for food, fuel or fabric. Everything which can be made edible serves as food for man or domestic animals. Whatever cannot be eaten or worn is used for fuel. The wastes of the body, of fuel and of fabric are taken back to the field; before doing so they are housed against waste from weather, intelligently compounded and patiently worked . . . to bring them into the most efficient form to serve as manure for the soil."[1]

This system of farming is more akin to gardening than to Western techniques of extensive farming. In the case of irrigated rice, the predominant crop in many areas of south China, Clifford Geertz has observed that output "can be almost indefinitely increased by more careful, fine-comb cultivation techniques" and that the capacity of small plots "to respond to loving care is amazing."[2]

1. F. H. King, *Farmers of Forty Centuries* (Emmaus, Pa.: Organic Gardening Press, n.d.), p. 25.
2. Clifford Geertz, *Agricultural Involution* (Berkeley: University of California Press, 1966), p. 35.

TABLE 4-1. PERCENTAGE DISTRIBUTION OF IDLE TIME, BY MONTH, 1929–33

Month	All regions	Rice region	Wheat region
January	32	32	32
February	12	12	13
March	3	3	3
April	2	1	2
May	1	2	1
June	3	3	2
July	3	4	3
August	2	2	2
September	2	2	2
October	4	4	5
November	11	10	11
December	25	25	24

Source: Survey of 15,013 farms in 140 counties and 22 provinces reported in John L. Buck, *Land Utilization in China* (Nanking: University of Nanking, 1937), p. 296.

This system of intensive farming supported a sevenfold population increase between 1400 and 1950 with no decline in availability of foodstuffs per capita. Although part of the rise in grain output came from newly settled lands, most came from higher yields.[3] By the twentieth century China possessed a highly developed farming system with few areas in which traditional reforms could bring about sharp increases in output in the absence of chemical fertilizer, machinery, and other moden farming inputs.

Despite its success in supporting growing numbers of inhabitants at constant living standards, traditional agriculture failed to provide full employment for the farming populace. Survey data from the 1930s show that seasonal idleness existed in all farming regions, with most regions clustering near the national average of 1.7 idle months per able-bodied rural male.[4] The seasonal distribution of idle time shown in Table 4-1 indicates a cluster of slack periods during the three months beginning in mid-November. During this interval, a typical male worker would be idle for $1.7 \cdot 30 \cdot .80$, or approximately 40 days. At the same time, the intensity of the farming cycle was restricted by seasonal periods of peak labor demand. The data reported in Table 4-2 show

3. Dwight H. Perkins, *Agricultural Development in China, 1368–1968* (Chicago: Aldine, 1969), chaps. 1 and 9.

4. John L. Buck, *Land Utilization in China* (Nanking: University of Nanking, 1937), p. 294.

TABLE 4-2. PERCENTAGE OF LOCALITIES REPORTING AGRICULTURAL LABOR
SHORTAGES, 1929–33

Farm operations hampered by shortages	All regions	Rice region	Wheat region
Harvesting	65	57	78
Planting	27	34	16
Irrigation	13	21	2
Cultivating	12	8	17
Plowing	2	1	3
No shortage	19.	22	15

Source: Survey of 260 localities in 169 counties and 20 provinces reported in John L. Buck,
Land Utilization in China (Nanking: University of Nanking, 1937), p. 301.

that more than four-fifths of the localities surveyed experienced
labor shortages at some point during the annual cropping cycle,
most often at harvest time.

This pattern of seasonal peaks and valleys in the demand for
farm labor shows both the potential and the danger of farm mechanization, which can allow further intensification of the cropping
cycle by breaking labor bottlenecks—but may also displace labor
and extend the phenomenon of seasonal idleness.

Major Developments: Collectivization and Supply
of Modern Farm Inputs

The success of China's agricultural sector in absorbing large cohorts of new workers and in raising output to accommodate unprecedented rates of population increase can be traced to two factors: collectivization and the infusion of industrial products into
farm production.

Collectivization

Following the extensive and violent land reform of the years
immediately after 1949, in which from 40 to 50 percent of arable
land was confiscated from its owners and redistributed to lower-
income farm households, family farming remained the dominant
form of agricultural organization until 1956. Within the context of

family farming, the government and the Chinese Communist Party encouraged the growth of cooperative units: at first, as mutual aid teams, then, as cooperatives in which members were remunerated on the basis of their contributions of both land and labor. In 1956 most farm households were grouped into higher-level cooperatives in which remuneration was based solely on contributions of labor.

In 1958, as part of the series of campaigns known as the Great Leap Forward, the rural populace was organized into large-scale collectives known as "People's Communes." These communes attempted to practice full communism. The consequent rupture of the link between peasant effort and income combined with general disorganization and bad weather to produce a series of disastrous harvests. This prompted in the early 1960s a policy of radical decentralization that abandoned the drive to attain full communism; instead, it returned control over agricultural production and income distribution to smaller units corresponding roughly to the lower-level cooperatives that had been formed before 1956.[5]

There have been no major reorganizations since this decentralization. The communes remain the basic unit of local government and administration in rural China. Chinese statements giving the numbers of communes and of their constituent production brigades and production teams yield the following rough estimates of the average size of these units:[6]

Type of unit	Number of units, 1978	Average size of units	
		Households	Persons
Commune	53,000	3,383	14,887
Production brigade	600,000	299	1,315
Production team	4,000,000	45	197

5. For one of many detailed accounts of collectivization, see Audrey Donnithorne, *China's Economic System* (London: Allen and Unwin, 1967), chaps. 2 and 3.

6. Numbers of units are reported in a "Briefing on China's Agriculture," distributed by the Bureau of Foreign Affairs, Ministry of Agriculture and Forestry, Peking, September 18, 1978, p. 2. Estimated unit sizes are based on a rural population of 789 million derived by projecting the estimated 1975 rural population (Table 2-6) forward at an annual rate of 2 percent and on rural household size of 4.4 persons estimated by Frederick W. Crook, "The Commune System in the People's Republic of China, 1963–1974," in U.S. Congress, Joint Economic Committee,

Involvement of communes in agriculture is now generally limited to management of fishing, forestry, animal husbandry, and horticulture. Communes do, however, exercise control over health care and secondary education. In addition, many communes manage a variety of industrial enterprises, especially in the fields of food and fiber processing. In recent years growing numbers of communes have moved into other industries such as metallurgy, machinery manufacture and repair, hydropower, and building materials.

Production brigades have grown in importance as centers of rural economic and political life. Many brigades now have headquarters buildings, communist party branches, and militia units. Brigade headquarters often house local branches of credit and supply-marketing cooperatives. Brigades also operate primary schools and cooperative health-care programs. "The brigade receives state plan targets, compulsory state procurement (grain) quotas, and schedules for delivering grain taxes and then works out plans with its teams to achieve these targets. Brigades continue to mobilize the rural labor force to build roads, canals, and water conservation projects."[7] Brigades also operate sideline activities such as piggeries, equipment repair shops, and food-processing workshops.

Production teams are the basic unit of agricultural production and income distribution. They are responsible for tilling most of China's farmland. After gathering the harvest and deducting the shares owing to the state (taxes and a compulsory grain delivery quota) and to the team itself (for purchase of current inputs, paying for investment projects, compensation of team leaders, repayment of loans, and replenishment of the team's welfare fund), the team distributes the remaining income to its members in proportion to the number of work-points accumulated by each person during the preceding year. Work-point systems are not uniform, but are generally based on labor-days adjusted by a coefficient reflecting the strength, experience, diligence, and in some cases class background, a factor used to discriminate against those

---

China: A Reassessment of the Economy (Washington, D.C.: U.S. Government Printing Office, 1975), p. 409. Discussion of the division of responsibilities among communes, brigades, and teams is based on Crook's account.

7. Crook, "The Commune System," p. 391.

whose families had been landlords or rich peasants before 1949.

The primacy of the small production team—with an average of several dozen households and somewhat less than 100 agricultural workers—in managing cultivation, accounting, and income distribution appears essential for preserving a close link between effort and reward in China's farm sector. Although some units have shifted the basis of crop and income management from the production team to the larger production brigade, a change that drew support from the Maoist wing of China's political elite before Mao Tse-tung's death, the constitution of 1975 includes a provision specifying the production team as the "basic unit of accounting." China's present administration strongly supports the concept of team autonomy and decries the negative effect of high-level interference with farming decisions. In a typical statement, Shensi leader Wang Jen-chung insisted in 1978 that "from now on the communes and the leading government departments will not be allowed to send orders on what to sow or how to assign production targets."[8]

In addition to the collective lands cultivated by commune members under the direction of production team leaders, rural households are permitted to maintain small private plots. The size of private plots has varied somewhat with the political climate. During the 1970s private plots occupied approximately 5 percent of arable farmland; they probably provided about one-fifth of the total income of farm households.[9]

The early problems encountered by communes were largely responsible for the disastrous harvests of 1959–61. They stemmed from unrealistic ambitions, inexperienced management, and the erosion of incentives associated with egalitarian distribution of income at the commune level. Growth of experience, abandonment of full communism, and the return of control over cultivation and distribution to the team level have overcome most but, as is

8. *China News Analysis*, no. 1,141 (1978), p. 6.

9. The size and importance of private plots are discussed by Crook, "The Commune System," pp. 402–05; Shahid Javed Burki, *A Study of Chinese Communes, 1965* (Cambridge, Mass.: Harvard University East Asian Research Center, 1969), p. 40; William L. Parish and Martin K. Whyte, *Village and Family in Contemporary China* (Chicago: University of Chicago Press, 1978), p. 365; and Christopher Howe, *China's Economy: A Basic Guide* (New York: Basic Books, 1978), p. 49.

evident from recent Chinese criticism of agricultural performance, not all of these difficulties. This in turn has allowed the commune system to exploit the advantages of collective agriculture, which include the following:

· Increased central control over rural life, and particularly over grain supplies, which increases state influence over rural savings and investment decisions.

· The possibility of mobilizing seasonally idle labor to participate in construction projects designed to raise farm output. This opportunity arises from the ability of the commune to internalize benefits from water conservancy, afforestation, road building, and the like, which individual households or small groups could not capture in a market economy.

· Development of a closely knit network of rural extension services that makes farmers more responsive to suggestions from research institutes and other scientific units. This has a potentially negative aspect if, as occurred often during 1958–60 and sometimes thereafter, these suggestions are inappropriate to local farming conditions.

· Development of a diversified rural economy, which may be stimulated by the ability of the commune to spread risks or start-up costs over a large population. Diversification may include creation of new industries, addition of new field crops, or development of insurance programs for human and animal health care.

· Improved allocation of resources in cultivation. This includes specialization and division of labor among the populace as well as such reforms as leveling boundaries between fields to increase plot size and sown area.

The existence of collectives does not ensure that these potential advantages will in fact be exploited. After the early period in which the net effect of collectivization on agricultural performance was strongly negative, however, the combination of growing managerial experience and sensible economic policies at all levels of government has allowed communes to make an increasingly positive contribution to agricultural development.

TABLE 4-3. GROWTH OF INDUSTRIAL INPUTS INTO CHINA'S RURAL ECONOMY, 1957–78

Year	Rural power consumption (billions of kilowatt-hours) (1)	Millions of tons		Inventory data (millions of horsepower)			Total for three categories	
		Small-scale cement output (2)	Chemical fertilizer output[a] (3)	Irrigation and drainage equipment (4)	Tractors (5)	Power tillers (6)	Millions of horsepower (7)	Horsepower per cultivated hectare (8)
1957	0.1	—	0.8	0.6	0.4	—	1.0	0.01
1962	1.6	1.6	2.8	5.8	1.5	—	7.3	0.07
1963	2.1	2.3	3.9	6.4	1.7	—	8.1	0.08
1964	2.5	2.2	5.8	7.3	1.8	—	9.1	0.08
1965	3.2	5.4	7.6	8.4	2.2[b]	—	10.6	0.10
1970	n.a.	11.5	14.0	16.9	4.5	0.3	21.7	0.20
1971	9.6[c]	12.4	16.8	20.0	5.6[b]	0.4	26.0	0.24
1972	n.a.	18.3	19.8	24.0	6.6	0.7	31.3	0.29
1973	n.a.	20.5	24.8	30.0	8.5	1.1	39.6	0.37
1974	n.a.	21.3	24.9	36.0	10.9	1.6	48.5	0.45
1975	14.4[d]	27.7	28.8	43.0	12.3	2.2	57.5	0.54
1976	n.a.	29.6	24.3	46.5[b]	14.6	3.2	64.3	0.60
1977	n.a.	36.0	38.0	60.0[e]	16.0[f]	5.6[b]	81.6	0.76
1978	27.0[g]	n.a.	48.0[h]	65.6[e]	19.1[c]	8.0[i]	92.7	0.87

— Negligible.
n.a. Not available.

80

a. Based on product weight, not nutrient weight.

b. Linear interpolation between figures for consecutive years.

c. Reported to be six times the figure for 1962; cited in Thomas B. Wiens, "Agricultural Statistics in the People's Republic of China," in *Quantitative Measures of China's Economic Output*, ed. Alexander Eckstein (Ann Arbor: University of Michigan Press, forthcoming), Table 17.

d. Based on increase for 1965–75 reported in *Peking Review*, no. 41 (1976), p. 17.

e. "Communique on Fulfillment of China's 1978 Economic Plan," *Beijing Review*, no. 27 (1979), p. 38. Tractor horsepower is assumed to have grown in proportion to the 19.3 percent increase in the number of tractors reported for 1977/78.

f. Previous year's inventory less 5 percent for retirements (assumed) plus 1977 output, as estimated in U.S. National Foreign Assessment Center, *China: Economic Indicators* (Washington, D.C.: 1978), p. 20.

g. Calculated from Nai-ruenn Chen, *Chinese Economic Statistics* (Chicago: Aldine, 1967), p. 186, and *China Reconstructs*, vol. 28, no. 4 (1979), pp. 8 and 56.

h. *Beijing Review*, no. 2 (1979), p. 7.

i. "Briefing on China's Agriculture" (Peking: Bureau of Foreign Affairs, Ministry of Agriculture and Forestry). p. 4, reports inventories of 800,000 power tillers. The average size of power tillers is assumed to be 10 horsepower.

Sources except as noted: Column 1, Kang Chao, *Agricultural Production in Communist China* (Madison: University of Wisconsin Press, 1970), pp. 139 and 151. *Columns 2 and 3*, U.S. National Foreign Assessment Center, *China Economic Indicators* (Washington, D.C.: Central Intelligence Agency, 1978), pp. 24–25. *Columns 4–6*, U.S. National Foreign Assessment Center, *China: Economic Indicators* (1977). *Column 8*, based on a constant total of 107 million cultivated hectares cited in Dwight H. Perkins, "Constraints Influencing China's Agricultural Performance," in U.S. Congress, Joint Economic Committee, *China: A Reassessment of the Economy* (Washington, D.C.: U.S. Government Printing Office, 1975), p. 353.

Increase of industrial inputs

The second major change that has contributed to the development of China's agricultural sector since 1957 is the presence of rapidly increasing and, by the 1970s, large supplies of industrial inputs, including power, machinery, building materials, steel, petroleum products, and chemical fertilizer. The pace of growth is illustrated in Table 4-3, from which average annual growth rates for flows and stocks of several products can be derived, as shown below:

Flows and stocks	Average annual growth rates (percent)
Rural power consumption, 1957–78	21
Small-scale cement output, 1962–77	23
Chemical fertilizer output, 1957–78	22
Stock of irrigation and drainage equipment, 1957–78	25
Stock of tractors (horsepower), 1957–78	20
Stock of power tillers (horsepower), 1970–78	50
Stock of three machinery types (horsepower per hectare), 1957–78	24

The magnitude of these product flows may be illustrated by observing that in 1977/78 power consumption and small-scale cement manufacture in rural areas alone surpassed the national output totals for power in 1957 and for cement in 1971.

The addition of growing quantities of chemical fertilizer, much of it manufactured in county-level plants, to traditional organic fertilizers has pushed China into "a class with some of the world's highest users of fertilizers including Japan."[10] Chemical manufacturers also provide the farm sector with large quantities of pesticides and plastic sheeting. Rural construction projects, including annual winter works campaigns involving more than 100 million peasants, depend on cement, steel, explosives, and other manufactured construction materials.

The expanded production of farm machinery has brought about

10. Dwight H. Perkins and others, *Rural Small-Scale Industry in the People's Republic of China* (Berkeley: University of California Press, 1977), p. 199.

a significant degree of agricultural mechanization. Table 4-3 presents inventory estimates for three types of farm equipment: irrigation and drainage machinery, tractors, and power tillers. These figures show that three types of equipment alone now provide Chinese farmers with mechanical power somewhat larger than the 0.69 horsepower per hectare of cultivated land available to Japanese farmers from all types of power machinery in 1955.[11] Since Chinese farmers also make use of large numbers of threshers as well as lesser quantities of other types of machines, it is possible to conclude that, despite the evident labor intensity of Chinese farm practices, agriculture will soon approach the levels of mechanization that prevailed in Japan in the early 1960s. Under these conditions China's present objective of achieving basic mechanization by 1980, although vague, is not unrealistic.

Rural electrification and farm machinery, both of which have spread rapidly through the Chinese countryside since the mid-1960s, illustrate the effect of industrial goods on the farm economy.[12] Perhaps the largest quantitative effect of electrification on rural employment patterns has resulted from the mechanization of grain processing, which has relieved women of a time-consuming chore. A knowledgeable county official in Kiangsu province informed members of the Rural Small-Scale Industry Delegation that before mechanization there were two ways of processing rice. One was by ramming with a stone rod (mortar and pestle), which might process five kilograms in two hours; the other was a pedal-operated device that could hull twenty-five kilograms of grain in three hours. If it is assumed that these data refer to the quantity of unhulled rice that can be processed in a given time period, the feeding of a family of five on a rice diet of 1,000 kilograms would require a housewife to process one ton of unhulled grain each

11. Japanese figures calculated from Keizo Tsuchiya, "Economics of Mechanization in Small-Scale Agriculture," in *Agriculture and Economic Growth: Japan's Experience,* ed. Kazushi Ohkawa, Bruce F. Johnston, and Hiromitsu Kaneda (Princeton, N.J.: Princeton University Press, 1969), p. 158; and Yujiro Hayami and Vernon W. Ruttan, *Agricultural Development* (Baltimore: Johns Hopkins Press, 1971), p. 340.

12. In addition to the power-consumption figures in Table 4-3, the spread of electricity in rural China can also be traced from the frequency of articles in farm journals warning of its hazards, emphasizing the need to keep power lines above ground level, and describing first-aid procedures for shock victims.

year. This would involve from 240 to 800 hours of work during the course of a year.

Although these figures refer only to rice processing, they give a rough idea of the amount of labor released by mechanization of grain processing, which may eliminate as much as 95 percent of the labor required in grain milling.[13] If the average rural housewife devoted only 250 hours a year to this task, and assuming 170 million peasant households, the annual premechanization labor input into household grain processing would be 42.5 billion man-hours—or, assuming a work-year of 275 eight-hour days, the equivalent of 19.3 million man-years. If the average rural household devoted 800 annual man-hours to the task of grain hulling, the full-time equivalent would amount to 61.8 million man-years.[14] These man-equivalents give only the order of magnitude of the released labor time, but they suffice to show that, in comparison with the estimated growth of agricultural labor force of 97.3 million persons during 1957–75, the labor time released by this one variety of mechanization was very large.

Mechanized spinning has also released large quantities of female household labor. According to one account from Honan province: "It had long been a tradition for women in China's cotton-growing areas to spend their spare time spinning yarn on home-made wheels, and then weaving cloth to their own taste. The weaving, on a wooden loom, is not so hard. A skilled housewife could turn out 10 to 20 feet of cloth a day. But it took four or five days to spin the yarn needed for a day's weaving. The spinning mill has been built by the commune to take this burden off the women."[15] In this case, mechanization reduces the direct labor input into home weaving by 80 percent; the superior quality of machine-spun yarn also lowers the amount of cotton required to produce each foot of cloth.

Irrigation, which absorbed from 12 to 17 percent of farm labor

13. One report implies that mechanization raises labor productivity in the manufacture of rice flour by a factor of twenty. See *China News Analysis*, no. 1,127 (1978), p. 6.

14. The figure of 170 million rural households is derived from the rural population figure for 1975 shown in Table 2-6 and average rural household size of 4.4 estimated by Crook, "The Commune System," p. 409.

15. Chu Li and Tien Chieh-yun, *Inside a People's Commune* (Peking: Foreign Languages Press, 1974), pp. 86–87.

in China's rice-growing areas during the 1930s,[16] is another major task that is being transformed by electrification and mechanization. Delivery of water to the fields by electric or diesel pumps is now standard practice throughout large areas of rural China. This eliminates the need for human and animal power formerly used by traditional methods of moving water. Wooden chain pumps of a type commonly used in prewar China enable one man to lift thirty-nine tons of water a distance of three feet in one ten-hour day. A longer lift reduced productivity: traditional waterwheels used to raise water from wells may have produced less than two tons per man-day. Improved manual waterwheels developed during the 1960s raised this figure to between 4.2 and 5 tons per man-day.[17] A five-horsepower gasoline-powered pump can move 570 tons of water a day; depending on the vertical distance involved, one horsepower of this type of machinery may perform the work of between 15 and 285 laborers.[18] A number of reports from several provinces indicate that one horsepower of pumping equipment, operating from 800 to 1,000 hours each year, can provide enough water to irrigate and drain from 30 to 40 mou of cropland.[19]

Mechanized irrigation does more than simply replace human and animal labor. Mechanical pumps can perform tasks that were previously impossible. They can service fields situated far above or far away from natural water courses; they can also exploit water deposits deep beneath the ground.[20] The land can be rapidly irri-

16. Buck, *Land Utilization*, p. 304.

17. Information on wooden chain pumps is from King, *Farmers of Forty Centuries*, p. 263; for improved manual waterwheels, see JPRS, no. 42,495 (1965), p. 7, which states that these devices raised working efficiency "more than twofold," implying that labor productivity for traditional waterwheels was only one-third of the level reached by improved versions.

18. See Table 4-4.

19. One mou is equivalent to 0.0667 hectare or 0.1647 acre. "Several Points About Mechanized Irrigation and Drainage in Kiangsu," *Chung-kuo shui-li* [Chinese Water Control], no. 1 (1957), p. 49, reports that in 1957 the province's 125,000 horsepower of irrigation and drainage equipment served 5.8 million mou of cropland, for an average of 46 mou per horsepower; most equipment was used between 800 and 1,000 hours a year. Similar averages for regions in Chekiang and Hupei as well as Kiangsu appear in JPRS, no. 15,657 (1962), p. 21; no. 16,268 (1962), p. 49; and no. 22,806 (1963), p. 72.

20. A report published in 1967 stated that a 3.5-horsepower lift pump can service 100 mou of land located 100 meters above water level, and a 7-horsepower lift

gated or drained with pumps that operate twenty-four hours a day. As a result, mechanization creates a potential not only for higher output within the traditional cropping pattern, but also for additional increases from the introduction of modified cropping systems that use greater quantities of resources but promise a higher output in return.

Mechanized threshing, which is now common in some parts of China, illustrates how machinery can create the opportunity for intensified farming cycles. Electric threshing machines come in various sizes: large models can remove 50 kilograms of grain a minute, and smaller units can handle 1,200 kilograms of wheat an hour.[21] These machines require from two to three workers to feed in the sheaves and remove stalks and grain; additional labor is needed to winnow the grain, sometimes aided by electric fans to blow away the chaff. Although this is still a labor-intensive process, it consumes less labor and is also less taxing than traditional methods of threshing. Reducing the length and intensity of labor requirements in the peak season clearly creates opportunities for intensification of farming.

Wheat threshing is also accomplished using stone rollers pulled by tractors. One report states that one tractor can perform the work of twenty-four draft animals, each of which consumes from 150 to 300 kilograms of food grains a year, along with quantities of fodder.[22] This shows that machinery can save land by freeing arable acreage from fodder crops as well as saving labor, here in the form of animal tending.

A variety of other machines are now used to process crops. Hsi-yang county in Shansi province reports that a corn-shucking machine can process 50,000 kilograms a day, whereas a strong worker can process only 250 kilograms by hand.[23] A cotton gin tested near Peking enabled three men to process six kilograms an hour—

---

pump can irrigate 200 mou of land situated 200 meters above water level (JPRS, no. 42,484 [1967], p. 8). High-pressure piston pumps made by county-level machinery plants in Honan province and raising water well over fifty meters were inspected by the Rural Small-Scale Industry Delegation in June 1975 (Rawski Trip Notes).

21. Perkins and others, *Rural . . . Industry,* pp. 130–34; and Rawski Trip Notes.

22. JPRS, no. 21,361 (1963), pp. 1 and 6.

23. *Yung Ta-chai ching-shen kao nung-yeh chi-hsieh-hua* [Use the Ta-chai Spirit to Raise Farm Mechanization] (T'aiyüan: Shan-hsi jen-min ch'u-pan-she, 1974), p. 25.

or, assuming an eight-hour day, sixteen kilograms per man-day, compared with from two to three kilograms for manual labor.[24] Other crop-processing machines used in rural China include fodder choppers, sugar-cane defoliators, winnowing machines, and small numbers of combine harvesters.

Transport is another area in which machines have influenced patterns of rural employment. Rural transport has been affected by the growth of national networks of rail, water, and highway transport and by the expansion of bicycle production, but the greatest effect has come from the growing substitution of tractors and power tillers for carrying poles and man- and animal-drawn carts.

Power tillers are manufactured in most provinces and cost approximately 2,000 yuan. They are powered by diesels of from seven to twelve horsepower, which are usually made in the same province as the tractor. One producer reports that when hitched to a trailer, a twelve-horsepower power tiller can haul one ton of cargo at a speed of fifteen kilometers an hour.[25] The increasing use of these vehicles releases labor for other tasks. The potential number of workers involved may be seen from a 1957 estimate of 10 million workers, or 4.3 percent of the agricultural labor force, engaged in traditional transport work.[26]

Tractors and power tillers are also used in land preparation. Machine plowing not only saves labor, but also may improve the quality of plowing in depth and timing. The overall effect of these machines is illustrated by the experience of a model unit in Shansi province: "The power tiller . . . is a multi-purpose machine. Each unit is used 345 days per year to plow 500 mou of land, transport 550 tons of grain, 3,500 tons of organic fertilizer, 50 tons of tax grain, 625 tons of ashes, 20 tons of threshed grain, deliver 100 tons of chemical fertilizer and cement, haul 500 tons of coal for the commune members, 390 tons of straw, also to fight drought by pumping 40,000 cubic meters of water and to haul 100,000 cubic meters of rock."[27]

24. JPRS, no. 44,251 (1968), p. 29.

25. Perkins and others, Rural . . . Industry, chap. 5; and Rawski Trip Notes.

26. Ta-chung Liu and Kung-chia Yeh, The Economy of the Chinese Mainland (Princeton, N.J.: Princeton University Press, 1965), p. 69.

27. Yung Ta-chai ching-shen, p. 56.

TABLE 4-4. AGRICULTURAL LABOR PERFORMANCE USING VARIOUS TECHNIQUES, 1959

Activity	Traditional implements	Improved implements	Mechanical implements
Plowing	One man, two animals, three mou a day	One man, two animals, ten mou a day	Two men, one 35-horsepower tractor, seventy mou a day
Seeding	One man, one animal, twelve mou a day	Two men, three animals, fifty mou a day	Two men, one 24-horsepower tractor, 240 mou a day
Irrigation	One man drawing from a well using bucket, five tons a day	One man using waterwheel, ten tons a day	Five-horsepower gasoline pump, 570 tons a day
Harvesting	Manual, one man, two mou a day	One man, one animal, sixty mou a day	Four men, one 40-horsepower tractor, 330 mou a day
Threshing	Stone rollers, one man, one animal, 750 kilograms a day	Animal-powered thresher, six men, one animal, 2,500 kilograms a day	One large 22-horsepower thresher, fourteen men, 20,000 kilograms a day

Source: JMJP, November 17, 1959, cited in Yamamoto Hideo, Chūgoku nōgyō gijutsu taikei no tenkai [Development of China's System of Agricultural Technology] (Tokyo: Ajia keizai kenkyūjo, 1965), p. 153.

China stands on the verge of major efforts to mechanize some basic field operations, principally the transplanting of rice. Mechanical transplanters are manufactured and used in the suburban regions surrounding Shanghai and Peking and in other regions as well. At Ma-lu Commune (Chia-ting county, Shanghai), experiments have shown that, with special paddy preparation, mechanical transplanting of rice can save labor without reducing yields.[28] At another model commune in Hupei, machine transplanting reduced labor requirements in transplanting from the previous level of from sixteen to seventeen man-days per mou for single-crop rice to the 1976 level of from eleven to twelve man-days per mou for transplanting two crops.[29] Experiments conducted in several regions during 1959 indicated that transplanting machines could increase labor productivity in this task by a factor of from five to seven; one commune near Shanghai reports a fifteenfold rise in labor productivity after transplanting was mechanized.[30] Nationally, the number of transplanters in use rose from 31,100 in 1966 to 277,000 in 1973.[31]

The results of a study made in 1959 are shown in Table 4-4; they summarize some of the ways in which mechanization can reduce human and animal labor requirements. These data illustrate the labor-saving nature of electrification and mechanization in China's farm economy. But what of the economic effect of these changes? Mechanical operations are often expensive in relation to manual labor. The purchase price alone for a power tiller is equivalent to the product of from six to seven man-years of farm labor; larger tractors cost up to ten times as much as power tillers; fuel costs, although subsidized, are not low. In perhaps an extreme case, a unit in Chekiang reported that bills for fuel, repairs, and

28. Perkins and others, *Rural . . . Industry*, pp. 128–29; and Rawski Trip Notes.

29. *Liu-chi kung-she nung-yeh chi-hsieh-hua* [Farm Mechanization At Liu-chi Commune] (Peking: Jen-min ch'u-pan she, 1976), p. 20.

30. JMJP, March 5, 1960, cited in Amano Motonosuke, *Chūgoku nōgyōshi kenkyū* [Studies in Chinese Agricultural History] (Tokyo: Ochanomizu shobō, 1962), pp. 462–63; and Peter Schran, "Farm Labor and Living in China," (Champaign: University of Illinois, processed, 1976), p. 14.

31. Leslie T. C. Kuo, *Agriculture in the People's Republic of China* (New York: Praeger, 1976), p. 224.

other costs associated with mechanical pumping amounted to one-fourth of all farm production costs.[32]

High costs imply that mechanization will not be profitable unless it leads to an increase in total farm output. The high yields developed under traditional systems of husbandry make it unlikely that substantial increases in output can be obtained merely by replacing human or animal labor with machines. Unless the labor released by mechanization is diverted to activities that contribute to further intensification of cultivation or create new income-earning opportunities, mechanization is likely to raise farming costs and reduce employment opportunities.

With the exception of mechanical irrigation, the direct and immediate effect of the innovations described above invariably reduces the demand for labor. Improved water supply acts in the opposite way by stimulating the growth of both crops and weeds and therefore raising labor requirements for weeding, cultivating, harvesting, threshing, and storage. Other types of mechanization, however, displace workers without creating new demands for labor. In an economy already troubled by seasonal idleness, the introduction of large quantities of machinery into a static farming system might therefore do more harm than good.

This unfavorable outcome has not occurred in China because the farming system has been modified in directions that permit mechanization to complement rather than compete with rural labor. The success of China's farm economy in raising production through the simultaneous absorption of both labor and machinery is best seen through a detailed review of recent changes in the agricultural sector. These shifts are grouped into four categories: intensification of cropping practices, intensification of the cropping cycle, shifts toward labor-using farm activities, and rural construction programs.

China's undeniable success in absorbing new cohorts of rural workers, however, has brought with it a substantial decline in the marginal product of labor. Although the rising number of workdays per farm laborer has prevented output per man-year from declining, both output per man-day and total factor productivity

32. JPRS, no. 15,657 (1962), p. 21.

in agriculture were considerably lower in 1975 than in 1957. The productivity dimension of labor absorption is discussed in the concluding section of this chapter.

Intensification of Cropping Practices

The phrase "intensification of cropping practices" refers to an increase in the resources applied to each unit of sown acreage in the absence of changes in the type of crops grown or in the rotation cycle. Chinese publications and visitors' accounts indicate that this type of intensification has absorbed considerable quantities of labor.

Land preparation

Chinese farm specialists advocate deeper plowing than was traditionally practiced. Although deep plowing, which is intended to raise crop yields, is often associated with mechanization, there has probably been some increase in human and animal labor devoted to plowing each unit of land that is not plowed by tractors.

The major increase in labor devoted to land preparation, however, has come in the use of organic fertilizers. These fertilizers, which include human and animal manure, plant wastes, ash, silt-bearing mud, and a variety of other materials, are applied in large quantity to arable lands throughout China. Two U.S. groups touring China in 1975 and 1976 visited a number of communes at which a minimum of 50 and a maximum of 225 metric tons of organic fertilizers were applied annually to each hectare of cultivated land (that is, from 5 to 22.5 kilograms a square meter).[33] Numerous other reports could be cited from visitor accounts or Chinese sources.

At the national level, Thomas Wiens has calculated the growth of nutrients supplied by organic and chemical fertilizers during 1957–71; his results are shown in Table 4-5. Estimated nutrient supplies rose by 40 percent, with virtually the entire increase com-

33. Perkins and others, *Rural . . . Industry*, Table 8.3; Virgil A. Johnson and Halsey L. Beemer, Jr., eds., *Wheat in the People's Republic of China* (Washington, D.C.: National Academy of Sciences, 1977), p. 163.

TABLE 4-5. ESTIMATE OF FERTILIZER SUPPLY, BY SOURCE, 1957–71
(million of tons of nutrient)

Nutrient source	1957	1962	1965	1971
Large animals	4.920	4.209	4.564	5.453
Hogs	3.150	3.008	4.632	6.768
Nightsoil	1.860	2.230	2.340	2.605
Green manure	0.274	0.440[a]	0.584	0.584[a]
Bean cakes	0.525	0.436[a]	0.390	0.390[a]
Other nonchemical	1.647	1.647	1.647	1.647
Chemical	0.384	0.836	2.095	4.347
Total nutrients	12.760	12.806	16.252	21.794
Kilograms per cultivated hectare	114.0	114.6	152.3	194.9
Organic	110.6	107.2	132.7	156.1
Chemical	3.4	7.4	19.6	38.8
Kilograms of nitrogen per cultivated hectare	51.1	53.5	69.8	92.8

a. Interpolated or assumed constant in original source.

Source: Taken or calculated from Thomas B. Wiens, "Agricultural Statistics in the People's Republic of China," in *Quantitative Measures of China's Economic Output,* ed. Alexander Eckstein (Ann Arbor: University of Michigan Press, forthcoming), Table 18.

ing during the decade 1962–71. China's hog population, which rose from 146 million in 1957 to 287 million in 1974 and to 301 million in 1978, provided much of the increased nutrients.[34] Indeed, Wiens' data show that, following a decline in the hog population caused by poor harvests and early commune mismanagement, growth of the hog population contributed more nutrients to China's farmlands during 1962–71 than the rapidly expanding supply of chemical fertilizers.

Taken together, the organic nutrient sources noted in Table 4-5 contributed 56.2 percent of increased nutrients during 1957–71 and 60.9 percent during the shorter period 1962–71. Despite the growing share of chemical products in the fertilizer total, evidence of widespread nutrient deficiency shows the continuing importance of organic fertilizers to raising the supply of nutrients as well as to maintaining soil structure.[35]

34. The figure for 1957 is from Nai-ruenn Chen, *Chinese Economic Statistics* (Chicago: Aldine, 1967), p. 340; for 1974, see Bureau of Foreign Affairs, "Briefing on Chinese Agriculture," p. 3; for 1978, see "Communiqué on Fulfillment of China's 1975 Economic Plan," *Beijing Review,* no. 27 (1979), p. 38.

35. Visiting plant scientists report that "on farmers' fields there was evidence in most areas visited of a nitrogen shortage for rice. It appeared that some nitrogen

In the present context, the most significant characteristic of organic fertilizer is the enormous labor input associated with its collection, preparation, and application. One pig produces an average of 1,642 kilograms of excreta annually. Nitrogen retention is substantially increased by mixing the excreta with dirt from the floor of the pigsty and burying this compost in covered pits to promote fermentation.[36] In Hai-ch'eng county of Liaoning province the peasants accumulate from 17,500 to 20,000 kilograms of manure (excreta plus earth) annually for each pig. This process requires the following amounts of labor:[37]

Process	Man-days	Animal-days
Earth transport	2.5–3.5	5–7
Dumping earth into pit	1.2–1.5	—
Paving pit with grass	1–2	—
Getting manure out of pit	1.5–3.5	—
Pulverizing manure	3–3.2	—
Manure transport	6.5–7.5	6.5–7.5
Manuring fields	1.5–2.5	—
Annual total for preparing and applying manure from one pig	18.2–23.7	11.5–14.5

I Ts'ai and Wang P'i-chang contend that although this process ensures a high rate of nitrogen retention, "it causes excessive expenditures of labor and animal power." They suggest that annual manure accumulation be reduced to 10,000 kilograms per pig by using less earth.[38] If it were assumed that reducing manure accumulation from about 18,750 kilograms (the midpoint of the data from Hai-ch'eng county) to 10,000 kilograms for each pig would reduce labor requirements proportionately, the labor requirement

had been applied, but the leaf color often suggested that this was inadequate" (*Plant Studies in the People's Republic of China* [Washington, D.C.: National Academy of Sciences, 1975], p. 46). For similar observations on north China, see Schran, "Farm Labor and Living," p. 20.

36. *Nung-yeh ch'ang-yung shu-tzu shou-ts'e* [Handbook of Common Agricultural Data] (Peking: Jen-min ch'u-pan she, 1975), p. 101; I Ts'ai and Wang P'i-chang, "Ways of Improving the Economic Effect of Fertilization," *Ching-chi yen-chiu* [Economic Research], no. 4 (1965), translated in ECMM no. 475 (1965), p. 30.

37. I and Wang, pp. 37–38.

38. Ibid.

for treating each pig's manure might be expected to decline from approximately twenty-one man-days and thirteen animal-days to about 53 percent of these amounts: that is, to about eleven man-days and seven animal-days.

Large animals—horses, mules, donkeys, cows, buffalo, and oxen—produce more excreta than hogs. An average of data for horses and oxen gives an annual total of 9,125 kilograms per head, or 5.6 times the output of one hog. If similar labor inputs are assumed for processing one ton of excreta for pigs and large animals, labor requirements for composting pig and large-animal manure in 1957 and 1975 may be calculated as follows:[39]

	Estimated animal population (millions)		Labor requirements for composting (millions)			
			Man-days		Animal-days	
	1957	1974/75	1957	1974/75	1957	1974/75
Hogs	146	287	1,606	3,157	1,022	2,009
Large animals	83	104	5,113	6,406	3,293	4,077

At 275 working days a year, the increased direct human labor (exclusive of animal tending) required to compost and process the manure of the enlarged animal population annually is equivalent to 11.5 million man-years for hogs and 23.3 million man-years for large animals. The combined total of 34.8 million man-years amounts to more than one-third of the rough total of 97.3 million workers added to China's agricultural labor force between 1957 and 1975.

Less is known about the growth of quantities applied and hence of labor absorbed in preparing other types of organic fertilizers. Application of human nightsoil is closely related to population growth. Availability of green manure and bean cakes depends on cultivation of green manure crops (which may have ex-

39. Animal population for 1957 from Chen, *Chinese Economic Statistics,* p. 340; for 1974/75 from "Briefing on Chinese Agriculture," p. 3 (for hogs) and from unpublished estimates made by Anthony Tang and Thomas Gottschang (for large animals). The reduced labor requirements mentioned in the text are used in these calculations.

panded more rapidly than is shown in Table 4-5) and of soybeans, respectively.[40] One might speculate that the category "other non-chemical"—which includes mud from the bottoms of canals, streambeds, reservoirs, fishponds, lakes, and rivers; ash, leaves, weeds, and plant refuse not used as animal feed; and manure from chickens, ducks, rabbits, and other domestic animals—has not remained constant, as shown in Table 4-5, but has increased along with such variables as the number of dams, fish ponds, trees, and irrigation canals, as well as household coal consumption and overall output of plant products.

In any case, there can be no doubt that collection, mixing, storage, transport, and application of various types of organic fertilizers account for a significant portion of the increased labor input into China's farm economy. One Chinese economist sees the accumulation and application of organic fertilizer as limited by the opportunity cost of the required labor: "[A]pplying fertilizers in layers and giving the field a greater number of dressings according to the dissimilar needs of agricultural crops . . . at different periods of growth definitely can yield good results technically. But applying fertilizers in layers and giving the field a greater number of dressings *will spend more labor*. This calls for the weighing of the advantages and disadvantages through comparing and analyzing the economic results before we can make a final decision."[41]

The significance of organic fertilizers in rural China's labor economy may be summarized by referring to the same author's observation that "under the present condition of having to supply an abundance of organic fertilizer, the amount of manpower and animal power spent in the accumulation, transportation and application of manure generally takes up *between 30 and 40 percent of the*

40. The area planted to green manure crops rose from 3.42 million hectares in 1957 to 6.78 million hectares in 1965 (Kang Chao, *Agricultural Production in Communist China* [Madison: University of Wisconsin Press, 1970], p. 312) and to 12.3 million hectares in 1977 or 1978 ("Briefing on China's Agriculture," p. 3). Since this area rose by 81 percent between 1965 and 1978, it is quite likely that supplies of green manure rose during 1965–71 rather than stagnating, as is shown in Table 4-5.

41. Yen Jui-chen, "Several Questions on Increasing the Economic Benefits of Fertilizers," *Ching-chi yen-chiu* [Economic Research], no. 6 (1964), translated in ECMM, no. 429 (1964), p. 24, with emphasis added.

total amount of manpower and animal power expended in the whole year."[42]

Planting and transplanting

Chinese farm specialists have advocated "close planting," which means raising the density of plants in the fields, since the early 1950s. Support for this labor-absorbing method has been eroded, however, by the memory of irrational implementation and consequent reductions of output during the years of the Great Leap Forward. Since then, Chinese agronomists have promoted "rational close planting," but recent disclosures indicate that this also has at times been counterproductive: for example, experiments in Hsiang-fen county, Shensi province, show that reducing the number of cotton plants from 4,000 to 2,000 per mou raises cotton yields and also permits vegetables to be grown between the rows of cotton plants.[43] Other districts have claimed positive results from close planting of cotton. In Hsin-hsiang county, Honan province, "Ch'i-li-ying Commune, after years of testing and popularization, has raised the density of its cotton plants from 2,000 to 7,000 and even 8,000 per mou"; with use of this method, yields rose by 250 percent between 1957 and 1973.[44] In Hsin-chou county, Hupei province, cotton was planted at a density of from 3,000 to 4,000 plants per mou during the mid-1960s, with good results.[45]

The contribution of close planting to output growth and labor absorption in other types of cropping is equally unclear. Closer planting of rice plants can raise yields, but only if accompanied by increased fertilization.[46] Specialists from the United States have observed that stunted produce may be the chief result of tighter spacing of vegetable plants.[47]

---

42. Ibid., with emphasis added. *1967 Fei-ch'ing nien-pao* [1967 Yearbook of Chinese Communism] (Taipei: Fei-ch'ing yen-chiu tsa-chih she, 1967), p. 1383, gives a national figure of 40 percent of labor power occupied with manuring for the 1950s.

43. *China News Analysis*, no. 1,141 (1978), p. 6.

44. Chu and Tien, *Inside a People's Commune*, pp. 16 and 40.

45. Ch'eng Chin-chieh, "The Way Liuchi Commune Wins Its Higher Grain and Cotton Yields," *Ching-chi yen-chiu* [Economic Research], no. 4 (1965), translated in ECMM, no. 473 (1965), p. 5.

46. I and Wang, "Fertilization," pp. 29–30.

47. *Plant Studies*, p. 87.

Transplanting of rice shoots from seed beds into the main field is a well-known feature of traditional Chinese agriculture. This procedure economizes on land and reduces the growing period in the main field, thus allowing an increase in the index of multiple cropping (sown area/cultivated area) within a fixed growing season. The highly labor-intensive practice of transplanting young shoots from seed beds into the fields has been adopted for a growing range of crops. In addition to rice, which is universally transplanted, and vegetables, which were commonly transplanted before 1949, some regions now transplant wheat, maize, cotton, soybeans, rape, and "such fiber crops as hemp, jute and abutilon avicennae."[48]

Crop management

The amount of labor devoted to each crop-hectare is now considerably larger than in the past. Buck's surveys of China's farming regions showed the following average human labor inputs per crop-hectare during 1929–33:[49]

Crop	National average	Average for region with highest labor inputs
Cotton	130.9	163.0
Maize	56.8	66.7
Rice	202.5	338.4
Wheat	64.2	123.5

The American Wheat Studies Delegation, which visited China in 1976 was told that:

. . . the cultivation of "high yield plots" of wheat required 225–450 days of work per sown hectare in the communes visited, the most frequent reference being to 300 days per hectare. Similar estimates were given for corn, rice, and cotton. This greater and more uniform effort per unit of cropped land appears to be attributable to the fact that all land—not only

---

48. Ibid., p. 86; G. F. Sprague, "Agriculture in China," *Science*, no. 188 (1975), p. 552; Johnson and Beemer, eds., *Wheat*, pp. 19 and 111; JPRS, no. 42,524 (1967), p. 12, and no. 44,014 (1967), p. 9.

49. Buck, *Land Utilization*, p. 302.

rice land—is being irrigated, that the same kind of heavy fertilizing is practiced on all crops, and that deep plowing and other forms of more intensive cultivation are used as a rule. The workdays per sown hectare reached 450 in two instances . . . where corn and wheat were being transplanted by hand. And they stayed—or had fallen below—150 in one case . . . where part of the work had been mechanized.[50]

This information, which comes from a sample of advanced farming regions, indicates that abundant supplies of organic and chemical fertilizers and water have created labor requirements (exclusive of composting) of roughly five times the prewar national average for each unit of land sown to wheat and maize, 2.3 times for cotton, and 1.5 times for rice (based on 300 man-days per sown hectare). These labor requirements do not take into account any increase in the index of multiple cropping. If the figure of 300 man-days per sown hectare for high-yield fields of irrigated maize, wheat, rice, and cotton is compared not with national averages, but with regions of peak prewar labor input for each crop, it is clear that the labor requirements of intensive cultivation in the 1970s outstrip even these higher figures for every crop except rice.

To what tasks is this extra labor assigned? In the case of cotton, Chinese reports allow an answer of some precision. The data in Table 4-6 permit comparison of unit labor requirements derived from Buck's nationwide surveys of the 1930s with reports from three units in Wu-kung county, Shensi province, for 1962. These comparisons show that the added labor applied to cotton in the unirrigated Wu-kung fields goes primarily to three activities: cultivating and pruning, harvesting, and indirect labor (probably composting).

Developments in Wu-kung may not be atypical. Chinese descriptions of cotton cultivation portray a highly labor-intensive system in which each plant receives individual attention. Farm journals report that "during the budding period of cotton, the best result is observed when the fertilizer is applied directly near the root" of the plant, rather than being broadcast.[51] Another source observes that "a usual process was to pluck the tips of cotton

50. See Johnson and Beemer, eds., *Wheat*, p. 111.
51. JPRS, no. 43,415 (1967), p. 42.

TABLE 4-6. LABOR REQUIREMENTS, YIELDS, AND PRODUCTIVITY
IN COTTON GROWING, 1929–33 AND 1962

| Survey data, 1929–33 | | Wu-kung, Shensi, 1962 | | |
| | | Individual units | | |
		A	B	C
Labor requirements, total (man-days per mou)	8.8	Labor requirements, total (man-days per mou)	40.28	35.90	34.57
Direct labor					
Plowing	0.3	Direct labor			
Digging	0.2	Land preparation	0.84	1.33	3.75
Harrowing	0.2	Planting	0.13	0.11	0.57
Planting	0.4	Cultivating and			
Cultivating	2.3	pruning	10.75	11.25	8.75
Fertilizing	0.6	Transport and			
Harvesting	3.0	apply fertilizer	1.88	2.00	2.50
Total	7.0	Plant protection	1.88	1.25	1.40
		Harvesting	13.37	11.87	13.00
Indirect labor		Total	28.85	27.81	29.97
Carrying	1.0				
Threshing	0.1	Indirect labor, total	11.43	8.09	4.60
Storage	0.1				
Drying	0.3				
Piling	0.1				
Other	0.2				
Total	1.8				
Yields (kilograms per mou)	12.6	Yields (kilograms per mou)	40.0	20.0	15.0
Output per man-day (kilograms)[a]	1.4	Output per man-day (kilograms)[a]	1.0	0.6	0.4

a. Output in kilograms of ginned cotton.

Sources: 1929–33 data, John L. Buck, Land Utilization in China (Nanking: University of Nanking, 1937), pp. 302–04; 1962 data, Wu Yung-hsiang, "Appraisal of the Economic Effect of Dryland Cotton Cultivation in Wu-kung County," Ching-chi yen-chiu [Economic Research], no. 10 (1963), p. 33.

plants. . . . A new method has been used since 1961 . . . the tips are pinched slightly."[52] A third source states that farmers in one area rely on constant plowing and loosening of the soil and timely cutting of leaves and branches to control growth during the crucial budding period.[53] Similar care is exercised at the final stages of plant growth, when "it is important to exterminate insect pests,

52. JPRS, no. 43,073 (1967), p. 18.
53. JPRS, no. 43,410 (1967), p. 32.

prune the cotton plants properly, and carry out weeding work just as carefully as at the early stage" of growth.[54] Harvesting is also done on a plant-by-plant basis. Chinese sources emphasize the delicacy of this task, and visitors report that cotton fields "are picked frequently and few open bolls are visible at any one time."[55]

How effective is this increase in the labor applied to preparing, cultivating, and harvesting in raising cotton yields? At the national level, average yields per mou are known to have risen from the figure of 12.6 kilograms reported by Buck for 1929–33 to 19 in 1957 and an estimated 24 for 1964/65, indicating some progress toward the regional yield targets of 20, 30, 40, and 50 kilograms per mou established during the mid-1950s.[56] At least some of this increase must be attributed to improved supplies of chemical fertilizer, water, and pesticides and to better seeds and mechanization—leaving the output effect of increased labor inputs uncertain. The data for Wu-kung county are no more revealing. The figures in Table 4-6 seem to indicate a positive association between labor intensity and both yield and output per man-day; here again, however, use of pesticides and machinery must be considered. Furthermore, data for seven production brigades within the commune described as "Unit A" in Table 4-6 show a distinctly negative association between labor application and output per man-day, suggesting diminishing marginal labor productivity. Again, the impact of higher labor input is indeterminate.

Scattered references indicate that similar labor-using methods are commonly applied to crops other than cotton:[57]

It is important to clean the peanut plant at the time of sprouting.

---

54. JPRS, no. 44,050 (1968), p. 1.

55. JPRS, no. 43,377 (1967), p. 34, and *Plant Studies*, p. 108.

56. National yield data from Thomas B. Wiens, "Agricultural Statistics," in *Quantitative Measures of China's Economic Output*, ed. Alexander Eckstein (Ann Arbor: University of Michigan Press, forthcoming), Table 22; regional yield targets from Kuo, *Agriculture*, pp. 110–11.

57. Quotations are from: JPRS, no. 42,495 (1967), p. 9, and no. 44,527 (1968), p. 26; *Plant Studies*, pp. 46, 65 and 116; and Harold Reynolds, "Chinese Insect Control Integrates Old and New," *Chemical and Engineering News* (March 15, 1976), p. 30.

Increase the production of broad beans by cutting tips and main stems.

Research in the northeast confirms results obtained elsewhere that a concentration of nitrogen fertilizers near the root zone of the rice plant gave a greater efficiency of utilization than broadcast applications.

[Maize] planting is done by hand. Weed control is almost exclusively done by hand hoeing. Herbicides are used to only a limited extent because of problems posed by both interplanting and crop sequences.

In the vegetable growing area around Shanghai . . . hand watering of individual plants helps assure success of the transplanted crop.

One of the biggest plant protection resources is their huge human labor force. . . . Some 1,500 people in one commune visited are involved in plant protection work. Of these, 65 raise and herd some 220,000 ducks—a traditional method of controlling paddy insects. . . . The country has the manpower to grow and deploy [wasps, fungi, bacteria, and other biological control agents] by methods economically infeasible here. . . . Masses of 300,000 wasps per acre are released . . .

Biological methods were used to control plant diseases and insect pests on 3.47 million hectares of land in 1976.[58]

Increasing use of chemical technology also requires a substantial labor input. Reynolds reports that in the field of insecticides, the Chinese have moved away from DDT, which bred resistance among target species, toward "narrower spectrum, less persistent organophosphorus insecticides," which require repeated applications.[59] Chinese sources also emphasize the desirability of multiple applications of chemical fertilizers, particularly for sandy soils, which do not retain unused nutrients.[60]

The materials presented in this section lead to the conclusion

58. *Peking Review*, no. 30 (1977), p. 31.

59. Reynolds, "Chinese Insect Control," p. 30.

60. I and Wang, "Fertilization," pp. 27–28; JPRS, no. 43,679 (1967), p. 4, no. 44,050 (1968), p. 4, and no. 44,527 (1968), p. 3.

that intensification of cropping practices—an increase in resources applied per crop-hectare of particular crops in the absence of changes in multiple-cropping or rotation patterns—has absorbed large amounts of labor during the past two decades. The largest sources of new labor demand within this category appear to have come from an increased application of organic fertilizers and from large increases in labor requirements for transplanting and cultivating cotton, wheat, maize, other northern grain crops, and, to a lesser extent, rice.

Intensification of the Cropping Cycle

The phrase "intensification of the cropping cycle" refers to an increase in the number of crops harvested per unit of cultivated land resulting from multiple cropping and intercropping. Multiple cropping and intercropping have long histories in China. Buck found that the overall index of multiple cropping (sown area divided by cultivated area) had reached 1.49 in the regions for which he collected survey data during 1929–33; for regions in which double cropping of rice was the chief farming system, the index was as high as 1.76. Since 1949 the national index of multiple cropping has risen from 1.31 in 1952 to 1.41 in 1957 and to more than 1.50 in 1977 or 1978.[61]

Multiple cropping

Raising the index of multiple cropping requires major increases in farm labor. In rice-growing areas, for example, a shift from one to two crops raises labor requirements by from 60 to 70 percent.[62] Extension of multiple cropping is feasible in many areas in China in which intensification is limited less by climate than by the supply of labor, water, and fertilizer.

61. Information on index of multiple cropping from Buck, *Land Utilization*, p. 274; Chen, *Chinese Economic Statistics*, pp. 284–85; and "Briefing on China's Agriculture," p. 4. The report that China's index of multiple cropping is more than 1.50 probably indicates a figure between 1.50 and 1.60.

62. "Evolution and Development of the Paddy Crop Situation in the Lake District," *Chung-kuo nung-pao* [China Agricultural Bulletin], no. 8 (1964), p. 27.

One way of raising the ratio of sown to cultivated acreage is to develop plant varieties that either mature in a shorter time or are more resistant to extreme weather conditions than existing varieties. In China reforms of this type are difficult because of the already intensive cropping system developed over the centuries. New varieties of rice developed at the International Rice Research Institute are unsuited to many parts of China because their growing period is too long to fit into existing patterns of double and triple cropping.[63] A review of the secondary literature suggests that Chinese efforts at seed development over the past twenty years have emphasized development of varieties that provide high yields while resisting common plant diseases, rather than development of fast-growing plant types. Recent reports indicate, however, that more attention is being given to development of early-maturing varieties of rice, wheat, and vegetables to expand the scope for multiple cropping.[64]

The major stimulus to expansion of multiple cropping since 1957 has come from changes that eliminate bottlenecks arising from seasonal shortages of farm inputs, notably human and animal labor. Buck found that 81 percent of 260 localities surveyed during 1929–33 reported seasonal labor shortages, most often during the harvest period (see Table 4-2). The following report from Hsin-chou county, Hupei province, illustrates the problems encountered by localities attempting to intensify the cropping cycle:

> This place harvests a cotton crop and a wheat crop each year. However, from planting to harvesting, wheat and cotton need a total of 428 days. . . . [T]his is the principal contradiction of the two-crop system. . . . It finds concentrated reflection in the two periods of "four quicks" and "three kinds of autumn work" during the summer harvest.
>
> First, the "four quicks" period [that is, quick in harvesting wheat, destroying the stubble, controlling insect pests, and

63. *Plant Studies*, p. 45.
64. General treatments include *Plant Studies*; Kuo, *Agriculture*, chap. 14; and Benedict Stavis, *Making Green Revolution* (Ithaca, N.Y.: Cornell University Rural Development Program, 1974). In 1976 the Wheat Studies Delegation observed that "the one major objective of all programs visited is early maturity" (Johnson and Beemer, eds., *Wheat*, p. 31).

dressing the land] lasts only about ten days, but there are eleven kinds of work to be done at the same time. The amount of work involved is huge, and there is a time limit.
. . .

Next, the period for "three kinds of autumn work" [that is, autumn harvesting, plowing, and planting] also lasts only about ten days. It is necessary to harvest cotton as well as to plant wheat. If the removal of cotton plants is postponed in order to ensure the cotton harvest, wheat cannot be sown in good time. If the cotton plants are removed earlier, cotton yield must suffer. This is the second hurdle which must be negotiated in order to ensure the two-crop system.[65]

If farmers attempt to complete a rotation cycle for which resources cannot meet peak demands, yields will fall. In Yuan-chiang county, Hunan province, a region in which double cropping of rice requires that four man-days of labor be devoted to each mou within a period of fifteen or sixteen days during July and August, reducing the area of two crop rice from 70 to 57 percent of the paddy field area raised average yields. Observers concluded that "[u]nder present conditions of labor supply and reliance on manual labor, it makes sense for the lake district to allocate about 50 percent of paddy land to double cropping."[66]

Under these conditions machines capable of replacing labor formerly devoted to irrigation, harvesting, threshing, transport, plowing, and transplanting during seasonal periods of peak labor demand can eliminate bottlenecks limiting the spread of multiple cropping. In the Hupei example described above, machinery performed tasks equivalent to 61 work-days for each of one commune's 2,205 workers. Use of threshing machines and power tillers ensured timely processing of the wheat harvest and sowing of the cotton crop. In the same unit, "the 'two-way rush' [that is, rushing through harvesting and planting] has for years been the critical period of time in which cotton and rice fight for labor power, fertilizer, and water supply. But in 1964, because machines were used to lift water, abundant labor power was saved. The

65. Ch'eng, "Liu-chi Commune," p. 3.
66. "Evolution . . . of the Paddy Crop," p. 28.

pressure of the 'two-way rush' on paddy fields was reduced, and there were special shifts responsible for fighting the drought and guarding against insect pests in cotton fields."[67] Mechanization allowed unprecedented harvests in this locale.

These anecdotes show that mechanization can create opportunities to add crops to the annual cycle without breaching the newly enlarged peak supplies of human, animal, and machine power. A recent report placing the 1977/78 index of multiple cropping above 1.50, an increase of about 10 percent over the 1957 figure of 1.41, indicates modest success in intensifying cropping patterns. New double-cropping areas have emerged in areas north of the Yellow River, including Hopei and Shansi provinces and parts of Shantung and Honan, and a shift from double to triple cropping is reported for the delta regions of Kiangsu and Kwangtung. Because the area planted to green manure crops, which Chinese sources exclude from calculations of the multiple cropping index, grew by 8.9 million hectares between 1957 and 1977/78, the overall sown area has risen by approximately 17 percent over a period of two decades, during which the cultivated area has remained near the 1957 level of 112 million hectares.[68]

Intercropping

Intercropping, or simultaneous cultivation of more than one crop in a single field, is common in many regions of China. Although foreign agricultural specialists report a wide variety of intercropping systems, the extent to which this represents a modification of traditional practice remains uncertain, as does the treatment of interplanting in estimates of multiple-cropping indexes.[69] It is worth noting, however, that intercropping raises

67. Ch'eng, "Liu-chi Commune," p. 4.

68. Information about the index of multiple cropping and area sown to green manure crops is from notes 40 and 61, above. The spread of multiple cropping is discussed in *Plant Studies*, pp. 114–15. Computation of the index of multiple cropping is discussed in Chen, *Chinese Economic Statistics*, p. 59. For cultivated area, see ibid., p. 285; Dwight H. Perkins, "Constraints Influencing China's Agricultural Performance," in U.S. Congress, Joint Economic Committee, *China: A Reassessment of the Economy* (Washington, D.C.: U.S. Government Printing Office, 1975), p. 353; and "Briefing on Chinese Agriculture," p. 2.

69. *Plant Studies*, pp. 85 and 115–16; Johnson and Beemer, eds., *Wheat*, pp. 16–20.

requirements for both direct and (through fertilizer, water, and so on) indirect labor input into the growing process.

A Shift toward Labor-Using Farming Activities

One way of raising agricultural manpower requirements is to increase the share of relatively labor-using activities in the total farming picture. Data presented in Tables 4-7 and 4-8 show that the years since 1957 have witnessed a modest but definite trend in this direction.

Buck gives the following data for main labor requirements for growing various crops during 1929–33:[70]

Grain crops	Man-days per crop-hectare	Other crops	Man-days per crop-hectare
Maize	57	Cotton	131
Wheat	64	Sugar cane	168
Kaoliang	87	Tobacco	218
Millet	99	Tea	312
Oats	141	Mulberry	
Rice	203	(for silk)	485

The five nongrain crops above can be regarded as labor intensive because they require more labor per acre than any grains except paddy rice. Cotton is included because of recent increases in its labor intensity. Other labor-intensive activities include vegetable growing and, because of the labor associated with the collection and treatment of manure, the raising of hogs and draft animals.

Table 4-7 summarizes available data on output growth for various sectors of China's farm economy between 1957 and (whenever possible) 1974. These data show a clear pattern of differential growth favoring labor-intensive products. With the exception of large animals (for which slow growth is associated with the growing availability of tractors) and silkworm cocoons, each labor-intensive activity has grown more rapidly than output of grain crops.

A rough calculation of the gross value of agricultural output for

70. Calculated from Buck, *Land Utilization*, p. 302.

TABLE 4-7. GROWTH OF AGRICULTURAL OUTPUT, 1957–74

Category	Gross value, 1957 (billions of 1952 yuan) (1)	Growth rate, post-1957 (percent) (2)	Period covered by data in (2) (3)
Grain	22.81	2.1	1957–74
Labor-intensive agriculture	12.22	3.5[a]	
Hogs	3.95[b]	4.1[c]	1957–74
Vegetables	3.91[b]	3.8[b]	1957–70
Cotton	2.78	2.5	1957–74
Large animals	0.57	0.9	1957–72
Tobacco	0.45	6.4	1957–74
Sugar	0.27	4.7[d]	1957–74
Silk cocoons	0.13	0.9	1957–73
Tea	0.16	2.7	1957–73
Other	2.12	2.2[a]	
Soybeans	1.41	2.4[e]	1957–74
Hemp	0.40	1.0	1957–74
Sheep and goats	0.31	2.8	1957–72
Total identified	37.15	2.6[a]	
Unidentified	9.93		
Total output, plant and animal products, 1957	47.08[f]		

a. Average of component growth rates weighted by 1957 gross output values.

b. Dwight H. Perkins, "Growth and Changing Structure in China's Twentieth-Century Economy," in *China's Modern Economy in Historical Perspective*, ed. Dwight H. Perkins (Stanford, Calif.: Stanford University Press, 1975), p. 154, converted from 1957 to 1952 prices using an index derived from Nai-ruenn Chen, *Chinese Economic Statistics* (Chicago: Aldine, 1967), p. 364.

c. Based on hog population figures shown in note 34 of this chapter.

d. U.S. Central Intelligence Agency, *People's Republic of China: Handbook of Economic Indicators* (Washington, D.C., 1976), p. 3.

e. U.S. Central Intelligence Agency, *China: Agricultural Performance in 1975* (Washington, D.C., 1976), p. 9.

f. Thomas B. Wiens, "Agricultural Statistics in the People's Republic of China," in *Quantitative Measures of China's Economic Output*, ed. Alexander Eckstein (Ann Arbor: University of Michigan Press, forthcoming), Table 8.

Sources (except as noted): *Column 1*, Ta-chung Liu and Kung-chia Yeh, *The Economy of the Chinese Mainland* (Princeton, N.J.: Princeton University Press, 1965), pp. 397–98. *Column 2*, Wiens, "Agricultural Statistics," Table 21, and, *for tea*, Wiens' note 81.

1974, presented in Table 4-8, shows that the incremental contribution of labor-intensive activities to farm output growth was nearly 50 percent more than their share in total output in 1957, whereas the incremental contribution of grain is only about three-fourths of its initial share of output. If data were available for dairying and horticulture, two labor-intensive sectors that appear to have

TABLE 4-8. SECTORAL CONTRIBUTIONS TO GROWTH
OF AGRICULTURAL OUTPUT, 1957–74
(billions of 1957 yuan)

| Sector | Gross value of output | | | | Contribution to growth of gross value of output, 1957–74 | |
| | 1957 | | 1974 | | | |
	Amount	Share	Amount	Share	Amount	Share
Total	53.700[a]	100.0	83.076[b]	100.0	29.376	100.0
Grain	29.970[a]	55.8	42.670[c]	51.4	12.700	43.2
Labor-intensive activities	10.873[d]	20.2	19.514[c]	23.5	8.641	29.4
Other	1.886[d]	3.5	2.731[c]	3.3	0.845	2.9
Unidentified[e]	10.971	20.4	18.161	21.9	7.190	24.5

a. Dwight H. Perkins, "Growth and Changing Structure in China's Twentieth-Century Economy," in *China's Modern Economy in Historical Perspective,* ed. Dwight H. Perkins (Stanford, Calif.: Stanford University Press, 1975), p. 154.

b. Based on the 1957 figure and the 2.6 percent annual growth rate for 1957–74 derived in Table 4-7.

c. Based on component growth rates derived in Table 4-7.

d. Converted from 1952 to 1957 prices using an index derived from Nai-ruenn Chen, *Chinese Economic Statistics* (Chicago: Aldine, 1967), p. 364.

e. Residuals.

Source: Table 4-7.

grown rapidly since 1957, the trend toward labor-using activities might be stronger than is shown in Tables 4-7 and 4-8.[71]

Strong performance of labor-intensive segments of the farm economy raises the present estimate of the gross value of agricultural output for 1974, shown below, above Perkins' results:[72]

| Year | Gross value of agricultural output (billions of 1957 yuan) | | |
	Perkins	Wiens	Present study
1957	53.700	53.7	53.700
1964	51.500	—	—
1965	58.960	—	—
1974	77.700	79.9	83.076
1975	—	—	83.907

71. Chi I-chai, "A Study of Food Output in Mainland China III," *Fei-ch'ing yueh-pao* [Chinese Communist Affairs], vol. 10, no. 9 (1967), translated in JPRS, no. 43,937 (1968), p. 17, estimates that production of powdered milk rose at an annual rate of 12.3 percent between 1957 and 1966.

72. Gross value estimates are from Dwight H. Perkins, "Growth and Changing

Perkins' estimate for 1964 is derived from the figure for 1974 using Premier Chou En-lai's statement that output rose by 51 percent during 1964–74. This shows the need for some upward revision of Perkins' figure for 1974 which implies that growth of output during 1964/65—a year of stagnant grain production—reached an impossibly high figure of 14.5 percent. Raising the figure for 1974 to 83.076 billion yuan lowers the 1964/65 increase to 7.2 percent. This is still excessive, suggesting that either Perkins' figure for 1965 is too high or the present figure for 1974 is too low.[73]

Further increases in labor requirements may have occurred as a result of shifts in the composition of grain output. Since "the manual labor required for working in paddy fields is 2–3 times that for wheat or [maize]," the northward spread of rice cultivation may have raised the average level of labor input for each unit of acreage sown to food grains.[74]

Rural Construction

Annual campaigns to build water-conservancy and land-improvement projects during the winter months have become a regular feature of Chinese rural life and one which has absorbed vast amounts of manpower during the past fifteen years. These campaigns, which encompass major projects coordinated in Peking, as well as local projects planned and carried out by communes and brigades, cover a wide range of activities including water encatch-

---

Structure of China's Twentieth-Century Economy," in *China's Modern Economy in Historical Perspective,* ed. Dwight H. Perkins (Stanford, Calif.: Stanford University Press, 1975), p. 155; Perkins, "Constraints," p. 351; Wiens, "Agricultural Statistics," Table 23; and Tables 4-8 and 4-11 in this chapter.

73. Although Perkins ("Growth and Changing Structure," pp. 117 and 155) and other analysts assume an unchanging rate of value added in agriculture, rapidly rising consumption of chemical fertilizer, electric power, insecticides, petroleum products, and other purchased inputs means that the ratio of value added to gross value of output has declined over time, and that the growth rate of value added is consequently lower than that of the gross value of agricultural output. This inference is confirmed by a sample survey of 2,162 production brigades, which found that between 1965 and 1976 output per mou rose by 36 percent while production costs increased by 54 percent ("Strengthen Scientific Research on the Farm Economy," *Kuang-ming jih-pao* [Kuang-ming Daily], December 7, 1978).

74. JPRS, no. 21,971 (1963), p. 37.

ment, afforestation, irrigation, flood control, hydroelectric stations, tubewells, and leveling, terracing, and reclamation of arable land.

In some regions, these programs have achieved dramatic results. One Chinese source says the following about the formerly grain-deficient northern provinces of Hopei, Honan, and Shantung:

> Each winter-spring season, tens of millions of people braved the biting wind and snow and worked on irrigation projects. They raised and reinforced 1,000 kilometers of dykes. . . . Several thousand rivers and tributaries were dredged . . . freeing more than 6.6 million hectares of low-lying land from the threat of flooding and waterlogging. At the same time the inhabitants went in for water conservancy and other farm improvement projects, concentrating on fighting drought. Reservoirs and terraced fields were built and trees planted on the hilly areas . . . to prevent soil erosion. Wells and ditches were dug on the plains and alkali leached from the soil, all of which involved a tremendous amount of work. By 1970, however, the three provinces were in the main self-sufficient in grain, while their record output in 1973 was 2.5 times that of . . . 1949, and an increase of 16,500 million kilograms over 1965.[75]

Available data on the overall size and results of these campaigns appear in Table 4-9. These data show the truly massive scale of China's winter works campaigns, which in recent years have involved 30 percent of the entire rural labor force. With more than half of the reported increase in irrigated area attributable to tubewells, the bulk of construction work is directed toward improving use of existing water supplies and reducing the vulnerability of crop yields to inadequate or excessive rainfall.[76]

The timing of these campaigns coincides with the pattern of seasonal idleness reported by Buck for the years 1929–33. Buck

75. *New China's First Quarter-Century* (Peking: Foreign Languages Press, 1975), p. 182.

76. James E. Nickum, *Hydraulic Engineering and Water Resources in the People's Republic of China* (Stanford, Calif: U.S.–China Relations Program, 1977), p. 28.

TABLE 4-9. WATER MANAGEMENT STATISTICS, 1930s TO 1977

Year	Winter works campaign Participants (millions of persons)	Earth and stone-work (billions of cubic meters)	Irrigated area Millions of hectares	Percentage of arable land	Number of powered tubewells (thousands)
1930s	—	—	26.5	27	—
1952	n.a.	n.a.	21.3	20	—
1957	n.a.	n.a.	34.7	31	—
1963	8–15	1.0–1.8	n.a.	n.a.	n.a.
1964	15–30	1.4–2.5	33	31	n.a.
1965	30–40	2.2–3.8	n.a.	n.a.	100
1966	40–60	2.5–4.5	n.a.	n.a.	n.a.
1967	40–60	3.0–4.5	n.a.	n.a.	n.a.
1968	30–45	1.0–2.5	n.a.	n.a.	n.a.
1969	50–60	2.0–3.0	n.a.	n.a.	n.a.
1970	60–80	3.0–4.5	n.a.	n.a.	n.a.
1971	90	5.0	n.a.	n.a.	600
1972	80–90	4.0–4.5	42.6	40	800–900[a]
1973	100[b]	n.a.	44.0	41	n.a.
1974	100[b]	n.a.	n.a.	n.a.	1,300
1975	100[b]	n.a.	47.4[c]	44[c]	1,700[d]
1976	100+[e]	n.a.	n.a.	n.a.	n.a.
1977	100+[f]	13[f]	n.a.	50−[f]	1,800+[e]

Note: Data for the winter works campaign of 1964/65 appear in the row labeled 1965, and similarly for other years.

n.a. Not available.

— Negligible.

a. Figure of 900,000 electrically powered wells in North China is from Robert Scalapino, "Trip Notes," (unpublished, 1972).

b. Annual average for the four campaigns from 1971/72 to 1974/75 reported in JMJP, October 21, 1975.

c. Based on average annual increase of 1.6 million hectares of irrigated land achieved during the campaigns of 1971/72 to 1974/75 (BBC, no. w881 (1976), p. A1). Total arable land is assumed to remain constant.

d. James E. Nickum, *Hydraulic Engineering and Water Resources in the People's Republic of China* (Stanford, Calif.: U.S.–China Relations Program, 1977), p. 28.

e. BBC, no. w955 (1977), p. A2.

f. Bureau of Foreign Affairs, "Briefing on China's Agriculture," pp. 3–4.

Sources (except as noted): *Estimates for winter works campaigns* from James E. Nickum, "A Collective Approach to Water Resources Development: The Chinese Commune System, 1962–1972" (Ph.D. dissertation, University of California, Berkeley, 1974), pp. 279 and 290–291; *estimates for other categories,* from Perkins, "Constraints Influencing China's Agricultural Performance," in U.S. Congress, Joint Economic Committee, *China: A Reassessment of the Economy* (Washington, D.C.: U.S. Government Printing Office, 1975), p. 360.

found that rural male workers were idle for an average of 1.7 months annually, with 80 percent of the idle time coming in the winter months November through February (see Table 4-1). In studying the winter works campaigns during 1962–72, James Nickum found that this "distribution of idle time corresponds closely to the recent winter-spring water conservancy activities" in which "the average participant . . . is active for $1^1/_2$ to 2 months during an active campaign."[77]

It therefore appears that even before the increase in scale suggested by the participation data for the 1970s, winter works campaigns have reduced or eliminated traditional slack periods in the farming calendar of a substantial segment of China's rural populace, particularly in the north.

Nickum's findings are consistent with Chinese reports that during the mid-1960s construction consumed about 20 percent of the time of the rural labor force.[78] The share of winter works in total labor input may have risen during the 1970s. This is suggested both by the participation data in Table 4-9 and by the findings of the American Wheat Delegation at advanced communes that had passed beyond the most intensive phase of construction: "During the initial construction phase, which seems to have been completed everywhere in two or three years, the communes invested . . . as much as 40–50 percent of their entire workdays. Even now, however, when what remains to be done is maintenance and improvement of the facilities, the communes visited reported allocations of 6–30 percent of their workdays to basic construction, the unweighted average being 20 percent." The delegation also observed, however, that "much if not most of the arable land of North and Central China has been leveled and is being irrigated as of now," which indicates that whole regions may be working mainly on maintaining and improving rather than constructing water-control facilities.[79]

Focus on maintenance and upgrading is not inconsistent with the rising participation shown in Table 4-9. This is because extension of water-control and irrigation facilities creates major new labor demands. A rising water supply and, equally important, a re-

77. James E. Nickum, "A Collective Approach to Water Resources Development: The Chinese Commune System, 1962–1972," (Ph.D. dissertation, University of California, Berkeley, 1974), pp. 172 and 293.

78. The 20 percent figure is from a 1966 report cited in ibid., p. 280.

79. Johnson and Beemer, eds., *Wheat*, p. 110.

duction in its variability raise yields and permit intensification of the cropping cycle (it has been seen how these changes increase the demand for labor). In addition, the irrigation system itself absorbs quantities of manpower for management and repair work.

The extent to which available water supplies actually fulfill the needs of crops in the fields depends heavily upon the construction and maintenance of ditches and gates, perfect leveling of fields, and other auxiliary projects. One survey found that the absence of auxiliary projects could lower the use of water supplies by as much as 40 percent.[80] Maintenance of water-control facilities necessitates frequent repair work, especially since most ditches are not lined or equipped with drainage tubing. The labor intensity of maintenance and repair work can be seen from the following suggestions for limiting leakage from irrigation channels: "loosening the dirt of the bottom and side slopes before releasing water, thus using the dirt to seal holes and crevices; tamping the soil with packers; covering the channels with clay; the use of small rocks and pebbles [that is, to seal holes] . . . and adding a certain amount of clay to the water to seal the crevices."[81]

Overall Results: The Supply of, and Demand for, Agricultural Labor

This chapter has surveyed various mechanisms for absorption of labor that have operated in China's farm economy during the past two decades. Any summary of the overall effect of these mechanisms on the balance between supply and demand for rural labor must recognize the mutual influence of the various components that create demand for labor. The following passage gives some indication of these relations: "Agricultural development, in the Chinese scheme, begins with water management and land improvement. . . . With the provision of timely and adequate supplies of water, it becomes possible to introduce fertilizer-responsive plant varieties together with the fertilizer needed to achieve high yields for these varieties. Effective water management may

80. Nickum, "Water Resources Development," p. 296.
81. JPRS, no. 44,050 (1968), p. 47.

also make it possible to increase the cropping index . . . and this increase will in turn require more fertilizer as well. All of the above steps raise the demand for rural labor."[82]

Rural industry can provide the tools and construction materials needed for water-control and land-development projects, which in turn stimulate local demand for pumps, fertilizer, threshers, electricity, and other industrial goods. Increased consumption of industrial products stimulates nonindustrial components of the farming cycle. Assured water supplies raise the returns to labor-intensive construction projects such as leveling of land, terracing, and construction of feeder ditches; and rising consumption of chemical fertilizers improves not only the crop yield, but also the yield and nutrient content of green manures and plant wastes that provide the raw material for organic fertilizers.

The dynamic process of rural development stemming from the introduction of collective organization and industrial inputs has enabled China's farm economy to support a growing population at low but modestly rising living standards with no increase in cultivated acreage. Vigorous reclamation efforts have barely managed to match the steady alienation of arable land for housing, industrial construction, irrigation projects, and roadbuilding. The growth of output recorded in Table 4-8 has come entirely from more intensive use of an essentially fixed land base.

The conclusion of this chapter is that during the past two decades collectivization and industrialization have modified the framework of China's rural economy in directions that have permitted rural labor as well as land to be used with increasing intensity. Intensification of cropping practices and of the cropping cycle, increasing adoption of labor-using plant and animal products, and massive farmland construction campaigns have contributed to agricultural development by a simultaneous raising of output and absorption of rural labor. The effect of these changes on the labor market is summarized by the data in Table 4-10, which contains estimates of the supply and demand for agricultural labor in 1957 and 1975.

Construction of estimates of labor demand for 1975 must avoid projecting conditions from atypical model units onto national to-

82. Perkins and others, *Rural . . . Industry*, p. 194.

TABLE 4-10. SUPPLY OF, AND DEMAND FOR, AGRICULTURAL LABOR, 1957 AND 1975
(billions of man-days)

| | | 1975 | |
Category	1957	Estimate A	Estimate B
1. Labor supply assuming 275 man-days of work a year			
A. Low population base	63.0	86.0	86.0
B. High population base	63.7	90.4	90.4
2. Labor demand, total	36.9	89.4	67.9
A. Farm work	27.4[a]	71.2	49.7
(i). Cultivation	n.a.	49.7	33.1
(ii). Organic manuring	n.a.	21.5	16.6
B. Subsidiary work	6.2[a]	9.9[a]	9.9[a]
C. Construction	2.3[a]	8.3	8.3
(i). Winter works campaign	n.a.	5.0	5.0
(ii). Other	n.a.	3.3[a]	3.3[a]
D. Other	0.9[a]	0	0
3. Degree of full employment			
A. Low population base			
(i). Total labor demand ÷ total supply	0.58[b]	1.03[b]	0.78[b]
(ii). Annual workdays per worker	160	284	215
B. High population base			
(i). Total labor demand ÷ total supply	0.58	0.99	0.75

n.a. Not available.

Note: Column totals may not add because of rounding.

a. Derived using the high estimate (line 1.B) of agricultural labor force.

b. Based on revised calculations of total labor demand using the low estimate (line 1.A) of agricultural labor force in deriving entries for lines 2.B and 2.C (ii). These adjustments reduce total labor demand by 0.3 and 0.6 billion man-days in 1957 and 1975, respectively.

Sources: For 1957; labor force totals are from Table 2-9. Number of man-days contributed by each worker in each category is calculated from Peter Schran, *The Development of Chinese Agriculture, 1950–1959* (Urbana: University of Illinois Press, 1969), pp. 64 and 75. Labor demand is the product of labor force and average days contributed in each category. Labor supply is the product of labor force and the assumed full-employment figure of 275 annual man-days. *For 1975; Line 1,* product of agricultural labor force from Table 2-9, version A (for line 1.A) or version B (for line 1.B) and the assumed full employment total of 275 annual workdays. *Line 2.A,* based on 1975 sown area of 165.7 million hectares. This is the product of estimated cultivated area of 107 million hectares (Perkins, "Constraints," p. 353) and a 1975 multicropping estimate of 1.549 sowings per cultivated hectare provided by Anthony M. Tang and Thomas Gottschang. *Line 2.A (i),* 165.7 million sown hectares times estimated labor input of 300 (Estimate A) or 200 (Estimate B) man-days per sown hectare. *Line 2.A (ii),* 165.7 million sown hectares times estimated labor input of 130 (Estimate A) or 100 (Estimate B) man-days per sown hectare. *Line 2.B,* product of agricultural labor force and assumed labor input of 30 annual man-days. *Line 2.C (i),* product of 100 million participants (Table 4-9) and average of 50 days' work per participant (based on James Nickum's finding that "the average participant . . . is active for 1.5 to 2 months," ["Water Resource Development," p. 293]). *Line 2.C (ii),* product of agricultural labor force and assumed labor input of 10 annual man-days. *Line 3.A (i),* line 2 (adjusted downward as explained in note b, above) divided by line 1.A. *Line 3.A (ii),* line 3.A (i) multiplied by the assumed full-employment total of 275 annual man-days. *Line 3.B (i),* line 2 divided by line 1.B. *Line 3.B (ii),* line 3.B (i) multiplied by the assumed full-employment total of 275 annual man-days.

tals. The critical assumption here concerns the number of man-days devoted to fertilizing and cultivating each hectare of sown area (line 2.A). In the report of the Wheat Studies Delegation, the most common observation for cultivation is 300 man-days per sown hectare, and use of organic fertilizer clusters around 75 tons per sown hectare, implying a labor requirement of from 75 to 188 man-days per sown hectare for fertilizing.[83] These observations are from advanced units, but most of these were located in northeast and north China, and not in the south, where labor inputs tend to be higher than in the north.

It is therefore not implausible that the national average labor input for cultivating and fertilizing each hectare of sown area is now as high as 430 man-days—300 for cultivating and 130 (the midpoint of the range cited above) for fertilizing. Labor inputs exceeding this level, which is equivalent to 29 man-days per mou, have been reported for dryland cultivation; in irrigated areas, reported labor inputs range as high as 765 or more man-days.[84] The figure of 430 man-days per sown hectare is used to derive the figures shown in estimate A for 1975 in Table 4-10. The table also includes an alternative calculation, estimate B, in which average labor input is reduced from 300 to 200 man-days for cultivating and from 130 to 100 man-days for fertilizing each sown hectare of land. The resulting estimates, in which the national average labor input for cultivation and fertilizing is assumed to rise from 196 to 300 man-days per sown hectare between 1957 and 1975, surely understate the spread of intensive farm practices.[85]

Other assumptions built into Table 4-10 do not exaggerate the growth of employment. In line 2.B each worker is assumed to spend thirty days annually in subsidiary tasks such as forestry, horticulture, pisciculture, household crafts, dairying, tending poultry, hogs, or draft animals, and marketing; comparable figures for 1957–59 were 26.9, 29.8, and 25.9 days.[86] Construction activity outside the winter campaign period (line 2.C (ii)) is as-

83. Johnson and Beemer, eds., *Wheat*, p. 111.

84. For dryland areas, see Table 4-6, above. For irrigated areas, see Johnson and Beemer eds., *Wheat*, p. 162.

85. The figure for 1957 is calculated from Peter Schran, *The Development of Chinese Agriculture, 1950–1959* (Urbana: University of Illinois Press, 1969), p. 107.

86. Ibid., pp. 64 and 75.

sumed unchanged from the level of 1957: ten days a year for each worker.[87] These assumptions yield shares of construction activity in total workdays considerably below the level of 20 percent reported for advanced units.[88]

In addition to allowing the different assumptions about the labor intensity of cultivation and manuring activities in 1975 that are incorporated in estimates A and B, the employment estimates derived in Table 4-10 allow also for the variations in the assumed size of China's population and labor force that were discussed in Chapter Two. Estimates assuming a low population base are derived from version A of the agricultural labor force estimates shown in Table 2-9; these in turn are based on the low national population figures published in Chinese sources and reproduced in Table 2-1. Estimates assuming a high population base are derived from version B of the agricultural labor force figures shown in Table 2-9, which is in turn based on John Aird's estimated population figures shown in Table 2-1. Aird's higher population figures appear more realistic than the low figures given by Chinese sources. Therefore, the estimates in Table 4-10 constructed on a low population base should overstate both the annual work-days per agricultural worker and the ratio of labor demand to labor supply in the farm sector during 1975.

In his study of Chinese farming during the 1950s, Peter Schran concluded that the average agricultural laborer worked only 159 days during 1957. Regardless of whether the estimates based on high or low population figures are found more reasonable, the results derived in Table 4-10 indicate that, between 1957 and 1975, China's farm sector not only absorbed close to 100 million new workers, equivalent to about 40 percent of the agricultural work force in 1957, but also raised the average number of days worked considerably above the levels observed before 1960.

The data in Table 4-10 show that, at the very least, the number of annual workdays in 1975 surpassed the estimated average of 175–190 achieved during the tumultuous early years of the communes in the late 1950s.[89] If the intensive cultivation practices observed by the Wheat Studies Delegation can be taken as represen-

87. Ibid.

88. Johnson and Beemer, eds., *Wheat*, p. 110.

89. Schran, *Chinese Agriculture*, p. 75.

tative of national averages (estimate A for 1975 in Table 4-10), the average number of workdays for each farm laborer is estimated at from 272 to 284 for 1975. This result would imply that China's rural development program has removed most of the seasonal idleness observed during the 1950s and has brought the agricultural labor force, with approximately 275 annual workdays a person, to a position of virtually full employment.

If labor input per sown hectare in advanced agricultural brigades stands well above the national average, as is assumed in estimate B for 1975 in Table 4-10, a rise is found in the annual number of workdays for each agricultural laborer, with the estimate for 1975 falling between 207 and 215 annual workdays. This alternative represents progress toward full employment, but it implies that seasonal idleness continues in most areas of China.

All factors being taken into consideration, it seems most likely that the nationwide average for 1975 is around 250 days. An average of less than 250 days would be difficult to reconcile with the certainty that leading communes in many areas of the country obtain 300 or more days of collective labor from their able-bodied members. Recent demands that rusticated urban youths spend a minimum of 250 days a year in collective work suggest that the average may not exceed 250, for despite their lack of farming skill these young men and unmarried women should be able to contribute more labor time than the average member of the commune.

Overall Results: Productivity Trends in Agriculture

At several points in the foregoing discussion there has been the suggestion that agricultural reforms that absorb labor may fail to increase or perhaps may even reduce total output. It is now possible to analyze the behavior of partial labor productivity between the benchmark years 1957 and 1975 and to probe more speculatively into trends in overall factor productivity in Chinese farming since 1957.[90]

90. All quantitative statements in the remainder of this chapter use the population, labor force, and employment estimates based on Aird's population figures compiled in Table 2-1.

Table 4-11 presents estimates of agricultural labor productivity for 1957 and 1975 in terms of gross value. Since, as is noted above, the rate of value added in agriculture has declined over time, these figures provide a more favorable view of productivity trends than would emerge from calculations using agricultural value added; the difference, however, appears small.[91]

The figures in Table 4-11 show that agricultural output per man-year increased by 10 percent between 1957 and 1975. Conversion of the results to a value-added basis, if possible, would eliminate some and perhaps most of this increase. It does appear safe to conclude, however, that annual output of the average member of China's rural work force did not decrease between 1957 and 1975 even though nearly 100 million workers were added to a labor force that already faced an extremely unfavorable man-land ratio. Absorption of this enormous incremental farm population without lowering average annual labor productivity must count as an important and impressive achievement of China's rural economy.

When productivity is measured in output value per man-day, the results are equally clear: output per man-day declined sharply between 1957 and 1975, with the fall ranging from 15 to 36 percent depending upon which assumptions are chosen with regard to the labor intensity of cultivation and fertilizer preparation. Since man-days provide a much better measure of labor use than man-years, these unambiguous results point to diminishing returns as a serious problem facing Chinese agriculture both during 1957–75 and, as population growth continues to enlarge the farm labor force, in the future.

The effect of diminishing returns can be seen in further detail through the highly tentative estimates of overall factor productivity in Chinese agriculture presented in Table 4-12. These calculations distinguish four categories of inputs: land, measured by

91. If the survey results cited in note 73, above, were typical of China's entire farm sector and if the net output ratio of 0.763 reported for 1957 were valid for 1965 as well, the rate of value added in 1976 would be 0.732, or 96 percent of the initial level. This suggests that the use of gross value to measure farm output may inflate a labor productivity index linking 1957 with 1975 by something of the order of 5 to 10 percent. Net output ratio for 1957 is reported in Shigeru Ishikawa, *National Income and Capital Formation in Mainland China* (Tokyo: Institute of Asian Economic Affairs, 1965), p. 56.

TABLE 4-11. LABOR PRODUCTIVITY IN AGRICULTURE, 1957 AND 1975

Category	1957	1975 Estimate A	Estimate B
1. Gross value of agricultural output (billions of 1957 yuan)	53.700	83.907	
2. Labor input			
Millions of man-years	231.5	328.8	
Billions of man-days	36.9	89.4	67.9
3. Labor productivity in gross value			
Yuan per man-year	232.0	255.2	
Yuan per man-day	1.46	0.94	1.24

Sources: Line 1, Table 4-8; the 1975 estimate is based on a 1 percent output increase during 1974/75 as shown in U.S. National Foreign Assessment Center, *China: Economic Indicators* (Washington, D.C.: Central Intelligence Agency, 1977), p. 3. Line 2, Table 2-9 and 4-10; these figures are based on the high population base described in the notes to Table 4-10.

TABLE 4-12. ESTIMATED FACTOR PRODUCTIVITY IN AGRICULTURE, 1957 AND 1975

Category	Weights[a]	Growth of total input 1957	1975
Labor	0.55	100.0	184.0–242.3[b]
Land	0.25	100.0	105.4[c]
Current inputs	0.11	100.0	202.6[d]
Capital	0.09	100.0	680.8[e]
Total input	1.00	100.0	211.1–243.2
Gross value of agricultural output	—	100.0	156.2[f]
Total factor productivity	—	100.0	74.0–64.2

a. Anthony M. Tang, "Input-Output Relations in the Agriculture of Communist China, 1952–1965," in *Agrarian Policies and Problems in Communist and Non-Communist Countries*, ed. W. A. Douglas Jackson (Seattle: University of Washington Press, 1971), p. 287.

b. Index of total labor demand in man-days, from Table 4-10, line 2.

c. Index of sown area. Data for 1957 are from Nai-ruenn Chen, *Chinese Economic Statistics*, (Chicago: Aldine, 1967), p. 285; for 1975, see the notes to Table 4-10.

d. Index of total nutrient assumed to grow throughout 1957–75 at the annual rate of 4.0 percent shown for 1957–71 in Table 4-5.

e. Index is the weighted average of the stock of large animals (weight 0.9), which grew at an annual rate of 0.9 percent after 1957 (Table 4-7) and aggregate horsepower of irrigation and drainage equipment, tractors and power tillers (weight 0.1), which grew at an annual rate of 25 percent during 1957–75 (Table 4-3).

f. Table 4-11.

sown area; labor, measured in man-days; current inputs, measured by total nutrients provided by organic and chemical fertilizers; and capital, measured by the stock of large animals (weight 0.9) and the stock in horsepower of tractors, power tillers, and irrigation machinery (weight 0.1). The weights used to aggregate these inputs are those proposed by Anthony Tang for calculations covering the period 1952–65.

The resulting index of farm inputs for 1975 is, if anything, too low. Plausible changes that would increase the growth of input include (a) enlarging the list of current inputs to include pesticides and other fast-growing manufactured items, which would lower the weight of organic fertilizer in the total and hence raise the index for this input; (b) assigning a larger share of the capital category to machinery, which would sharply increase the index for this input; and, most important, (c) shifting the weights in favor of current and capital inputs to reflect their growing importance in China's farm economy.

Even with a low index of input growth, the figures in Table 4-12 reveal a distinct downward trend in agricultural factor productivity during the years 1957–75. If output were measured by value added rather than gross value of output, the decline would be slightly steeper. In the present version, the annual rate of decline ranges between 1.7 and 2.4 percent depending upon the assumption made regarding the labor intensity of cultivation and fertilization in the terminal year. These calculations, though tentative, show convincingly that agricultural factor productivity declined after 1957 and suggest that the decrease was at least from one-quarter to one-third between 1957 and 1975.

On the basis of similar though more detailed estimates for 1952–65 published by Anthony Tang, it can be seen that declining factor productivity has been a regular feature of China's farm economy since 1952:[92]

92. Estimates for 1952–65 are from Anthony M. Tang, "Input-Output Relations in the Agriculture of Communist China, 1952–1965," in *Agrarian Policies and Problems in Communist and Non-Communist Countries*, ed. W. A. Douglas Jackson (Seattle: University of Washington Press, 1971), pp. 289 and 295. Data for 1975 are from Table 4-12.

Year	Estimated factor productivity (1957 = 100)	Harvest conditions
1952	107.0	Good
1957	100.0	Average
1965	91.4	Average
1975	64–74	Average

The rather smooth pattern of decline shown by Tang's results for 1952–65 suggest a Malthusian explanation focusing on diminishing returns to a growing farm labor force rather than one which emphasizes problems associated with rural collectivization. The seeming acceleration of the decline in productivity after 1965 raises several possibilities, including an intensification of diminishing returns as farm employment rises, as well as continuing organizational deficiencies in China's system of rural collectives. These issues will be explored further in the following chapter.

Chapter Five

Retrospect and Prospect

This study has shown that the People's Republic of China has made major strides in the direction of full employment for its enormous labor force, numbering well above 400 million men and women. Although the absence of regular statistical publications hampers quantitative investigation of the relation between economic growth and the supply of and demand for labor in China, available materials do allow a detailed comparison of labor market conditions in the benchmark years of 1957 and 1975.

Employment and Unemployment in China

On the basis of John Aird's relatively high estimates of China's population, which, as was shown in Chapter Two, appear to provide the most realistic picture of current demographic conditions, the results of this study may be summarized as follows.[1]

Growth of the labor force

China's labor force expanded during 1957–75 at an estimated annual rate of 2.4 percent, which slightly exceeds the estimated annual population growth rate of 2.2 percent. By 1975 the labor

1. Quantitative statements in this chapter are based on labor force and employment figures derived from John Aird's population estimates shown in Table 2-1. Substitution of lower population figures would reduce the estimated growth of the agricultural work force and improve the balance between the supply of, and demand for, agricultural labor in the benchmark year of 1975.

force comprised an estimated 430 million persons, or 46 percent of the entire population.

Demand for labor outside agriculture

Both the urban labor force (growing at 4.8 percent annually) and nonagricultural employment (growing at 4.9 percent annually) rose more rapidly than the labor force as a whole during 1957–75. Although the absolute increment in nonagricultural employment amounted to nearly 60 million persons, representing an increase of 150 percent above the employment level in 1957, the growth rate of nonfarm employment remained well below the growth rate of nonagricultural output, which Perkins estimates at 7.3 percent a year during the period 1957–74.[2]

The modest growth of nonagricultural employment relative to output stems largely from official policies and institutional arrangements that have moved industry, the sector of China's economy with the largest contribution to aggregate output, in the direction of increased capital intensity and rising labor productivity. The low priority attached to industrial labor absorption is evident from the relative growth rates of industrial output (9.7 percent annually, including handicrafts) and industrial employment (5.7 percent annually, including handicrafts), and also from the low and declining share of labor-intensive consumer manufacturers in the industrial output total.[3]

The factors underlying industry's relatively slow absorption of labor were discussed in Chapter Three. They include a development strategy that emphasizes the promotion of basic industries at the national and regional levels, resource allocation rules that lead enterprises to favor the use of capital rather than labor to expand

2. Dwight H. Perkins, "Estimating China's Gross Domestic Product," *Current Scene*, vol. 15, no. 3 (1976), p. 16.

3. Ibid., p. 15; Table 2-8; and Thomas G. Rawski, *China's Transition to Industrialism: Producer Goods and Economic Development in the Twentieth Century* (Ann Arbor: University of Michigan Press, forthcoming), chap. 4. The declining share of consumer products in industrial output is a result of their low priority in China's investment planning. The share of light industry in state budgetary investment was only 5.4 percent in 1978; for 1979 an increase to 5.8 percent is anticipated. See "China's National Economy (1978–79)," *Beijing Review*, no. 26 (1979), p. 9.

output, specific technological conditions at various types of enterprises, and a general reliance on foreign technologies that are
based on relatively high ratios of capital to labor.

This last point is worth some emphasis. China has developed
individual manufacturing processes, such as the production of
ammonium bicarbonate fertilizer, that are not found in other
countries. China has also achieved a certain degree of success in
combining labor-intensive ancillary operations with capital-intensive core technologies to produce sophisticated commodities
with relatively low capital inputs. In the main, however, China's
industrial products, materials, and processes are familiar to Western engineers. Automation is limited and labor intensity is much
higher in China than in the advanced industrial nations, but the
direction of movement is unquestionably toward technical arrangements resembling those in the industrial West.

Labor absorption in agriculture

Limited creation of employment outside agriculture has forced
much of labor absorption onto the farm sector, which is broadly
defined to include water conservancy and land improvement, as
well as farming and animal husbandry. Agriculture is estimated to
have absorbed 97.3 million workers between 1957 and 1975, or
about two-thirds of the overall labor force increase during those
years (Table 2-9). Even though the 2 percent annual growth rate of
China's farm labor force during 1957–75 was high by international
standards—World Bank estimates place the average growth rate of
the farm labor force in South Asia at only 1 percent a year during
1950–70—China's farm sector seems to have experienced relatively
little difficulty in absorbing an enlarged labor force of this magnitude.[4]

Agricultural labor absorption was facilitated by two principal
changes in China's rural economy. The first has been the collectivization of agriculture, which was begun with the formation of
cooperatives in 1956 and was taken a step further with the creation
of communes in 1958. China's rural communes have rebounded

4. World Bank, "Rural Enterprise and Non-Farm Employment," World Bank
Sector Policy Paper (Washington, D.C., January 1978), Table A-1.

from early difficulties to become reasonably effective managerial units. In recent years communes have succeeded in mobilizing labor to implement projects in water conservancy, land improvement, roadbuilding, and irrigation without severing the indispensable link between individual (or household) effort and income.

The second fundamental change has been the growth, beginning in the mid-1960s, of industrial support for agriculture, much of it from plants located in county seats, market towns, or within the communes themselves. Such small-scale industry brings together growing technical skills and a more intimate understanding of rural needs than is often present in large urban factories.

A review of the past two decades of rural development shows that the direction and the labor mobilization provided by the communes has complemented the growing availability of industrial products and skills, and that together they have promoted a multifaceted intensification of China's farm economy. More widespread use of organic as well as chemical fertilizers, intensive tilling, expanded multiple cropping, water conservancy and land improvement projects, and other measures described in Chapter Four not only absorbed nearly 100 million new entrants into the rural work force, but also substantially raised the average number of days of employment for the entire farm labor force of more than 300 million men and women.

Progress toward full employment

China has made long strides toward full employment during the past two decades. In this area, as in such fields as health, education, housing, and regional development China's achievements compare favorably with those in other large and populous developing nations.

Involuntary unemployment in China's cities is limited by controls over peasant migration that include a system of travel permits and location-specific grain rations. Most peasants are expected to participate in winter construction projects in the countryside. Those who travel in search of seasonal nonfarm jobs often must pay substantial monthly fees to their home units while they are gone, thus removing the economic motive for seasonal migration by those with little prospect of finding regular work.[5]

The only sizable urban group who could be described as unemployed consists of young men and women who have abandoned rural assignments without permission. Thomas Bernstein's careful study concludes that "judging from various estimates that have been made, there may be several hundred thousand" of these youths "living a kind of semilegal life between town and country." Some of these youths manage to obtain regular urban jobs; others "sustain themselves by engaging in petty crime or in black market activities."[6] Even if, as some observers believe, the number of returnees who have become "unemployed" by abandoning their rural jobs includes several million of the 12 million young people transferred from urban to rural locations since 1966, the resulting scale of unemployment among an urban labor force of close to 100 million persons is not severe when compared with conditions in other large and populous low-income countries.

In the rural sector there can be no doubt of a general increase in the availability of work. The national average of annual workdays per agricultural worker has risen from fewer than 200 days during the 1950s to approximately 250 days in the mid-1970s. Although there are no aggregate data to confirm this hypothesis, it appears that rural incomes have risen as well. The estimates of population and of gross domestic product shown in Table 1-1 imply an increase of 50 percent in per capita output between 1957 and 1974. Part of this increased output has been used to raise the share of total output devoted to investment and to military spending. But a portion has remained available for supporting rising levels of personal consumption. Since the real income levels of urban workers, although substantially above farm incomes, did not increase and may even have fallen slightly between 1957 and 1974, these aggregate data suggest a perceptible rise in per capita consumption in the countryside between 1957 and 1975. Part of this increase may

5. William L. Parish and Martin King Whyte, *Village and Family in Contemporary China* (Chicago: University of Chicago Press, 1978), p. 120.

6. Thomas P. Bernstein, *Up to the Mountains and Down to the Villages* (New Haven: Yale University Press, 1977), pp. 93 and 261.

have come from the small rise in farm output per agricultural worker recorded in Table 4-11. Additional contributions have come from relative price shifts favoring the agricultural sector and from governmental fiscal policies intended to reduce regional inequality in the distribution of health, education, and welfare benefits.[7]

Costs and benefits

These significant achievements have not been without cost. As was noted in Chapter Four, the modest rise in the average value of output per man-year in agriculture occurred only because the increase in the number of days worked by commune members offset the reduction in the average value of output per man-day in agriculture. In addition, available data show that overall factor productivity dropped substantially between 1957 and 1975 in China's agricultural sector.

The finding that the average level of gross output value per man-day in agriculture declined by from 15 to 36 percent between 1957 and 1975 (see Table 4-11) provides clear-cut evidence of Malthusian diminishing returns. Chinese sources confirm this result: a survey of 2,162 production teams in several provinces found that the average value of a labor-day declined by 20 percent, from 0.7 to 0.56 yuan, between 1965 and 1976.[8] Indeed, with the total number of man-days lavished on a fixed land base rising since 1957 at nearly 4.6 percent annually from a high initial level, it is perhaps sur-

7. Christopher Howe, *China's Economy: A Basic Guide* (New York: Basic Books, 1978), pp. 174–76, estimates that consumption per capita at the national level increased at an annual rate of 1.66 percent between 1952 and 1974; among urban workers, real wages declined by an estimated 12 percent between 1957 and 1974. In their detailed study of Kwangtung province, Parish and Whyte identify a variety of indicators that "point toward increasing output and slowly improving living standards" in the countryside (see *Village and Family*, p. 124). Terms of trade and fiscal policies are discussed in Nicholas R. Lardy, *Economic Growth and Distribution in China* (Cambridge, England: Cambridge University Press, 1978), chaps. 4 and 5.

8. "Strengthen Scientific Research on the Farm Economy," *Kuang-ming jih-pao* [Kuang-ming Daily], December 7, 1978. These figures are smaller than those in Table 4-11 because the former represent cash income per labor-day and are net of taxes, input costs, and other charges deducted from total output before distributing income to team members.

prising that the average output per man-day did not decline more rapidly.[9]

If an increase of roughly 125 percent in the aggregate number of man-days devoted to agricultural labor between 1957 and 1975 forced the nationwide level of average productivity down by from 15 to 36 percent, the marginal productivity of agricultural labor in many farming regions must be far below the reduced level of average productivity recorded in 1975. This inference is reinforced by observations of visitors. Surely, the effect on current output of the marginal bucket of earth moved on construction projects, the marginal seedlings planted for afforestation, the marginal silt collected as organic fertilizer, or the marginal effort of plowing, weeding, or pruning is often extremely small.

What significance should be attached to the indubitable fact of low marginal labor productivity in agriculture? One possibility is that low marginal labor productivity in farming reveals a serious error in China's economic strategy. Instead of "manicuring the countryside" with labor-intensive farming techniques that add little to total output, new entrants to the work force could have been assigned more productively to labor-intensive consumer industries producing for export. Recent policy changes show that many Chinese would agree that the foreign sector can contribute more to China's development than it did during the years 1957–75. But even leaving aside limitations on the demand side, expansion of industrial exports is narrowly constrained by capacity limitations and by the slow growth in supplies of agricultural raw materials used to produce the textile products and processed foodstuffs that account for a large proportion of China's manufactured exports. Although it is easily possible to imagine alternative policies that might have enabled consumer manufacturing to absorb several million additional workers, no industrial strategy could have spared China's farm sector from the task of absorbing nearly 100 million new workers during 1957–75 or from the consequent downward trend in average and marginal labor productivity.

For most new entrants into China's labor force, agriculture was

9. Annual increase of 4.6 percent in labor-days between 1957 and 1975 is calculated from the agricultural labor force figures in Table 2-9 by assuming 159 workdays per person for 1957 (Table 4-10) and 250 days for 1975.

the only possible source of employment. Under these conditions, the government faced the choice of using available farm labor either more or less intensively. On the one hand, fuller employment raises farm output and contributes to external balance of trade by reducing net food imports. On the other hand, intensive use of labor lowers the marginal product of labor and curtails peasant leisure. Since the government places a low value on leisure relative to higher farm output, the decision to mobilize available labor for tasks with a low and declining—but positive—effect on farm output was probably not difficult to reach. From the peasants' viewpoint, the falling value of each workday brought about by a rising man-land ratio meant that, with migration and private plots closely restricted, increased collective labor was the only way to protect existing living standards; to attain higher incomes, further extra work was unavoidable. Resistance arose only when the peasants perceived that extra work would not lead to higher real incomes because of shortages of consumer goods in rural fairs and sales outlets.[10]

Despite the increased availability of employment, it would be premature to claim that China's agricultural labor force is fully employed. This is because nationwide figures conceal important regional variations. In areas with long growing seasons and abundant supplies of water and organic manures the average number of workdays per man-year certainly exceeds 300. These conditions were observed in north and central China by the Wheat Studies Delegation; they must also exist over substantial areas of south and southwest China as well.

These regions of high labor demand probably coincide with the regions that Benedict Stavis has identified as the beneficiaries of complete packages of modern farm inputs. Stavis estimates that as of the late 1960s these areas of high and stable yields, widespread mechanization, and high multiple cropping indexes included 20 percent of China's cultivated land.[11] These areas have undoubtedly expanded in the past decade. Since they also include some of

10. See, for example, Ross H. Munro, "Why China's Peasants Don't Want to Work," *San Francisco Chronicle* (July 29, 1977), p. 12.

11. Benedict Stavis, *Making Green Revolution* (Ithaca: Cornell University Rural Development Program, 1974), pp. 1–3.

China's most densely populated regions, up to one-quarter of China's agricultural population may live in regions in which farm workers are expected to work for 300 or more days each year.

If the demand for labor substantially exceeds the estimated average of 250 annual workdays in large areas of the country, it follows that "there may still be absorption problems in the northern plains" where the agricultural environment includes both a relatively short growing season and limited and uncertain water supplies.[12]

Despite these remaining problems of seasonal idleness, China during the past two decades has unquestionably made major gains in overcoming rural underemployment. The spread of modern farm inputs, which has caused serious employment problems elsewhere, has been accompanied in China by a general increase in labor demand large enough to boost labor input per worker by approximately 50 percent in two decades.

Gains in employment opportunities and the resulting growth in income have benefited poor as well as prosperous farming regions. Furthermore, universal collectivization of farming means that underemployed agricultural workers are not cut off from the land. Adverse conditions may prevent certain localities from joining in the general rise in farm output, but all households continue to enjoy a share in the income of their commune, brigade and production team.

In conclusion, the situation of employment in China may be summarized as follows: Open unemployment appears limited largely to illegal urban residents. Many of these are voluntarily idle, having chosen to abandon rural employment that would have allowed them to support themselves. In the countryside there has been a general rise in the availability of work over the past two decades. Seasonal idleness still exists in some areas, but its extent and duration are much reduced in comparison with the 1950s. Recent news reports suggest new problems of voluntary rural idleness, but these may be localized and are in any case amenable to solution by administrative changes or improved supplies of consumer goods. Despite these problems, the improved availability

12. Peter Schran, "Farm Labor and Living in China," (Champaign: University of Illinois, 1976; processed), p. 11.

of work is an impressive achievement for a densely populated country with a fixed land base, substantial labor force growth, and an average annual income of about US$400 (at 1977 prices) per capita.[13]

Prospects for China's Labor Market

The uncertainty surrounding existing estimates of the size and age structure of China's population makes it difficult to attempt a forecast of future trends in the supply of, and demand for, labor. Nonetheless, it is possible to draw some broad inferences regarding probable trends in the size and structure of the labor force and in the balance between supply and demand.

Labor force projections

Table 5-1 contains projections based on the simplest of assumptions. China's labor force is projected from 1975 to 1990 using an annual growth rate of 2.7 percent. Even though the rate of population growth may soon fall below 2 percent, the present age structure is dominated by young people; as the share of economically active age cohorts in the population total rises, the growth rate of the labor force may be expected to accelerate until around 1990, after which it will slow down. The assumed annual growth rate for the labor force is identical with the average growth rate of the working age cohorts (16 to 60 years for males, 16 to 55 years for females) in John Aird's intermediate model of China's population during the years 1975–90.[14]

Nonagricultural employment increased at an annual rate of 4.9

13. U.S. National Foreign Assessment Center, *China: Economic Indicators* (Washington, D.C.: Central Intelligence Agency, 1978), p. 1.

14. In his intermediate population model, John S. Aird projects average growth rates for the working-age population at 2.6 percent for 1970–80, 2.9 percent for 1980–90, and 1.3 percent for 1990–2000. See his "Population Growth in the People's Republic of China," in U.S. Congress, Joint Economic Committee, *Chinese Economy Post-Mao* (Washington, D.C.: U.S. Government Printing Office, 1978), vol. 1, p. 472. The figures for 1975 were provided separately by Dr. Aird.

TABLE 5-1. LABOR FORCE PROJECTIONS, 1975–90

Year	Total labor force	Nonagricultural employment	Urban unemployment	Agricultural labor force
	Absolute figures (millions)			
1957	281.6	42.3	7.8	231.5
1975	430.1	100.3	1.0	328.8
1990				
Version A	641.4	208.5	1.0	431.9
Version B	641.4	296.8	1.0	343.6
	Average annual growth rate (percent)			
1957–1975	2.4	4.9	−10.8	2.0
1975–1990				
Version A	2.7	5.0	0	1.8
Version B	2.7	7.5	0	0.3
	Annual increment (millions)			
1974–75	10.7	4.7	0	5.4
1989–90				
Version A	16.9	9.9	0	7.0
Version B	16.9	20.7	0	−3.8

Note: The basis for projections is explained in the text.
Source: Table 2-9.

percent between 1957 and 1975. Future employment expansion in this area depends largely on trends in industrial employment, which expanded at an average rate of 5.7 percent over the same period. It is likely that the need to increase supplies of consumer goods to bolster incentives among both urban and rural workers will lead the government to step up investment in relatively labor-using consumer manufactures. Rising imports may spur expansion of consumer industries directed toward foreign markets as well. These developments suggest that the growth of industrial employment may accelerate. But recent policy statements emphasizing modernization and increased technological sophistication suggest a continuing emphasis on deepening of capital to raise productivity. Imports of whole plants, equipment, and designs from Western suppliers point in the same direction.

Given this uncertainty and the absence of information on demand for employment in other nonfarm sectors, nonagricultural employment is projected forward to 1990 under two assumptions: first, a 5 percent growth rate reflecting continuation of past trends;

and, second, a growth rate of 7.5 percent that may be taken as an upper limit for growth in employment outside agriculture. [15]

Under the additional assumption of constant urban unemployment, the projected agricultural labor force may be derived as a residual. These projections are simple but not implausible. They show that, with nonagricultural employment rising at an annual rate of 5 percent, China's agricultural labor force will continue to rise until 1990. If the growth of nonfarm employment accelerates to 7.5 percent, the farm labor force will peak five years sooner. More important is the implication that accelerated employment growth outside agriculture could reduce the eventual maximum size of the farm labor force by approximately 80 million workers. Thus, it is evident that the magnitude of the labor absorption requirements facing agriculture during the coming decade depends heavily on the growth rate of nonfarm employment. Small changes in the latter will raise or lower the influx of new farm workers (or, alternatively, of jobless urban dwellers) by tens of millions.

The data on agricultural productivity that are summarized in Tables 4-11 and 4-12 emphasize the importance of lowering the annual increments to the agricultural work force—and eventually its size—as quickly as possible. Growing supplies of modern inputs, intensification of the farming system, and rising numbers of labordays per worker have jointly maintained the average annual value of output per agricultural worker betwen 1957 and 1975. But with few remaining opportunities to intensify peasant work schedules, further growth of the farm labor force may reduce the average level of output per worker in agriculture. Further relative price changes favoring agriculture, such as those announced early in 1979, can support farm incomes. If, however, the urban prices of farm products are not increased, the resulting subsidies to urban residents will represent a drain on the state budget and act to reduce investment and, as a result, the growth of nonagricultural employment. [16]

Therefore, it is reasonable to expect that China's agricultural

15. If nonagricultural employment were to rise by more than 7.5 percent annually, the investment requirements for capital widening in industry alone would take up an inordinate proportion of total capital formation.

16. "Communiqué of the Third Plenary Session of the 11th Central Committee of the Communist Party of China," *Peking Review*, no. 52 (1978), p. 13.

labor force will continue to grow at least during the late 1970s and early 1980s. Whether this growth will raise the eventual peak level of the agricultural work force by 10 million or 100 million above the estimated 1975 total of 329 million farm workers depends on whether the annual growth of nonagricultural employment remains near the historic level of 5 percent a year or accelerates to an annual rate of 7.5 percent. It is not possible to predict which of these rates is most likely to approximate the actual growth of nonagricultural employment opportunities. In either case, the most pressing questions concerning labor market conditions in China will continue to center on the effect of employment growth on the marginal product of labor in agriculture. Can the marginal product of farm labor be raised enough to reverse the recent downward trend in average output and earnings per labor-day?

The income prospects of China's farming population are inextricably linked with the fate of China's current drive to raise the annual growth rate of agricultural output from the rate of approximately 2.6 percent achieved between 1957 and 1974 (Table 4-7) toward an unprecedented target level of between 4 and 5 percent a year between now and 1985. Even if nonfarm employment fails to grow more rapidly than the 5 percent annual rate achieved during 1957–75, a 4 percent annual growth of gross agricultural output would ensure modest growth in the net value of the farm workday even with a 1.8 percent annual increase in farm labor (Table 5-1), further increases in annual workdays, and a falling ratio of value added to the gross value of agricultural output. Continued output growth in the 2.5 percent range recorded during 1957–74 (Table 4-7), however, is likely to cause incomes to fall unless the growth of nonfarm employment is rapid. Since growth in nonfarm employment depends on investment outlays whose import component is limited by China's trade balance in farm products, a weak agricultural performance and a spectacular nonfarm growth represent an extremely unlikely combination.

Prospects for rapid growth of agricultural output

Can China push the annual growth rate of agricultural output above 4 percent in the near future? Several foreign specialists have expressed reservations about the prospects for accelerated agricultural growth.[17] Nicholas Lardy disagrees, arguing that "because of the large investments that have already been made in irrigation systems and the ability of the Chinese to diffuse rapidly higher yielding seed varieties, the average rate of agricultural growth may approach 4 percent per year, given average weather conditions."[18] This controversy need not be reviewed in detail, but factors can be described that are likely to push the farm economy either toward or away from the ambitious target of from 4 to 5 percent annual growth in agricultural output.

On the positive side, large regions of China have not yet begun to reap the full benefits from an integrated package of modern farm inputs. Continuing increases in the supply of fertilizer, machinery, and other manufactured producer goods may pave the way for intensification of cropping patterns, rising demand for labor, and increased output in these regions, of which the north China plain is the largest. Of particular importance is the imminent jump in supplies of chemical fertilizers as new plants incorporating Western technology begin to operate. Since foreign observers agree that the "level of fertilization is still far from adequate," expanded fertilizer use may permit growing numbers of communes to imitate the pattern of expanded double and triple cropping heretofore confined to model units with preferential access to scarce resources.[19] Continued growth in the output of farm machinery, another objective receiving high priority in current economic plans, may have a similarly beneficial effect.

The prospects for agricultural intensification may become constrained, however, by the difficulty of attaining large increases in

17. Authors stressing the difficulty of accelerating the growth of farm output include Dwight H. Perkins, "Constraints Influencing China's Agricultural Performance," in U.S. Congress, Joint Economic Committee, *China: A Reassessment of the Economy* (Washington, D.C.: U.S. Government Printing Office, 1975), pp. 350–65; Walter P. Falcon and Gerald C. Nelson, "Prospects for China's Agriculture," (unpublished draft, 1978); and Robert F. Dernberger and David Fasenfest, "China's Post-Mao Economic Future," in U.S. Congress, Joint Economic Committee, *Chinese Economy Post-Mao* (Washington, D.C.: U.S. Government Printing Office, 1978), vol. 1, pp. 21–26.

18. Nicholas R. Lardy, "Recent Chinese Economic Performance and Prospects for the Ten-Year Plan," ibid., p. 61.

19. Schran, "Farm Labor and Living," p. 13.

the supply of water. Two decades of effort may have enabled the Chinese to tap most readily available water sources; in many localities the returns to construction of additional small- or medium-scale water conservancy projects may now be quite low. If so, major improvements in availability of water must await progress in such massive and long-term endeavors as control of silting in the Yellow River and diversion of Yangtze River waters to the north. In the meantime, as one specialist observed, "[I]mproving water management in China would get very little increase in production" because "the level of water management in China is exceptionally high" already.[20]

Another potentially positive contribution may come from improvements in farm-oriented scientific work. In contrast to their favorable evaluations of other economic sectors, visiting experts have criticized China's agricultural research establishment severely:

> One gets the impression that much Chinese agricultural research is currently stagnant. . . . In general scientists were not aware of work in other provinces. . . . China's scientists have been, and still are, out of contact with the mainstream of international scientific activity. . . . Consequently, we found scientists generally unaware of advances occurring elsewhere, many that could be of great benefit to Chinese agriculture. . . . [T]he absence of active field and laboratory work on some of the major agronomic problems was noticeable at all institutions visited.[21]

The question here is how quickly Chinese scientific institutions can reverse the weak state of the agricultural sciences noted by foreign visitors in 1974 and 1976.[22] Recent emphasis on science and technology has swept away one obstacle noted by visitors in 1974, the "lack of conviction of central authorities that more funda-

---

20. Dwight H. Perkins, "A Conference on Agriculture," *China Quarterly*, no. 67 (1976), p. 605. Preliminary plans for one major project are sketched in Kao Hsia, "Yangtze Waters Diverted to North China," *Peking Review*, no. 38 (1978), pp. 6–9.

21. *Plant Studies in the People's Republic of China* (Washington, D.C.: National Academy of Sciences, 1975), pp. 119–21.

22. Ibid., and Ramon H. Myers, "Wheat in China—Past, Present and Future," *China Quarterly*, no. 74 (1978), pp. 317–18.

mental research is important."[23] Peking is now keenly aware of
the vital role of research in supporting agriculture as well as other
sectors of the economy. If official encouragement, enlarged fund-
ing, and foreign contacts can quickly stimulate a flow of useful
innovation, agricultural science could contribute substantially to
both growth of output and absorption of labor:

> Soil classification studies are still unknown at the commune
> level, but when this new information becomes available it
> should be possible for production teams to use the new
> chemical fertilizers more efficiently. Hydrological work to
> measure the proper amount of irrigation for different soils is
> still in its infancy at the commune level. As this development
> progresses, communes gradually should be able to make op-
> timal application of water to wheat and other crops when
> applications of chemical fertilizer are used. Such scientific
> developments will most certainly continue to raise wheat
> yields in even the advanced farming areas, and most as-
> suredly in the backward farming areas if the present wheat
> science research system can be encouraged to produce
> them.[24]

The rapidity with which China's farm sector can take advantage
of existing opportunities to raise output depends not only on
technical conditions but also on the analytic capabilities of policymakers and the rationality of farm management. Reports of diminishing returns appear as early as 1964, when one group of authors
pointed out that "what needs attention is that some production
units, though raising output through a change in the cropping
rotation system, have had to invest excessively, with the result
that per unit cost of product and labor productivity are [adversely]
affected."[25] As Marxists, however, Chinese economists found it
difficult to recognize the extent of diminishing returns:

> The general tendency is that with continued advancement
> made in science and technology and with more fertilizer and

23. *Plant Studies*, p. 119.

24. Myers, "Wheat in China," p. 330.

25. Liu Chih-cheng et al, "The Relations Between the Four Transformations
and Economic Effects," *Ching-chi yen-chiu* [Economic Research], no. 2 (1964), translated in ECMM, no. 424 (1964), p. 4.

other investment put into each unit area of land, the output will also increase gradually. This is where we fundamentally differ from the pseudo-scientists of the bourgeoisie concerning the law of "diminishing returns from land." But under given conditions of science and technology, when other measures for increase of production fail to catch up, each unit of investment in fertilizer will yield lower results.[26]

This commentator, also writing in 1964, admits that the marginal product of individual inputs may decline as their application is increased, but he expects that returns from packages of complementary inputs will not decline under conditions of "continued advancement made in science and technology."

A decade of strongly diminishing returns and a change of leadership have encouraged Chinese social scientists to subject these problems to objective empirical study:

> Today, our country's agricultural mechanization shows great development, but there are many problems. For instance . . . [there is] the problem of raising output and incomes. According to a multi-province survey of 2,162 production teams, average yield of six grains rose from 232 chin per mou in 1965 to 316 chin in 1976, an increase of 36 percent. But costs per mou rose from 26.2 yuan per mou to 40.5 yuan, an increase of 54 percent, and the value of one labor-day declined from 0.7 to 0.56 yuan. The main reason why these problems arise is because in the course of farm mechanization we have ignored objective laws, failed to clarify economic accounting, and failed to improve economic efficiency. These conditions are directly linked to the long-term interruption of research on agricultural technology and economics.[27]

If this type of blunt, factually based analysis maintains its current popularity, China's agricultural growth will not be retarded by failure to recognize the extent and significance of current problems.

The question of managerial rationality at the microeconomic

26. Yen Jui-chen, "Several Questions on Increasing the Economic Benefits of Fertilizers," *Ching-chi yen-chiu* [Economic Research], no. 6 (1964), translated in ECMM, no. 429 (1964), p. 20.

27. "Strengthen Scientific Research." One chin equals 0.5 kilograms.

level, however, is more difficult. Most foreign analysts, including the present author, have assumed that the return of control over production and distribution decisions to small production teams removed the chief element of economic irrationality from China's commune system during the early 1960s. Pessimistic foreign appraisals of China's agricultural prospects do not refer to managerial incompetence as a reason for expecting a low growth rate for output. If incentives are inadequate, higher farm prices and increased allocation of consumer products to rural areas are cited as appropriate policy responses.

Recent criticism of agricultural operations appearing in the Chinese press suggests, however, that foreign appraisals of the commune management system may be overoptimistic. Numerous instances are cited of counterproductive management practices: farm machines in disrepair, afforestation projects nullified because seedlings are not tended, ill-conceived irrigation projects creating alkaline soil, seeds and livestock imported from distant regions without preliminary experimentation, irresponsible and corrupt financial administration, forced shifts to double cropping despite inadequate resources, prosperous units burdened with ceilings on personal incomes, peasants denied monthly holidays, and so on.[28] Do these reports, which recall the excesses of the Great Leap Forward, merely reflect the inevitable weak points in a system whose decisionmaking units number in the millions? Or is it possible that a high incidence of defective management in agriculture has significantly retarded China's agricultural growth?

A review of available evidence tends to support the first view. Despite the difficulties caused by managerial incompetence, higher-level interference, and internal strife in some units, collective organization does not appear to pose a major obstacle to agricultural growth. Since peasants participate in the selection of production team leaders and "have some fairly effective means of expressing dissatisfaction" with decisions made at the lowest administrative level, the general orientation of production team efforts would be expected to coincide with the income-seeking as-

28. Examples of critical reports on these topics appear in FBIS, February 10, 1978, E11-12, and November 30, 1978, G-5; *China News Analysis*, no. 1,124 (1978), no. 1,135 (1978), and no. 1,141 (1978); and *Peking Review*, no. 48 (1978), pp. 21–22.

pirations of peasant households.[29] Unless shackled by contrary instructions from above, production teams should push for rapid growth of output. An extensive and detailed inquiry by Parish and Whyte confirms this expectation: "In the Kwangtung country-side the emphasis on . . . rewarding the most productive . . . and on efficiency (retaining flexibility and initiative in the hands of those making the daily farming decisions) have clearly been fore-most in the minds of Chinese planners."[30]

Transferability of China's Experience to Other Countries

The success China has had in raising the levels of employment for growing urban and rural populations naturally brings to the fore the question of how this experience is relevant to the problems of countries whose political, social, and economic systems may differ widely from China's.

Several fundamental features of China's political economy do appear to stand in the way of wholesale application of Chinese methods to problems confronting other developing countries. China's climate, topography, farm technology, and agricultural population are all well suited to the system of intensive agriculture built up over the centuries and further developed over the past several decades. China's farming technology, and especially the wet-rice culture of the south, proved its ability to adjust to large increases in population density centuries before 1949. Recent re-forms in cultivation practices consist to a large extent of in-troducing the technology of rice culture—with its transplanting, irrigation, heavy fertilization, and intensive plant care—into the northern and central regions in which irrigation was previously the exception rather than the rule.

Pursuit of intensive farming patterns presupposes a farm labor force that is prepared to devote long hours to careful tillage during

29. Parish and Whyte, *Village and Family,* p. 109; see also John P. Burns, "The Election of Production Team Cadres in Rural China, 1958–74," *China Quarterly,* no. 74 (1978), pp. 273–96.

30. Parish and Whyte, *Village and Family,* p. 117.

the growing season and to composting, land leveling, and maintenance of irrigation works in the off-season. Progressive intensification of farming also requires widespread entrepreneurship among the farm populace. Even a casual acquaintance with
conditions in various regions of the Third World provides frequent instances in which socioeconomic conditions make it difficult to foresee the calculating and aggressive response to economic
opportunity that seems typical of both urban and rural populations not only in China but throughout East Asia.

Effective administration at all levels of government is another
inheritance from China's past that provides an essential link in the
current economic system. In the countryside, substantial male literacy, a tradition of reporting local price and output data for major
crops, and keeping of records in connection with irrigation and
marketing networks formed a foundation upon which commune
administration could be built.[31] The strength of rural administrative capacity was evident soon after 1949, when the new government succeeded in establishing a wide array of financial and marketing organizations operated by non-elite rural dwellers who
were not among the victims of the extensive and violent campaign
for land reform.[32]

The communes that succeeded these early cooperatives have occupied a significant role in the process of labor absorption described in the previous chapters. Water conservancy and greater
attention to animal husbandry, horticulture, and forestry are aspects of agricultural intensification that owe their existence to rural collectivization. Local industry requires administration and organization of both production and distribution—and, for machinery, of maintenance and repair work as well. This industry is
another component of China's rural development program that appears virtually inseparable from collectivization.

Some features of recent agricultural reforms such as increased
inputs per acre of organic fertilizer and manpower could easily
have developed under a system of family farming. But others rang-

31. Thomas G. Rawski, "On the Reliability of Chinese Economic Data," *Journal
of Development Studies*, vol. 12, no. 4 (1976), p. 439.

32. Vivienne Shue, "Reorganizing Rural Trade," *Modern China*, vol. 2, no. 1
(1976), pp. 104–34.

ing from livestock insurance and road building to rural power grids and canal systems could hardly have developed as rapidly in a market economy as under the present system of socialized farming.

More generally, China has benefited from a tradition of social control that has been reshaped to meet the goals of a new leadership. Social control enables the Chinese government to implement policies that might be difficult or impossible elsewhere: for example, steeply rising investment proportions; restriction of peasant migration to the cities; enforced migration of educated urban youth to agricultural communities; and intense propaganda efforts directed at training local leaders to adhere to central policy guidelines without close supervision. A whole series of programs with the goal of reducing rural-urban differences has helped China to achieve a well-integrated administrative system in which the combined bureaucratic and practical skills of local officials contribute to effective policy implementation at the grass-roots level.

An unusually large, well-established, and widely distributed industrial sector is a final feature of China's economic life that is not often duplicated in other low-income countries. Industry replaced agriculture as the largest contributor to China's aggregate product during the 1960s, and economists agree that this is not a statistical illusion caused by price distortions. The scale of industry is large by any standard. Industry is no longer concentrated in a few coastal centers, but is widely dispersed throughout China's provinces, counties, and even communes. This change has far-reaching implications:

> A hand tractor imported from Japan would have the same physical productivity as one made in China, but it will certainly not have the same impact as one made in a Brigade or Commune machine shop where every peasant knows someone who helped built it. By pushing the production of particular agricultural machinery all the way to the Brigade level, China has removed the "foreignness" from new technology. Not only will this speed adoption of the technology, but the presence of the factory and machine shop locally means spare parts and repairs are readily available. The level of utilization of machinery locally produced is thus likely to be far higher

than of machinery imported from higher levels or abroad for which no such capability exists.[33]

Finally, decades of experience both before and after 1949 led to an accumulation of problem-solving capabilities within industry. These skills are in part the fruit of China's isolation from trade and outside aid. They represent another crucial ingredient in recent economic gains that will be difficult for many developing countries to match.

These observations underline Donald Keesing's view that the unique features and integrated nature of China's socioeconomic system make it difficult to envision wholesale transfers of the strategies and mechanisms that have contributed to China's economic achievements into the economic milieu of other developing countries.[34] Even so, China's relatively successful experience in absorbing large new labor force cohorts despite limited non-agricultural employment opportunities and an unchanged stock of farmland suggests a variety of opportunities for other countries facing similar combinations of circumstances.

Recent developments in Chinese agriculture show that an initially labor-intensive system of farming can be modified in directions that facilitate the absorption of additional labor. Although some of the labor-using methods advocated by Chinese officials have turned out to be counterproductive, there can be no doubt of the beneficial effects on both output and employment of increased application of organic manures, the northward spread of transplanting and multiple cropping, more intensive tillage, the shift toward labor-using farm activities, vast efforts to improve the network of water control and irrigation facilities, and other measures described in Chapter Four.

In China growing supplies of manufactured farm inputs, both chemical and mechanical, appear to have contributed to a growing demand for farm labor. Although rural industry occupies only a small fraction of the rural work force, the indirect contribution of its output of fertilizer, cement, and machinery to the growth of

33. Dwight Perkins and others, *Rural Small-Scale Industry in the People's Republic of China* (Berkeley: University of California Press, 1977), p. 73.

34. Donald B. Keesing, "Economic Lessons from China," *Journal of Development Economics,* vol. 2 (1975), pp. 1–32.

rural employment opportunities has been substantial. In contrast to the pessimistic view of mechanization expressed by some observers, the influx of tractors, power tillers, irrigation equipment, and other types of labor-saving machinery into China's farm economy has stimulated rather than curtailed the overall demand for agricultural labor.

Finally, China's experience illustrates the potential of a multilayered system of economic administration. Although China's economy includes strong elements of central planning and control, the past two decades have witnessed a considerable expansion of economic authority at the provincial, county, municipal, commune, brigade, and even production team level. Central officials certainly retain the power to constrain, review, and countermand policies determined at lower levels, but there are substantive areas in which economic policy in the countryside is determined and implemented by rural people.

It is possible, of course, that some of the elements that in the past have contributed to China's achievements in providing increased employment opportunities to a growing labor force may no longer do so in the future. Further progress toward agricultural mechanization, for example, may reduce rather than raise the demand for farm labor. Recent reports suggest that relaxation of pressures obliging urban school graduates to settle in rural areas may lead to new problems of joblessness among urban youth. Other elements of China's successful employment record may be linked with social or economic conditions established before 1949, with the existence of effectively managed agricultural collectives or with other aspects of the Chinese scene that may find no counterparts in other developing countries.

On the other hand, John Mellor's proposed strategy for India's economy illustrates the potential value of Chinese experience as a guide to policy elsewhere. Although Mellor's analysis does not consider the Chinese case, his suggestions for an agriculturally based, employment-oriented development policy closely parallel many of the Chinese programs described in the present study.[35] This shows that, despite the unique aspects of China's

35. John W. Mellor, *The New Economics of Growth* (Ithaca, N.Y.: Cornell University Press, 1976). The long list of proposals that resemble actual Chinese programs

social, political, and economic arrangements, China's success in enlarging employment opportunities for the world's largest national labor force can offer an instructive as well as an encouraging example to those persons concerned with employment problems throughout the developing world.

---

includes rural infrastructure investment in health, education, electrification, communication, transport, water control, and agricultural research; increased supplies of chemical fertilizer, water, credit, and risk-sharing arrangements for farm households; diversification of agriculture in the direction of labor-using activities; expansion of rural industry centered on light engineering; indirect taxation of rising farm incomes; and administrative decentralization to foster local resource mobilization. Mellor's principal deviations from Chinese methods are his advocacy of lower foodgrain prices and his suggestion that investment in capital-intensive urban industries should be curtailed, at least in the short run, to free resources for rural investment.

Appendix A

Chinese Economic Statistics

ANY STUDY THAT SETS OUT to provide a detailed quantitative analysis of China's economy must consider the accuracy, veracity, and international comparability of Chinese economic data. The purpose of this brief discussion is to acquaint nonspecialist readers with the major issues and to explain why, despite undeniable difficulties of compilation and interpretation, available data do permit construction of meaningful estimates that provide broadly accurate quantitative information about the size, structure, and evolution of China's economy.[1]

Statistical Capacity

The statistical capacity of the present Chinese government compares favorably with the achievements of other nations with similar levels of per capita income. This is not a recent phenomenon, but stems in part from the high level (relative to other nonindustrial societies) of administrative and statistical competence inherited from the period before 1949. As a bureaucratic state, the Chinese imperial government maintained statistical records of population, prices, and fiscal information long before the twentieth century. The Republican period (1912–49) produced a rich variety of statistical materials at all levels of government and in the

1. This discussion is based on Thomas G. Rawski, "On the Reliability of Chinese Economic Data," *Journal of Development Studies*, vol. 12, no. 4 (1976), pp. 438–41.

private sector as well. These include detailed farm survey investigations, a competent and comprehensive industrial census, and attempts to construct estimates of national income and its components.[2] Statistical work after 1949 benefited from this data base and from the experience of the individuals and organizations that had created it.

The tradition of gathering and recording quantitative information extended into rural as well as urban areas. Evelyn Rawski has shown that male literacy in imperial China approximated the high levels found in Japan at the end of the Tokugawa period (1600–1868); this tradition continued into the twentieth century, when rural surveys found that 45 percent of all males above seven years of age had received some schooling and 30 percent were literate.[3] Before 1949 widespread literacy facilitated regular reporting of local price and output data for the principal crops and maintenance of records in connection with irrigation systems and marketing networks.[4]

To these foundations the new communist government added its own program of recruiting and training statistical personnel, standardizing the format for recording and reporting economic data and developing a national system of communicating, compiling, and checking quantitative information. Again, this effort was not limited to a few cities. The regime's concern with rural development and the presence of widely dispersed literacy and adminis-

2. Many of these studies are described and evaluated in Ta-chung Liu and Kung-chia Yeh, *The Economy of the Chinese Mainland* (Princeton, N.J.: Princeton University Press, 1965).

3. Evelyn S. Rawski, *Education and Popular Literacy in Ch'ing China* (Ann Arbor: University of Michigan Press, 1979), pp. 151–52, and Dwight H. Perkins, "Introduction: The Persistence of the Past," in *China's Modern Economy in Historical Perspective*, ed. Dwight H. Perkins (Stanford, Calif.: Stanford University Press, 1975), p. 4.

4. Han-sheng Chuan and Richard A. Kraus, *Mid-Ch'ing Rice Markets and Trade* (Cambridge, Mass.: Harvard University Press, 1975), chap. 1; Endymion P. Wilkinson, "Studies in Chinese Price History," (Ph.D. dissertation, Princeton University, 1971); and Ramon H. Myers, "Economic Organization and Cooperation in Modern China: Irrigation Management in Xing-tai County, Ho-bei Province," in *Chūgoku no seiji to keizai* [The Polity and Economy of China], ed. The Late Professor Yuji Muramatsu Commemoration Board (Tokyo: Tōyō keizai shimpō sha, 1975), pp. 199–204.

trative skills meant that, even without the participation of former elite households who had been stripped of property and authority soon after the communist takeover, the regime could find personnel capable of implementing land reform, collecting taxes, enforcing compulsory quotas for grain delivery, and administering increasingly complex cooperative and collective arrangements for producing and marketing farm products. The same personnel and skills made it possible to obtain increasingly serviceable agricultural statistics.

As a result of these efforts, the end of the First Five-Year Plan period (1953–57) found China in possession of a national statistical system that could be classed as quite respectable by the standards of other low-income nations.[5] There were, of course, wide variations in the quality of data for different localities, sectors, and functional areas. Statistics relating to the physical output of large-scale urban industries, for example, were vastly superior to data on production costs, labor requirements, or even physical output in the farm sector.

The Great Leap Forward years (1958–60) brought an abrupt reversal of the trend toward growing statistical competence. With the politicization of statistical work, plans became dreams, and the latter were reported as achievements to superiors who were either too credulous or too frightened to resist false reporting. This episode culminated in the publication of vastly exaggerated national harvest figures that later had to be retracted—at considerable political cost.

The collapse of the Great Leap Forward brought strenuous efforts to rebuild and later to develop China's statistical system further. In the urban sector, where resistance to the erosion of professionalism continued throughout the Great Leap Forward, reinstatement of specialist personnel soon restored the statistical system to its former level of competence, which then became a base for further improvements. In the countryside the people's communes have since the policy reversals of the early 1960s experienced strong and continuous pressure to produce comprehen-

5. For a detailed evaluation of China's statistical system between 1949 and 1960, see Choh-ming Li, *The Statistical System of Communist China* (Berkeley: University of California Press, 1962).

sive and reliable statistics. At that time, China's nationwide food shortage made accurate measurement of farm output a task of the utmost importance. Units suspected of statistical malpractice were subjected to searching investigations in both rural and urban areas.[6] Isolated instances of statistical anarchism during the Cultural Revolution (1966–68) drew sharp criticism, and the 1970s have seen a steady flow of articles stressing the importance of accounting and excoriating political interference in harsh terms.[7]

These incentives have been matched by a steady increase in the competence of statistical workers, especially in rural areas. The spread of peasant literacy, migration of an estimated 12 million urban graduates to the countryside, creation of training courses for rural accountants, expansion of telephone and other communication links, and the government's increased awareness of agriculture's central place in China's economy all point to a vastly improved apparatus for monitoring the rural sector.[8]

As a result of these developments, there is no longer any serious doubt of the Chinese government's ability to collect reasonably accurate data on commodity output, production costs, employment, investment, and other magnitudes used in the present study. Even in the case of population, an area in which China's statistical capability is notoriously weak, the gap between official statements and the most plausible outside estimate is less than 5

6. An example involving the famous Tachai brigade is in *New China's First Quarter-Century* (Peking: Foreign Languages Press, 1975), pp. 169–70. More generally, see Michel Oksenberg, "Methods of Communication Within the Chinese Bureaucracy," *China Quarterly*, no. 57 (1974), pp. 21–28.

7. For example: "We often encounter . . . comrades . . . who chant slogans about giving prominence to proletarian politics and speeding up socialist construction. But they could not give an answer when asked how much money a certain project would require, when the project would be completed for production, and how its economic effect could be developed to the fullest extent" (SCMP, no. 4,949 [1971], p. 61).

8. For details on some of these areas, see Leo A. Orleans, "China's Science and Technology: Continuity and Innovation," in U.S. Congress, Joint Economic Committee, *People's Republic of China: An Economic Assessment* (Washington, D.C.: U.S. Government Printing Office, 1972), pp. 216–19; Jack Craig, "China: Domestic and International Telecommunications, 1949–74," in U.S. Congress, Joint Economic Committee, *China: A Reassessment of the Economy* (Washington, D.C.: U.S. Government Printing Office, 1975); and SCMP, no. 5,310 (1973), pp. 76–79.

percent of the total (see Table 2-1). Chinese statistical competence is visible at the microeconomic level, at which technical and managerial personnel impress well-informed foreign guests with detailed and precise accounts of their units' affairs, as well as at the macroeconomic level, at which consistency checks regularly confirm the internal coherence of Chinese statements about production, acreage, yields, consumption, and trade.[9]

Statistical Veracity

There is absolutely no evidence that Chinese government offices or economic enterprises maintain separate books for internal administration and for external publicity. Consistency between national and regional figures for industrial and agricultural output value, grain output, cultivated area, and other magnitudes means that, if falsification exists, it cannot be confined to a few offices in the capital but must permeate the entire statistical network. Tens of thousands would know if published information were false, an inference that underlines the significance of Perkins' observation that "of all the people who daily go in and out of China, not one has produced evidence of the existence of two sets of books."[10]

Many of Peking's recent economic claims imply trends in per capita commodity supplies that can be verified by any reader. China's numerous bookstores are filled with cheap pamphlets that often contain time series data on grain yields, fertilizer input, mechanization, food consumption and reserves, household and per capita incomes, personal savings, and other magnitudes at the provincial, county, commune, brigade, team, or even household levels. Given the corrosive effect of exaggeratedly optimistic economic claims on public opinion during and after the Great Leap, it is inconceivable that the Peking government would knowingly release false data of this sort. Since information obtained by foreigners either comes from, or is repeated in, domestic Chinese-lan-

9. Many of these consistency tests are mentioned in Nai-ruenn Chen, "An Assessment of Chinese Economic Data: Availability, Reliability and Usability," in U.S. Congress, Joint Economic Committee, *China: A Reassessment*, pp. 57–60.

10. Dwight H. Perkins, *Market Control and Planning in Communist China* (Cambridge, Mass.: Harvard University Press, 1966), p. 222.

guage sources, confidence in the veracity of Chinese statistical statements extends to materials directed at foreign as well as domestic audiences.

International Comparability

Even if it is agreed that available economic data represent the fruits of Peking's increasingly successful efforts to measure various aspects of economic activity, it is not always easy to fit Chinese data into a format suitable for international comparison. Chinese statistics are often incomplete. The Chinese may not collect or may choose not to publish certain types of information. Published data may be difficult to interpret because of the possibility of unreported changes in statistical concepts: "industry," "foodgrains," "chemical fertilizers," and "sown acreage" are some of the many statistical categories for which the exact meaning of the data is uncertain for this reason.

A third difficulty arises from China's adherence to statistical procedures derived from Marxist economic theory and Soviet statistical conventions. Output data, for example, normally refer only to commodity production and exclude services. Value totals are presented in gross (or global) figures that include the value of interindustry purchases. This means that the measured growth rate of output value is affected not only by changes in physical output and prices, but by changes in the average degree of vertical integration as well. Increased specialization and division of labor among producing units will artificially inflate, and increased verticalization will artificially deflate, an index of gross value of output.

In trying to overcome these difficulties, foreign specialists have benefited from certain features of China's economy that simplify the task of measurement. Low per capita income and the associated simplicity of economic structure permit the analyst to track the performance of important segments of China's economy by use of only a few variables. Thus, output figures for grain and cotton can be used to project farm output; cotton production and imports determine the output of cotton textiles; until the recent expansion in the manufacture of man-made fiber, output of food and cotton textiles largely determined the level of personal consumption as well as output of manufactured consumer goods. The output mix in producer industries is less homogeneous than in the consumer sector, but here there are relatively plentiful output data in Chinese sources.

Some of the difficulties encountered in quantitative studies of socialist economies in the Soviet Union and Eastern Europe appear muted or absent in China. Changes in the degree of vertical integration that, as noted above, can distort time series of gross value of output, and have done so in the Soviet Union, do not appear as a significant influence in the Chinese data. As a result, data on gross value give good approximations to the growth of value added in industry.[11] Artificial inflation of industrial output figures because of overpricing of new products is another distortion encountered in Soviet, but not in Chinese, figures for industrial output.[12] Although Chinese prices are largely administered by the government and are not immediately responsive to market forces, price changes have moved the structure of relative values in the directions indicated by scarcity relations, with the relative (and sometimes absolute) prices of fast-growing manufactures declining while farmgate prices increase.[13]

Aided by these favorable circumstances, specialists willing to immerse themselves in the intricacies of reconstructing Chinese economic magnitudes from scattered fragments of information have produced estimates that stand up well to tests of consistency; they frequently anticipate reports from Chinese sources or visitor accounts. Gradual accumulation of both data and experience have

11. Thomas G. Rawski, "China's Industrial Performance, 1949–1973," in *Quantitative Measures of China's Economic Output*, ed. Alexander Eckstein (Ann Arbor: University of Michigan Press, forthcoming); and U.S. National Foreign Assessment Center, *China: Economic Indicators* (Washington, D.C.: Central Intelligence Agency, 1978), p. 17.

12. Thomas G. Rawski, "Chinese Industrial Production, 1952–71," *Review of Economics and Statistics*, vol. 55, no. 2 (1973), pp. 173–75; and "Industrial Performance," in *Quantitative Measures*.

13. Dwight H. Perkins, "Growth and Changing Structure of China's Twentieth-Century Economy," in *China's Modern Economy in Historical Perspective*, ed. Dwight H. Perkins (Stanford, Calif.: Stanford University Press, 1975), pp. 128–47, and "Issues in the Estimation of China's National Product," in *Quantitative Measures of China's Economic Output*.

narrowed conceptual and empirical disagreements, resulting in a broad consensus among specialists regarding the quantitative dimensions of growth and structural change in China's economy since 1949.[14]

The evolution of the field of Chinese economic studies shows that, despite problems of collecting, compiling, and assessing statistical information, detailed empirical studies of China's economy can produce meaningful results. This does not mean that studies such as the present one are free of statistical error. Error can arise from deficiencies in China's statistical system, from gaps in published information, and from the assumptions required to construct reasonably complete sets of data. Readers familiar with studies of other countries will recognize that these problems are not unique to studies of China, but arise in all empirical studies of economic development. For China, as for India, Indonesia, Meiji Japan, or preindustrial Europe, careful research can and does produce results that are not guesses but estimates of actual economic magnitude.

---

14. This change can be seen by comparing the broad agreement within the *Quantitative Measures* volume with the sharp controversy evident in the discussion inspired by Ta-chung Liu, "Economic Development of the Chinese Mainland, 1949–1965," in *China in Crisis,* eds. Ping-ti Ho and Tang Tsou (Chicago: University of Chicago Press, 1968), vol. 1, bk. 2, pp. 609–90.

Appendix B

Derivation of Estimated Nonagricultural Employment, 1957 and 1975

Sectoral estimates for nonagricultural employment were summarized in Table 2-8. A more detailed compilation, in which nonagricultural employment in various sectors is divided between workers and employees and other laborers, appears in Table B-1. The Chinese concept of workers and employees "implies a contractual relationship between the employed person and his employer and payment of cash wages in return for labor."[1] Although it is possible that unannounced changes have occurred since 1960 in this definition, the availability of a statement giving a total of 90 million workers and employees in 1978 provides a standard against which to evaluate the estimates of nonagricultural employment in 1975.[2] Since the total for 1975 comes to 88.8 million workers and employees, or within 2 percent of the reported total (which probably refers to 1977), the present estimate does appear to approximate the order of magnitude of actual employment conditions for 1975.

---

1. John P. Emerson, *Nonagricultural Employment in Mainland China: 1949–1958* (Washington, D.C.: U.S. Government Printing Office, 1965), p. 3. Further information on this concept may be found in the translations included in ibid., Appendix C.
2. FBIS, October 24, 1978, p. E2.

TABLE B-1. NONAGRICULTURAL EMPLOYMENT BY SECTOR, 1957 AND 1975 (millions of workers)

	1957			1975		
Sector	Workers and employees	Other	Total	Workers and employees	Other	Total
Industry						
State sector[a]	8.0	0	8.0	25.0	0	25.0
Collective sector	0	0	0	0	14.3	14.3
Handicrafts	0	6.6	6.6	0	0.3	0.3
Construction[b]	1.9	0	1.9	6.5	0	6.5
Transport, posts, and communication	1.9	2.5	4.4	6.4	2.5	8.9
Trade, food and drink, finance banking and insurance	5.6	2.8	8.4	12.0	6.0[c]	18.0
Personal services	0	0.5	0.5	0	1.1[c]	1.1
Health	0.5	1.4	1.9	3.1	3.5	6.6
Education and culture	2.7	0	2.7	7.6	0	7.6
Government administration and mass organizations	2.9	0	2.9	6.2[c]	0	6.2
Salt	0	0.5	0.5	0	1.1	1.1
Fishing	0	1.5	1.5	0	1.2	1.2
Civilian nonagricultural employment	23.5	15.8	39.3	66.8	30.0	96.8
Military personnel	0	3.0	3.0	0	3.5	3.5
Total nonagricultural employment	23.5	18.8	42.3	66.8	33.5	100.3
State farms, forestry and water conservancy	0.9	0	0.9	22.0	0	22.0
Total nonagricultural employment plus workers and employees in farming, forestry, and water conservancy	24.4	18.8	43.2	88.8	33.5	122.3

a. Includes large-scale utilities.

b. Excludes employment in farmland improvement and water conservancy.

c. Assumed to have grown at the 4.3 percent annual rate derived for workers and employees in trade, food and drink, and finance.

Sources: For 1957, see Table 2-8. For 1975, see text.

Nonagricultural Employment in 1957

There are three separate studies of nonagricultural employment for 1957. Their authors estimate civilian nonagricultural employment for that year as follows: John P. Emerson, 39.7 million; Ta-chung Liu and Kung-chia Yeh, 60.6 million; and Chi-ming Hou,

47.7 million.[3] The present study relies on Emerson's results for
two reasons. First, Emerson's is the most detailed, careful, and
comprehensive review of available information on nonagricultural
employment during the 1950s. Second, Emerson's compilation excludes part-time workers, and his results are therefore more consistent with the present estimates of full-time nonagricultural employment in 1975 than the results of the studies by Liu and Yeh
and by Hou. The differences between the three estimates of nonagricultural employment for 1957 arise primarily from the following factors:

First, Liu and Yeh include 5.6 million members of work brigades in their total.[4] These workers are excluded from Table B-1
because most of them are farm workers who are recruited into
work brigades for short periods of time. Both Emerson and Hou
exclude these workers from their estimates of nonagricultural employment.

Second, Hou's estimate of handicraft employment exceeds
Emerson's by 1.4 million because Hou attempts to estimate the
number of craftsmen who joined advanced producer cooperatives
in 1956. His procedure leads to double counting because some of
these craftsmen joined industrial enterprises and thus appear in
both industrial and handicraft employment. The Liu and Yeh estimate for handicrafts includes both craftsmen who joined cooperatives and an additional 4.6 million workers as an estimate of the
full-time equivalent of part-time craftsmen.[5]

Third, employment in nonmodern transport is extremely difficult to quantify because of the paucity of detailed information either before or after 1949. Emerson's figure of 2.5 million workers is
smaller than Hou's estimate of 4.8 million or the Liu and Yeh fig-

---

3. Employment estimates from Emerson, *Nonagricultural Employment*, p. 128;
Ta-chung Liu and Kung-chia Yeh, *The Economy of the Chinese Mainland* (Princeton,
N.J.: Princeton University Press, 1965), p. 208; and Chi-ming Hou, "Manpower,
Employment and Unemployment," in *Economic Trends in Communist China*, eds. Al-
exander Eckstein, Walter Galenson, and Ta-chung Liu (Chicago: Aldine, 1968), p.
362.

4. Liu and Yeh, *The Economy*, p. 206.

5. Chi-ming Hou, "Manpower," pp. 356 and 384–86; Liu and Yeh, *The Economy*,
pp. 193–96.

ure (again, including a full-time equivalent of part-time workers) of 10.0 million.[6]

Fourth, trade, food, and drink is another problematic sector because of the difficulty of estimating numbers of rural peddlers. Emerson's employment total for this sector includes 6.7 million workers in trade and 1.1 million in food and drink. Liu and Yeh estimate employment in these categories at 5.0 and 6.4 million, respectively.[7] Hou's figures are ambiguous because he lists employment in trade, food, and drink at 5.374 million for 1957 but also identifies this as an estimate for the traditional segment of these activities alone, with another 5.245 million workers allocated to the modern segment of trade, food, and drink.[8]

Fifth, the number of domestic servants is assumed by Liu and Yeh to have remained at the 1933 level of 2.3 million; Hou uses the same figure.[9] The present study follows Emerson in omitting this category because there are no data whatsoever.

Handicrafts, trade, and transport, each of which includes large numbers of unorganized rural workers whose numbers are difficult to estimate, form the weakest segment of the estimates for 1957. In each case Emerson's figures, which are used here, fall below alternative totals suggested by Hou and by Liu and Yeh. Accordingly, it is possible that the total of 42.3 million persons shown in Tables 2-8 and B-1 underestimates full-time nonagricultural employment in 1957. The actual total could be as high as the figure of 50 million implied by Hou's results (47.7 million civilians plus 3 million military personnel). The figure of 50 million appears, however, to provide an upper limit to the level of full-time nonagricultural employment in 1957. The remaining difference between this and the higher Liu and Yeh figures arises from their inclusion of part-time workers in the total. Any tendency for the present estimates to understate the level of nonfarm employment in 1957 would lead to an overestimate of the subsequent absorption of labor outside agriculture, which in turn would result

6. Liu and Yeh, *The Economy*, pp. 198–99; Chi-ming Hou, "Manpower," pp. 356 and 387–89.

7. Liu and Yeh, *The Economy*, p. 200.

8. Chi-ming Hou, "Manpower," pp. 356 and 366.

9. Liu and Yeh, *The Economy*, pp. 203 and 608; Chi-ming Hou, "Manpower," p. 356.

in a small downward bias in the estimate of labor absorption in the agricultural sector between 1957 and 1975.

Nonagricultural Employment in 1975

The point of departure for the present estimates of nonagricultural employment for 1975 is an article by Günter Kohrt, former ambassador to China from the German Democratic Republic, which refers to "the workers in industry, construction and transportation—about 55 million in a total population of 800 million."[10] This statement, together with independent estimates of employment in transportation and construction, leads to an estimate of the level of industrial employment in 1975.

Transport, post, and communications

An index of freight transport by rail, water, and highway compiled in Table B-2 shows an annual average growth rate of 5.4 percent a year between 1957 and 1973. Assuming that other transport modes grew at a similar pace and making some allowance for rising productivity as a result of improved highways, more powerful locomotives, substitution of motor for sailing vessels, and so on, employment in this sector can be assumed to have expanded at an annual rate of 4 percent after 1957. This assumption results in the employment figure of 8.9 million workers in 1975 shown in Table B-1. It is assumed that all incremental workers in this sector are regular wage-earners, all of whom are classified as workers and employees.

Construction, excluding farmland improvement and water conservancy

The present estimate of growth of employment in this sector is based on an index of construction activity developed by U.S. government analysts. This index shows that construction activity in 1975 was 4.04 times the level in 1957, implying an average annual

10. Günter Kohrt, "Maoism's Permanent Crisis and Growing Threat," *Horizont,* vol. 9, nos. 33–37 (1976), translated in JPRS, no. 68,303 (1976), p. 94.

TABLE B-2. GROWTH OF DOMESTIC TRANSPORT, 1949–73

Transport mode	Index of freight volume			Freight turnover in 1957 (millions of ton-kilometers)
	1949	1957	1973	
Railways	100	491	1,400	134,590
Shipping	100	990	1,100	34,390
Highway	100	1,446	4,500	3,940
Aggregate freight volume[a]	100	612	1,411	172,920

a. Weighted average of indexes for three transport modes, using 1957 freight turnover statistics as weights.

Sources: For 1949 and 1957: Nai-ruenn Chen, *Chinese Economic Statistics* (Chicago: Aldine, 1967), pp. 373–76. For 1973: Cheng Shih, *A Glance At China's Economy* (Peking: Foreign Languages Press, 1974), p. 35. The figure for highway transport compares 1973 with the peak year before 1949.

increase during 1957–75 of 8.1 percent.[11] With some allowance made for possible increases in labor productivity, an annual growth rate for construction employment of 7 percent can be assumed for the period 1957–75. This results in an employment estimate for 1975 of 6.5 million for the construction sector. It is assumed that, as in 1957, workers in this sector are all classified as workers and employees.

Industry

With an employment figure of 55 million for industry, transport, and construction, industrial employment may be derived as a residual total of $55 - (8.9 + 6.5) = 39.6$ million workers. According to the formerly prominent Chang Ch'un-ch'iao, now disgraced as a member of the "Gang of Four": "Industry under ownership by the whole people accounted for 97 percent of the fixed assets of industry as a whole, 63 percent of the industrial population, and 86 percent of the value of total industrial output [for 1973]. Besides these, individual handicraftsmen made up 0.8 percent of the industrial population."[12]

11. U.S. National Foreign Assessment Center, *China: Economic Indicators* (Washington, D.C.: Central Intelligence Agency, 1977), p. 5.

12. Chang Ch'un-ch'iao, "On Exercising All-Round Dictatorship over the Bourgeoisie," *Peking Review*, no. 14 (1975), p. 6.

Application of these figures to the estimate of industrial employment yields the following results:

State-owned industry : $39.6 \cdot 0.63 = 25.0$ million employees
(approximately)
Collective industry   : $39.6 \cdot 0.362 = 14.3$ million employees
Individual craftsmen : $39.6 \cdot 0.008 = 0.3$ million craftsmen

It is assumed that, as in the 1950s, only the personnel of state-owned industry are classified as workers and employees.[13]

The state sector includes plants that derive their fixed assets from, and return most of their profits to, the state. This category includes enterprises administered by offices of the central, provincial, municipal, and county governments. Collective industry is made up of enterprises that derive their assets from the saving of a distinct community: an agricultural commune, one of the constituent brigades or teams of a commune, or an urban neighborhood. Collective enterprises retain most of their profits.[14]

The significance of the employment figure for collective industry is not entirely clear because many employees of rural collective industry are described as "both workers and peasants," which suggests the possibility that the present estimate considerably overstates the level of full-time employment in collective industry. But a subsequent report that commune members who work in enterprises operated by brigades, communes, or townships "work in the small factories most of the year and go to the fields in the busy farming season" indicates that most employees of collective indus-

13. Ch'en Chih-ho, "The Question of Groups Included in Labor Force Statistics," *Chi-hua yü t'ung-chi*, no. 11 (1959), translated in Emerson, *Nonagricultural Employment*, states that all personnel of state enterprises are "workers and employees" and ridicules the suggestion that laborers in commune industry should be included in this category (pp. 195 and 197).

14. The borderline between collective and state-owned urban industries is not distinct. *Peking Review*, no. 20 (1976), p. 22, gives examples of urban factories switching from collective status into the state sector. Visitors to the Peking West District Optical Meter Plant, a unit employing 520 workers that shifted into the state sector in 1969, were told that the distinction between the two types of units is not great because urban collective units may receive partial support from the state sector through grants of equipment, material, and other resources (Rawski Trip Notes).

try can fairly be described as fullly employed in the industrial sector.[15]

A report stating in 1978 that the rapidly growing industrial activity associated with China's rural communes and brigades employs a total of 17 million people fits well with the figure of 14.3 million workers in collective industry in 1975. This suggests that the estimates in Table B-1 capture the order of magnitude of employment changes in industry. In view of the circuitous derivation of these results, however, further substantiation of their order of magnitude is desirable; it can be found by investigating industrial employment and output figures for Shanghai and for Liaoning province.

Data in Table B-3 show that industrial labor productivity in these two regions averaged 23,235 yuan per man-year for 1975 in 1957 prices. If this figure is applied to the gross value of national industrial output in 1975, 378.480 billion 1957 yuan, overall employment in industry and handicrafts for 1975 would appear to be 16.3 million, far less than the total of 39.6 million derived above.[16]

But Shanghai and Liaoning are China's most advanced industrial regions. Dividing national gross value of output by average labor productivity in these two regions is certain to understate total employment because of the implicit assumption that labor productivity in these two regions approximates the national average. In fact, the advanced state of factory industry and the small share of low-productivity handicraft activity in the industrial output of these regions means that the productivity figures shown in Table B-3 must exceed the national average by a large margin.

The extent of this deviation is calculated for 1955 in Table B-4, which shows that with industry defined to include handicrafts, as has been the case since 1958, industrial labor productivity in Shanghai and Liaoning was 2.40 times the national average. If this differential has persisted over the subsequent two decades, the national employment figure for industry (including handicrafts) in 1975 would be $378.480 \cdot 2.40 \cdot 10^9 / 23.235 \cdot 10^3$, or 39.1 million work-

---

15. FBIS, January 6, 1978, E17.
16. Robert M. Field, Nicholas R. Lardy, and John P. Emerson, *Provincial Industrial Output in the People's Republic of China: 1949–75* (Washington, D.C.: U.S. Department of Commerce, 1976), p. 17.

TABLE B-3. INDUSTRIAL OUTPUT, EMPLOYMENT, AND PRODUCTIVITY, IN SHANGHAI AND LIAONING PROVINCE, 1975

Region	Gross value of industrial output (billions of 1957 yuan)[a]	Industrial employment (millions of workers)	Gross value per worker (yuan)
Shanghai	55.707[a]	2.3[b]	24,220
Liaoning	44.202[a]	2.0[c]	22,101
Combined total	99.909	4.3	23,235

a. Robert M. Field, Nicholas R. Lardy, and John P. Emerson, *Provincial Industrial Output in the People's Republic of China: 1949–75* (Washington, D.C.: U.S. Department of Commerce, 1976), p. 11.

b. There are 3 million employees in Shanghai city (BBC, no. W825 [1975], pp. A1–2). References to 2 million industrial workers therefore appear to include the entire municipality, not just the city proper. *Peking Review*, no. 27 (1975), p. 17, states that "in Shanghai . . . the number of female industrial workers has increased from 180,000 in 1949 . . . to over 800,000 or 35 percent of that metropolis' total work force today." Assuming that "work force" refers to industry alone, Shanghai industrial employment becomes 800,000 ÷ 0.35, or about 2.3 million.

c. BBC, no. W825 (1975), p. A1.

TABLE B-4. INDUSTRIAL LABOR PRODUCTIVITY FOR 1955, SHANGHAI, LIAONING PROVINCE, AND NATIONWIDE

Region	Gross value of output (billions of 1952 yuan)			Employment (thousands of workers)			Gross value of output per worker for all industry (yuan)
	Factories	Handicrafts	Total	Factories	Handicrafts	Total	
Shanghai	8.763[a]	0.284[b]	9.047	430	169[c]	599	15,104
Liaoning	7.532[d]	0.397[b]	7.929	754	242[c]	996	7,961
Combined total	16.295	0.681	19.976	1,184	411	1,595	10,643
Nationwide figures	44.748	10.123	54.870	4,152	8,202[e]	12,354	4,441

a. Robert M. Field, Nicholas R. Lardy, and John P. Emerson, *A Reconstruction of the Gross Value of Industrial Output by Province in the People's Republic of China: 1949–73* (Washington, D.C.: U.S. Department of Commerce, 1975), pp. 20–21.

b. Calculated from data in ibid. by assuming that the ratio of handicraft to factory output was the same in 1955 as in 1956 (for Shanghai) or 1957 (for Liaoning).

c. Calculated from the gross value of handicraft output and from average productivity per gainfully occupied handicraftsman in 1954: 1,677 yuan (Shanghai) and 1,642 yuan (Liaoning). Productivity data from Peter Schran, "Handicrafts in Communist China," *China Quarterly*, no. 21 (1964), p. 172.

d. Arithmetic average of 1954 and 1956 figures shown in Thomas G. Rawski, "Regional Distribution of Industrial Production," (unpublished, 1971; available from the author).

e. John P. Emerson, *Nonagricultural Employment in Mainland China, 1949–1958* (Washington, D.C.: U.S. Government Printing Office, 1965), p. 128.

Source: Except as noted, Nai-ruenn Chen, *Chinese Economic Statistics* (Chicago: Aldine, 1967), pp. 210 and 483.

ers, a figure that is within 2 percent of the comparable figure reported in Table B-1.

Although it is not possible to check the validity of the assumption that interregional productivity differentials have persisted through a period that has seen major shifts in the level, structure, and regional distribution of industrial activity, the close agreement between employment figures derived from entirely different sources suggests that the results shown in Table B-1 give a broadly accurate picture of employment trends in industry, construction, and transport.[17]

Trade, food and drink, finance, banking, and insurance

There is relatively little quantitative information regarding the growth of China's service sector. In July 1978, however, it was stated that the work force in commerce, the service trades, foreign trade, and banking amounted to 12 million persons.[18] This figure is 1.35 times the (possibly low) 1957 employment total for these sectors shown in Table B-1 and 2.14 times the figure of workers and employees in these activities for 1957.

It is known that the volume of transactions in commerce and finance has risen rapidly since 1957. "China's total retail sales of commodities in 1973 rose more than sevenfold compared with the early post-Liberation days."[19] This statement apparently compares 1973 with 1950 or 1951 (no retail sales figures for 1949 were ever published). If retail sales for 1973 are 8 times the 1950 level, then with 1957=100, retail volume for 1973 is 239–289, depending

17. In an article entitled "Observe Economic Laws, Speed Up the Four Modernizations," *Peking Review*, no. 46 (1978), p. 22, Hu Ch'iao-mu, president of the Chinese Academy of Social Sciences, presents information on labor productivity that can be used to estimate industrial employment for 1977. Although the exact categories underlying Hu's statement cannot be determined, his figures appear to imply an industrial labor force in 1977 of about 51 million workers, or 12 million more than the present estimate for 1975. Since it is doubtful that industrial employment rose by as much as 12 million persons in only two years, these figures suggest that the present estimate of 1975 industrial employment may be too low. Further inquiry must await clarification of the calculations on which Hu's statement is based.

18. *Peking Review*, no. 30 (1978), p. 1.

19. Chi Ti, "Stable Prices and the Reasons—Part 1," *Peking Review*, no. 19 (1975), p. 17.

on which of two trade indicators is used. If 1951 is the base, trade volume in 1973 becomes 341–395 with 1957=100.[20] The annual growth rate for domestic retail sales implied by these comparisons falls between 5.6 and 9.0 percent. Foreign trade flows rose at an annual rate of 5.4 percent between 1957 and 1974 (Table 1-1). Scattered data on savings deposits show even faster increases in turnover at bank branches:

Province	Period	Increase in deposits (percent)	Annual growth rate (percent)
Chekiang	1966–75		
Urban		76.8	n.a.
Rural		103.3	n.a.
Fukien	1965–75	89	6.6
Heilungkiang	1965–75	230	12.7
Kiangsi	1974–75	11	11
Kirin	1965–75		
Urban		160	10.0
Rural		390	17.2

Sources do not indicate whether the foregoing figures refer to stocks or flows. Chekiang data compare increases recorded during 1966–75 with comparable figures for 1956–65.[21]

In the absence of information suggesting implementation of productivity-enhancing innovation in these service trades, it seems reasonable to assume substantial increases in employment. Accordingly, the figure of 12 million persons has been taken as an estimate of the number of workers and employees in trade, food and drink, finance, banking, and insurance during 1975. This assumption implies an annual growth rate of 4.3 percent for this category of employment during 1957–75. The number of personnel in these activities who are not classified as workers and employees is assumed to have grown at the same 4.3 percent annual rate during 1957–75, leading to an overall total of 18.0 million persons in this sector in 1975.

20. The trade series for 1949–57 covering total retail volume and retail volume of commercial organizations are shown in Nai-ruenn Chen, *Chinese Economic Statistics* (Chicago: Aldine, 1967), pp. 394–95.

21. Data for Fukien, referring to reserves and savings of cities and villages, are from BBC, no. W873 (1976), p. A1; the remaining figures are from BBC, no. W867 (1976), p. A3.

Personal services

Employment in this sector, which includes such personal services as barbering, is assumed to have grown during 1957–75 at the same rate of 4.3 percent derived for workers and employees in trade, food and drink, finance, banking, and insurance.

Health

Employment for health care in 1975 is derived from the following statement: "The rural medical network has six million medical personnel, including 1.5 million barefoot doctors [paramedics] and 3 million spare time public health workers who work in the fields an average of 100 days/year. In addition, 1.1 million urban medical personnel visit rural areas in mobile teams."[22] It is assumed that the 4.5 million paramedics and part-time public health workers are not counted as workers and employees, but that the remaining 1.5 million rural medical personnel are full-time wage-earners who are so classified, along with 1.1 million urban medical personnel who visit rural areas and an additional (assumed) category of 0.5 million urban medical personnel who do not visit rural areas in mobile teams. The estimate of employment in health care for 1975 thus includes 3.1 million workers and employees and, assuming that the typical part-time public health worker spends two-thirds time in medical activities, 3.5 million other personnel, for a sectoral total of 6.6 million workers.

Education and culture

The number of teachers is estimated from school enrollment figures by assuming constant class size:

	1957 data		1977 data and estimates	
Type of school	Students (millions)	Teachers (thousands)	Students (millions)	Teachers (thousands)
Elementary	64.3	2,010	146.1	4,567
Middle	7.1	190	67.0	1,793
Higher education	0.4	60	0.6	90
Total	71.8	2,260	213.7	6,450

22. BBC, no. W885 (1976), pp. A3-A4.

The number of teachers at each level is assumed in the foregoing tabulation to have risen in proportion to the number of students.[23] It is also assumed that the number of teachers did not change between 1975 and 1977. Under the further assumption that the share of teachers in total employment in education and culture remained at the 1957 level of 84.8 percent, employment in this field in 1975 may be estimated at 7.6 million persons, all of whom are assumed to be classified as workers and employees.[24]

Government administration and mass organizations

Employment in this category is assumed to have increased during 1957–75 at the 4.3 percent annual rate established for workers and employees in trade, food and drink, finance, banking, and insurance. This may prove controversial, but in view of the rapid growth of state revenue and the proliferation of economic planning and administrative activities at the provincial, county, and commune levels, it is difficult to doubt that employment in this area is now substantially above the level reached in 1957.

Total state revenue and expenditure have grown as follows:[25]

| | Billions of current yuan | | | | |
	1950	1957	1973	1977	1978
Revenue	6.5	31.0	91.0	87.4	112.1
Expenditure	6.8	29.0	81.6	84.4	111.1

23. Data for 1957 are from *Ten Great Years* (reprint edition, Bellingham: Western Washington State College, 1974), p. 133. Recently published enrollment figures, which are assumed to relate to 1977, are from *Peking Review*, no. 36 (1978), p. 15, and FBIS, July 20, 1978, p. E14.

24. Data on the number and composition of employees in education and culture for 1957 appear in Emerson, *Nonagricultural Employment*, pp. 93 and 128.

25. Data for 1950 and 1957 are from Chen, *Chinese Economic Statistics*, pp. 441 and 446; 1973 data, expressed as multiples of 1949 that are applied to the figures for 1950, are from *Cheng-chih ching-chi-hsüeh chi-ch'u chih-shih* [Basic Knowledge about Political Economy] (Shanghai: Shanghai jen-min ch'u-pan she, 1975), p. 406. Data for 1977 and 1978 are from "China's National Economy (1978–79)," *Beijing Review*, no. 26 (1979), p. 12.

Both revenue and expenditure have risen at an annual rate of from 6 to 7 percent since 1957.

The spread of government activity is not as easy to document as the growth of fiscal aggregates. It is certainly a mistake, however, to take literally the statements made during the Cultural Revolution about reductions in the number of central government officials, which Subraminian Swamy uses to argue that "the total effect of the Cultural Revolution was a sharp decline in the net value added of the trade and services sector."[26] Merely listing some of the areas into which government administration and mass organizations have penetrated during the past two decades is perhaps enough to justify an assumption of substantial employment growth: rural communes, rural and urban small-scale industry, delegation of planning authority to provinical and county governments, formation of new administrative bodies within industrial units, expansion of the "down to the countryside" movement, and increased foreign contacts. As in the 1950s, all personnel in this sector are assumed to be classified as workers and employees.

Salt

China's output of salt increased from 8.3 million tons in 1957 to 19.5 million tons in 1978, implying an average annual growth rate of 4.2 percent.[27] A 4.2 percent annual increase in employment is assumed for 1957–75, which leads to an employment estimate of 1.1 million persons in 1975. As in the 1950s, these personnel are assumed to be excluded from the category of "workers and employees."

Fishing

The employment figure for this sector in 1975 is taken from a lecture by Robert Hart, chief adviser to the International Fisheries

26. Subraminian Swamy, "Economic Growth in India and China 1952–1970: A Comparative Appraisal," *Economic Development and Cultural Change,* vol. 21, no. 4, part 2 (1973), p. 58.

27. Output figures are from Chen, *Chinese Economic Statistics,* p. 189, and "Communiqué on Fulfillment of China's 1978 National Economic Plan," *Beijing Review,* no. 27 (1979), p. 38.

and Marine Directorate, Canadian Department of the Environment. In addition to these full-time fishermen, there are also 4.25 million part-time fishermen. As in the 1950s, fishermen are assumed to be excluded from the category of "workers and employees."

Military

China's regular armed forces were reported to consist of 3.5 million men in 1976. This figure is used for 1975, and it is assumed that, as in the 1950s, military personnel are not classified as workers and employees.[28]

State farms, forestry, and water conservancy

In 1978, China's state farms employed 5 million agricultural workers.[29] Data from 18 of China's 29 province-level units showed that 17 million workers were occupied in 1977 in full-time projects "involving building water conservancy projects, terracing hillsides, improving the soil and other basic measures for expanding the cultivated area and increasing per hectare yields."[30] It is thus assumed that these categories, together with forestry, employed a total of 22 million persons in 1975, and that, as in the 1950s, full-time members of state farms and rural construction brigades continued to be classified as workers and employees.

28. Personnel total is drawn from Drew Middleton, "Visit to China's Forces: Big But Poor in New Arms," *New York Times*, December 1, 1976, p. 1. Ch'en Chih-ho, "Labor Force Statistics," p. 196, states that military workers are "not included in the worker and employee universe."

29. "Briefing on China's Agriculture," distributed by the Bureau of Foreign Affairs, Ministry of Agriculture and Forestry, September 18, 1978.

30. Chou Chin, "A Year of Advance Amid Storms," *Peking Review*, no. 7 (1977), p. 9.

Appendix C

Employment in Leading Small-Scale Producer-Goods Industries, 1975

THE ESTIMATES OF LEVEL OF EMPLOYMENT for 1975 in Table C-1 cover small-scale plants and mines in the following industries: cement, chemical fertilizer, coal, ferrous metallurgy, machinery, and electric power. Chinese sources combine coal and power under the rubric of energy and refer to these sectors as the "five small industries." The purpose of this appendix is to explain the derivation of the figures in Table C-1.

Cement

Estimates based on Chinese sources indicate that China produced 47.1 million tons of cement in 1975, of which 27.7 million tons came from small plants.[1] Visits to three leading plants in the small-scale cement sector in 1975 elicited productivity figures averaging 145.0 tons per man-year.[2] Employment in the small-scale cement industry may therefore be estimated at 27.7 million tons ÷ 145 tons per man-year, or approximately 191,000 workers. If, as is

1. U.S. National Foreign Assessment Center, *China: Economic Indicators* (Washington, D.C.: Central Intelligence Agency, 1977), p. 23.
2. Dwight H. Perkins and others, *Rural Small-Scale Industry in the People's Republic of China* (Berkeley: University of California Press, 1977), p. 88. Labor productivity is the quotient of the combined 1974 output and combined 1975 employment totals at the three plants.

TABLE C-1. ESTIMATED EMPLOYMENT IN SMALL-SCALE PRODUCER-GOODS INDUSTRIES, 1975

Industry	Employment (thousands of workers)
Cement	191
Chemical fertilizer	223
Coal	1,720
Ferrous metallurgy	280
Machinery	2,046
Power	29
Total	4,489

Source: See text.

likely, productivity at the plants visited was above average, this figure understates actual employment.

Chemical Fertilizer

The output of chemical fertilizers in 1975 is estimated at 27.875 million tons, of which 10.276 million tons of nitrogenous fertilizers and 6.471 million tons of phosphates came from small plants.[3] Small plant output of 10.276 million tons of nitrogenous fertilizers containing 20 percent nitrogen is equivalent to 2.055 million tons of nitrogen. Pooled output and employment data for three plants visited in 1975 indicate average labor productivity of 18.3 tons of ammonia per man-year or, using a conversion factor of 0.82, 15.0 tons of nitrogen per man-year.[4] If these plants are representative, small-scale nitrogenous fertilizer production appears to have occupied approximately $2.055 \cdot 10^6 \div 15.0$, or 137,000 workers in 1975.

In the absence of detailed information, employment in small-scale manufacture of phosphate fertilizers is estimated by assuming that employment per ton of standard product in 1975 was the same as in small nitrogenous fertilizer plants. The latter group ac-

3. U.S. National Foreign Assessment Center, *China: Economic Indicators* (1977), p. 22.

4. Perkins and others, *Rural . . . Industry*, p. 96. Labor productivity is the quotient of pooled 1974 output and 1975 employment totals at the three plants.

counted for 36.9 percent of standard product weight in 1975, whereas small phosphate plants produced 23.2 percent of standard product weight. It can therefore be estimated that employment in small phosphate plants was 137,000 · (23.2 ÷ 36.9), or 86,135 workers in 1975.

Potassium fertilizers, which contributed only 1.8 percent of 1975 fertilizer output, are ignored. The estimate of employment for 1975 in small-scale production of chemical fertilizers is therefore 223,135, or 223,000 workers in round figures.

Coal

Production of coal in 1975 is estimated at 480 million tons, of which approximately 149 million tons came from small mines and 331 million tons from large mines.[5] A report in 1976 stated that "there are 3,000,000 staff and workers in China's coal industry," a figure that can be taken as valid for 1975 as well.[6]

Labor productivity at the large K'ai-lan mine complex in Hopei province, a model industrial unit, may be calculated as follows: Output obtained by K'ai-lan's 100,000 miners from January 1 to December 23, 1975, amounted to 25.2 million tons.[7] Labor productivity for 1975 is thus 25.2 · 10 · (365 ÷ 357), or 257.6 tons per man-year. Assuming 300 annual days of work, average daily output is 0.859 tons per worker, which is less than the figure of 0.978 tons per man-day for the entire coal industry in 1957.[8]

If K'ai-lan's performance may be taken as typical of large mines, employment at large mines may be estimated at 331 million tons ÷ 257.6 tons per man-year, or 1.28 million workers. This leaves a total of about 1.72 million workers associated with small mines. Productivity at small mines then becomes approximately 149 million tons ÷ 1.72 million workers, or 86.6 tons per man-year. This implies that the bulk of the output from small coal mines comes

5. U.S. National Foreign Assessment Center, *China: Economic Indicators* (1978), p. 22.

6. BBC, no. W906 (1976), p. A1, repeated in *Peking Review*, no. 49 (1976), p. 10.

7. BBC, no. W870 (1976), p. A9, and no. W882 (1976), p. A7.

8. The figure for 1957 is from Nai-ruenn Chen, *Chinese Economic Statistics* (Chicago: Aldine, 1967), p. 263.

from county units that are better equipped than the primitive commune facility visited by Ward Morehouse, at which labor productivity appeared to be approximately 31.8 tons per man-year.[9]

Iron and Steel

In 1973 small and medium-size plants produced an estimated 28 percent of pig iron and 13 percent of crude steel output.[10] It can be assumed that in 1975 small plants accounted for 20 percent of gross value of output in ferrous metallurgy. Gross value of output in this industry for 1974 is estimated at 23.170 billion 1952 yuan. If this total rose in proportion to the 14.3 percent rise in crude steel output estimated for 1974/75, the gross output for 1975 becomes 26.483 billion 1952 yuan, or, since steel prices for 1975 are estimated at 60.9 percent of the 1952 levels, 16.128 billion 1975 yuan, of which 20 percent, or 3.226 billion yuan, is linked to small plants.[11]

Labor productivity is estimated on the basis of a single observation: a Wu-hsi (Kiangsu) county plant whose 805 workers produced steel ingots, reinforcing rods, and angle irons valued at over 9 million yuan during 1974.[12] Estimated labor productivity is thus 9 million ÷ 805, or 11,180 yuan per man-year. Estimated employment in small-scale iron and steel plants is therefore approximately 280,000 workers.

Machinery

Estimating employment in small-scale machinery plants is not easy. Most small plants concentrate on producing farm machines,

9. Ward Morehouse, "Notes on Hua-tung Commune," *China Quarterly*, no. 67 (1976), p. 588.

10. U.S. National Foreign Assessment Center, *China: Economic Indicators* (1978), p. 23.

11. Estimated steel output is from ibid. Gross output and price estimates are from Thomas G. Rawski, "China's Industrial Performance, 1949–1973," in *Quantitative Measures of China's Economic Output*, ed. Alexander Eckstein (Ann Arbor: University of Michigan Press, forthcoming), Tables 27 and H-1.

12. Perkins and others, *Rural . . . Industry*, p. 103.

making parts for farm machines, or performing repair work. The present estimate is compiled by assuming that small machinery plants devote themselves exclusively to these activities. Agricultural machinery and equipment accounted for from 6 to 7 percent of overall machinery output in 1956.[13] This share has risen considerably since then. It is assumed that the share of farm equipment in machinery output in 1975 was 15 percent. Two-thirds of farm machinery produced in China came from small plants in 1966; it is assumed that the relevant proportion had risen to 75 percent by 1975.[14]

Chinese statements indicate that total output of all types of machinery in 1972 was 86.725 billion 1952 yuan. If output in 1975 was 45.4 percent above the 1972 level, the figure for 1975 becomes 126.098 billion 1952 yuan for all machinery, 15 percent of this amount, or 18.915 billion yuan, for farm machinery, and 75 percent of this latter amount, or 14.186 billion 1952 yuan, for small plant output of farm machinery—which can be equated with total machinery output from small plants.[15]

Labor productivity is estimated on the basis of information obtained from ten agricultural machinery enterprises in 1975; these data appear in Table C-2. Productivity at the Shanghai Fengshou Tractor Plant is far above the levels observed elsewhere; the performance of this large enterprise has no relation to average productivity at small plants. If this plant is excluded, average output value per man-year is 6,374 yuan. Even this is a high figure; it must be assumed that the inclusion of data from model units and regions often shown to foreign visitors (for example, Red Star Commune and Hsi-yang and Lin counties) and of enterprises in China's most advanced industrial region (Shanghai and Wu-hsi) results in productivity figures that substantially exceed the national average.

Accordingly, average labor productivity for 1975 is placed

13. Chao I-wen, *Hsin Chung-kuo ti kung-yeh* [Industry of New China] (Peking: T'ung-chi ch'u-pan she, 1957), p. 43.

14. The figure for 1966 is from Carl Riskin, "Small Industry and the Chinese Model of Development," *China Quarterly*, no. 46 (1971), p. 271.

15. Gross output and price estimates are from Rawski, "Industrial Performance," in *Quantitative Measures*, Tables 7 and H-1. Estimated growth of machinery production during 1972–75 is from U.S. National Foreign Assessment Center, *China: Economic Indicators* (1978), p. 1.

TABLE C-2. LABOR PRODUCTIVITY AT SELECTED FARM MACHINERY PLANTS

Plant and location	Gross output, 1974 (thousands of yuan)	Employment, 1975	Labor productivity (yuan)
Municipal plants			
1. Hsinhsiang fertilizer equipment[a]	1,300	330	3,939
2. Hsinhsiang water pump	7,100	680	10,441
3. Shanghai Feng-shou tractor	80,000	1,300	51,538
County plants			
4. Hsiyang (Shansi) tractor	1,044	310	3,368
5. Lin (Honan) Tung-fang-hung	1,000+	300	3,333+
6. Shanghai Chia-tung county	1,800	450	4,000
7. Wuhsi (Kiangsu) tractor	6,000	661	9,077
Commune plants			
8. Red Star (Peking)	575	261	2,203
9. Yang-shih (Wuhsi, Kiangsu)	1,600	192	8,333
10. Yao-ts'un (Lin, Honan)	450	90	5,000
Total	100,869	4,574	22,053
Total excluding plant 3	20,869	3,274	6,374

a. Administered by Hsinhsiang prefecture, Honan.

Source: Dwight H. Perkins and others, *Rural Small-Scale Industry in the People's Republic of China* (Berkeley: University of California Press, 1977), pp. 64–69.

arbitrarily at 4,000 yuan, and employment for 1975 in small-scale machinery plants is estimated at 8.185 billion ÷ 4,000, or 2.046 million workers.

Power

Small hydroelectric stations account for 20 percent of China's hydropower capacity, which in turn produced an estimated 25 percent of total output of 121 billion kilowatt-hours of electricity in 1975.[16] Of the hydroelectric output of 30 billion kilowatt-hours in 1975, 20 percent, or 6 billion kilowatt-hours, is attributed to small plants.

In 1975 visitors to a county power station in Lin county (Honan) were told that the 2,500 kilowatt installation employed 43 persons

16. Capacity figure is from *Peking Review*, no. 21 (1975), pp. 30–31; the output estimates, which appear to be considerably below actual performance, are from U.S. National Foreign Assessment Center, *China: Economic Indicators* (1978), p. 22.

and produced an annual total of 9 million kilowatt-hours of electricity.[17] If the implied labor productivity figure of 209,302 kilowatt-hours per man-year is typical of all small hydroelectric plants, employment in these plants for 1975 can be estimated at approximately 29,000 persons.

17. Perkins and others, *Rural . . . Industry*, p. 109.

Bibliography

Note: Titles of Chinese- and Japanese-language articles are given in translation only. Chinese language materials written by corporate authors are identified by their titles only.

Aird, John S. *Population Estimates for the Provinces of the People's Republic of China: 1953 to 1974.* International Population Reports, Series P-95, no. 73. Washington, D.C.: U.S. Department of Commerce, 1974.

_____. "Population Growth and Distribution in Mainland China." In U.S. Congress, Joint Economic Committee, *An Economic Profile of Mainland China,* vol. 2, pp. 341–401. 2 vols. Washington, D.C.: U.S. Government Printing Office, 1967.

_____. "Population Growth in the People's Republic of China." In U.S. Congress, Joint Economic Committee, *Chinese Economy Post-Mao,* vol. 1, pp. 439–75. Washington, D.C.: U.S. Government Printing Office, 1978.

_____. "Recent Provincial Population Figures," *China Quarterly,* no. 73 (1978), pp. 1–44.

Banister, Judith. "China's Demographic Transition in the Asian Context." From "The Current Vital Rates and Population Size of the People's Republic of China and its Provinces." Ph.D. dissertation, Food Research Institute, Stanford University, 1977.

Barnett, A. Doak. *Uncertain Passage: China's Transition to the Post-Mao Era.* Washington, D.C.: Brookings Institution, 1974.

Beijing Review (weekly). Formerly *Peking Review.* Peking.

Bernstein, Thomas P. *Up to the Mountains and Down to the Villages.* New Haven, Conn.: Yale University Press, 1977.

"Briefing on China's Agriculture." Distributed by the Bureau of Foreign Affairs, Ministry of Agriculture and Forestry, Peking, September 18, 1978.

British Broadcasting Corporation (BBC). *Summary of World Broadcasts: Part 3, The Far East, Weekly Economic Report.*

Buck, John L. *Land Utilization in China.* Nanking: University of Nanking, 1937.

Burki, Shahid Javed. *A Study of Chinese Communes, 1965.* Cambridge, Mass.: East Asian Research Center, Harvard University, 1969.

Burns, John P. "The Election of Production Team Cadres in Rural China: 1958–74." *China Quarterly,* no. 74 (1978), pp. 273–96.

Chang Ch'un-ch'iao. "On Exercising All-Round Dictatorship over the Bourgeoisie." *Peking Review,* no. 14 (1975), pp. 5–11.

Chao I-wen. *Hsin Chung-kuo ti kung-yeh* [Industry of New China]. Peking: T'ung-chi ch'u-pan she, 1957.

Chao, Kang. *Agricultural Production in Communist China.* Madison: University of Wisconsin Press, 1970.

Ch'en Chih-ho. "The Question of Groups Included in Labor Force Statistics." *Chi-hua yü t'ung-chi* [Planning and Statistics], no. 11 (1959). Translated in John P. Emerson, *Nonagricultural Employment in Mainland China: 1949–1958* (q.v.), pp. 195–99.

Chen, Nai-ruenn. "An Assessment of Chinese Economic Data: Availability, Reliability, and Usability." In U.S. Congress, Joint Economic Committee, *China: A Reassessment of the Economy,* pp. 52–68. Washington, D.C.: U.S. Government Printing Office, 1975.

———. *Chinese Economic Statistics.* Chicago: Aldine, 1967.

Chen, Pi-chao. "Overurbanization, Rustication of Urban-Educated Youths, and Politics of Rural Transformation." *Comparative Politics,* April 1972, pp. 361–86.

Cheng-chih ching-chi hsueh chi-ch'u chih-shih [Basic Knowledge About Political Economy]. 2d edition. Shanghai: Shang-hai jen-min ch'u-pan she, 1975.

Ch'eng Chin-chieh. "The Way Liuchi Commune Wins Its Higher Grain and Cotton Yields." *Ching-chi yen-chiu* [Economic Research], no. 4 (1965). Translated in ECMM, no. 473 (1965), pp. 1–7.

Cheng Shih. *A Glance at China's Economy.* Peking: Foreign Languages Press, 1974.

Chi I-chai. "A Study of Food Output in Mainland China III." *Fei-ch'ing yueh-pao* [Chinese Communist Affairs] vol. 10, no. 9 (1967). Translated in JPRS, no. 43,937 (1968), pp. 17–24.

Chi-lin jih-pao [Kirin Daily]. Ch'angch'un.

Chi Ti. "Stable Prices and the Reasons—Part 1." *Peking Review,* no. 19 (1975), pp. 17–20.

Chieh-fang jih-pao [Liberation Daily]. Shanghai.

China Business Review (bimonthly). Washington.

China News Analysis (weekly). Hong Kong.

China Reconstructs (monthly). Peking.

"China's National Economy (1978–79)," *Beijing Review*, no. 26 (1979), pp. 8–12.

Ching-chi tao-pao [The Economic Reporter] (weekly). Hong Kong.

Chou Chin. "A Year of Advance Amid Storms." *Peking Review*, no. 7 (1977), pp. 6–10.

Chu Li and Tien Chieh-yun. *Inside a People's Commune*. Peking: Foreign Languages Press, 1974.

Chuan, Han-sheng, and Richard A. Kraus. *Mid-Ch'ing Rice Markets and Trade*. Cambridge, Mass.: Harvard University Press, 1975.

Chūgoku kagaku gijutsu no genjō bunseki [Analysis of the Current State of China's Science and Technology]. Tokyo: Shokoku kagaku gijutsu ken-kyūkai, 1965.

Chūgoku kōgyō tsūshin [China Industrial Bulletin] (monthly). Tokyo.

Chūgoku shiryō geppō [China Materials Monthly]. Tokyo.

Chung-kung yen-chiu [Studies on Chinese Communism] (monthly). Taipei.

"Communiqué of the Third Plenary Session of the 11th Central Committee of the Communist Party of China." *Peking Review*, no. 52 (1978), pp. 6–16.

"Communiqué on Fulfillment of China's 1978 National Economic Plan," *Beijing Review*, no. 27 (1979), pp. 37–41.

Craig, Jack. "China: Domestic and International Telecommunications, 1949–74." In U.S. Congress, Joint Economic Committee, *China: A Reassessment of the Economy*, pp. 289–310. Washington, D.C.: U.S. Government Printing Office, 1975.

Crook, Frederick W. "The Commune System in the People's Republic of China, 1963–74." In U.S. Congress, Joint Economic Committee, *China: A Reassessment of the Economy*, pp. 366–410. Washington, D.C.: U.S. Government Printing Office, 1975.

Dernberger, Robert F. and David Fasenfest. "China's Post-Mao Economic Future." In U.S. Congress, Joint Economic Committee, *Chinese Economy Post-Mao*, vol. 1, pp. 3–47. Washington, D.C.: U.S. Government Printing Office, 1978.

Donnithorne, Audrey. *China's Economic System*. London: Allen and Unwin, 1967.

Eastern Horizon (monthly). Hong Kong.

Eckstein, Alexander. *China's Economic Development.* Ann Arbor: University of Michigan Press, 1975.

———. *China's Economic Revolution.* Cambridge, England: Cambridge University Press, 1977.

Emerson, John Philip. *Nonagricultural Employment in Mainland China: 1949–1958.* International Population Statistics Reports, Series P-90, no. 21. Washington, D.C.: U.S. Department of Commerce, 1965.

"Evolution and Development of the Paddy Crop Situation in the Lake District." *Chung-kuo nung-pao* [China Agricultural Bulletin], no. 8 (1964), pp. 27–30.

Falcon, Walter P., and Gerald C. Nelson. "Prospects for China's Agriculture." *Unpublished draft,* 1978.

Far Eastern Economic Review (weekly). Hong Kong.

1967 Fei-ch'ing nien-pao [1967 Yearbook of Chinese Communism]. Taipei: Fei-ch'ing yen-chiu tsa-chih she, 1967.

Field, Robert Michael. "Civilian Industrial Production in the People's Republic of China: 1949–74." In U.S. Congress, Joint Economic Committee, *China: A Reassessment of the Economy,* pp. 146–74. Washington, D.C.: U.S. Government Printing Office, 1975.

———. "Real Capital Formation in the People's Republic of China, 1952–1973." In *Quantitative Measures of China's Economic Output.* Edited by Alexander Eckstein. Ann Arbor: University of Michigan Press, forthcoming.

———, and James A. Kilpatrick. "Chinese Grain Production: An Interpretation of the Data." *China Quarterly,* no. 74 (1978), pp. 369–84.

———, Nicholas R. Lardy, and John Philip Emerson. *Provincial Industrial Output in the People's Republic of China: 1949–75.* Foreign Economic Report no. 12. Washington, D.C.: U.S. Department of Commerce, 1976.

———. *A Reconstruction of the Gross Value of Industrial Output by Province in the People's Republic of China: 1949–75.* Foreign Economic Report no. 7. Washington, D.C.: U.S. Department of Commerce, 1975.

First Five-Year Plan for Development of the National Economy of the People's Republic of China in 1953–1957. Peking: Foreign Language Press, 1956.

Furui, Yoshimi, and others. *Hōchū shoken* [A Visit to China]. Tokyo: n.p., 1959.

Geertz, Clifford. *Agricultural Involution.* Berkeley: University of California Press, 1966.

Hayami, Yujiro, and Vernon W. Ruttan. *Agricultural Development.* Baltimore: Johns Hopkins Press, 1971.

Hou, Chi-ming. "Manpower, Employment and Unemployment." In *Economic Trends in Communist China*, pp. 329–96. Edited by Alexander Eckstein, Walter Galenson, and Ta-chung Liu. Chicago: Aldine, 1968.

Howe, Christopher. *China's Economy: A Basic Guide.* New York: Basic Books, 1978.

_____. *Employment and Economic Growth in Urban China, 1949–1957.* Cambridge, England: Cambridge University Press, 1971.

Hsiang Lin. "How to Implement the Principle of Frugal National Construction." *Chi-hsieh kung-yeh* [Machinery Industry], no. 11 (1957), pp. 18–21 and 23.

Hsiao Han. "Developing Coal Industry at High Speed." *Peking Review*, no. 8 (1978), pp. 5–7.

Hsin Hu-nan pao [New Hunan News] (daily). Ch'angsha.

Hu Ch'iao-mu. "Observe Economic Laws, Speed Up the Four Modernizations." *Peking Review*, no. 45 (1978), pp. 7–12, no. 46 (1978), pp. 15–23, and no. 47 (1978), pp. 13–21.

Hu-pei jih-pao [Hupei Daily]. Hankow.

Huang Ching [Chairman, National Technological Commission]. "On Agricultural Mechanization in China." *Chi-hsieh kung-yeh* [Machinery Industry] no. 21 (1957). Translated in ECMM, no. 120 (1958), pp. 34–43.

I Ts'ai and Wang P'i-chang. "Ways of Improving the Economic Effect of Fertilization." *Ching-chi yen-chiu* [Economic Research], no. 4 (1965). Translated in ECMM, no. 475 (1965), pp. 23–31.

Ishikawa, Shigeru. *National Income and Capital Formation in Mainland China.* Tokyo: Institute of Asian Economic Affairs, 1965.

Jen-min jih-pao [People's Daily]. Peking.

Johnson, Virgil A., and Halsey L. Beemer, Jr., eds. *Wheat in the People's Republic of China.* Washington, D.C.: National Academy of Sciences, 1977.

Kao Hsia. "Yangtze Waters Diverted to North China." *Peking Review*, no. 38 (1978), pp. 6–9.

Keesing, Donald B. "Economic Lessons From China." *Journal of Development Economics*, no. 2 (1975), pp. 1–32.

King, F. H. *Farmers of Forty Centuries.* Emmaus, Pa.: Organic Gardening Press, n.d.

Kohrt, Günter. "Maoism's Permanent Crisis and Growing Threat." *Horizont*, vol. 9, no. 33–37 (1976). Partially translated in JPRS, no. 68,303 (1976), pp. 62–96.

Kuang-ming jih-pao [Kuang-ming Daily]. Peking.

Kuo, Leslie T. C. *Agriculture in the People's Republic of China*. New York: Praeger, 1976.

Lardy, Nicholas R. "Centralization and Decentralization in China's Fiscal Management." *China Quarterly*, no. 61 (1975), pp. 25–60.

———. *Economic Growth and Distribution in China*. Cambridge, England: Cambridge University Press, 1978.

———. "Recent Chinese Economic Performance and Prospects for the Ten-Year Plan." In U.S. Congress, Joint Economic Committee, *Chinese Economy Post-Mao*, vol. 1; pp. 48–62. Washington, D.C.: U.S. Government Printing Office, 1978.

Li, Choh-ming. *The Statistical System of Communist China*. Berkeley: University of California Press, 1962.

Liu-chi kung-she nung-yeh chi-hsieh-hua [Agricultural Mechanization at Liu-chi Commune]. Peking: Jen-min ch'u-pan she, 1976.

Liu Chih-cheng and others. "The Relations Between the Four Transformations and Economic Effects." *Ching-chi yen-chiu* [Economic Research], no. 2 (1964). Translated in ECMM, no. 424 (1964), pp. 1–15.

Liu, Ta-chung. "Economic Development of the Chinese Mainland, 1949–1965." In *China in Crisis*, vol. 1, bk. 2, pp. 605–90. Edited by Ping-ti Ho and Tang Tsou. 2 vols. Chicago: University of Chicago Press, 1968.

——— and Kung-chia Yeh. *The Economy of the Chinese Mainland*. Princeton, N.J.: Princeton University Press, 1965.

MacFarlane, Ian H. "Construction Trends in China, 1949–74." In U.S. Congress, Joint Economic Committee, *China: A Reassessment of the Economy*, pp. 311–23. Washington, D.C.: U.S. Government Printing Office, 1975.

Mellor, John W. *The New Economics of Growth*. Ithaca, N.Y.: Cornell University Press, 1976.

Meng Chih-chien. "On Mechanization of Casting Shops." *Chi-hsieh kung-yeh* [Machinery Industry], no. 13 (1957), pp. 5–8.

Middleton, Drew. "Visit to China's Forces: Big but Poor in New Arms." *New York Times*, December 1, 1976.

Morawetz, David. *Twenty-five Years of Economic Development, 1950 to 1975*. Baltimore and London: Johns Hopkins University Press, 1977.

Morehouse, Ward. "Notes on Hua-tung Commune." *China Quarterly*, no. 67 (1976), pp. 582–95.

Motonosuke, Amano. *Chūgoku nōgyōshi kenkyū* [Studies on China's Agricultural History]. Tokyo: Ochanomizu shobō, 1962.

Munro, Ross H. "Why China's Peasants Don't Want to Work." *San Francisco Chronicle,* July 29, 1977.

Myers, Ramon H. "Economic Organization and Cooperation in Modern China: Irrigation Management in Xing-tai County, Ho-bei Province." In *Chūgoku no seiji to keizai* [The Polity and Economy of China] pp. 189–212. Edited by The Late Professor Yuji Muramatsu Commemoration Board. Tokyo: Tōyō keizai shimpōsha, 1975.

_____. "Wheat in China—Past, Present and Future." *China Quarterly,* no. 74 (1978), pp. 297–333.

Nan-fang jih-pao [Southern Daily]. Canton.

New China's First Quarter-Century. Peking: Foreign Languages Press, 1975.

Nickum, James E. "A Collective Approach to Water Resource Development: The Chinese Commune System, 1962–1972." Ph.D. dissertation. University of California, Berkeley, 1974.

_____. *Hydraulic Engineering and Water Resources in the People's Republic of China.* Stanford, Calif.: U.S.–China Relations Program, 1977.

Nung-yeh ch'ang-yung shu-tzu shou-ts'e [Handbook of Common Agricultural Data]. Peking: Jen-min ch'u-pan she, 1975.

Oksenberg, Michel. "Methods of Communication within the Chinese Bureaucracy." *China Quarterly,* no. 57 (1974), pp. 1–39.

Orleans, Leo A. "China's Population: Can the Contradictions be Resolved?" In U.S. Congress, Joint Economic Committee, *China: A Reassessment of the Economy,* pp. 69–80. Washington, D.C.: U.S. Government Printing Office, 1975.

_____. "China's Science and Technology: Continuity and Innovation." In U.S. Congress, Joint Economic Committee, *People's Republic of China: An Economic Assessment,* pp. 185–219. Washington, D.C.: U.S. Government Printing Office, 1972.

_____. *Every Fifth Child: The Population of China.* Stanford, Calif.: Stanford University Press, 1972.

Ōzaki Shotarō. "Visit to Mukden No. 1 Machine Tool Plant." *Ajia keizai jumpō* [Asian Economic Weekly], no. 475 (1960). Translated in JPRS, no. 10,434 (1961), pp. 8–12.

Pai Ou. "Brief Discussion of the Direction and Tasks of the Machinery Industry." *Chi-hsieh kung-yeh* [Machinery Industry], no. 12 (1957), pp. 2–8.

P'an Kuang-chi. "Opinions on the Development of Basic Chemical Industries." *Hua-hsueh kung-yeh* [Chemical Industry], no. 8 (1957), pp. 33–35.

Parish, William L., and Martin King Whyte. *Village and Family in Contemporary China.* Chicago: University of Chicago Press, 1978.

Peking Review (weekly). Now *Beijing Review.* Peking.

Perkins, Dwight H. *Agricultural Development in China, 1368–1968.* Chicago: Aldine, 1969.

_____. "A Conference on Agriculture." *China Quarterly,* no. 67 (1976), pp. 596–610.

_____. "Constraints Influencing China's Agricultural Performance." In U.S. Congress, Joint Economic Committee, *China: A Reassessment of the Economy,* pp. 350–65. Washington, D.C.: U.S. Government Printing Office, 1975.

_____. "Estimating China's Gross Domestic Product." *Current Scene,* vol. 15, no. 3 (1976), pp. 12–19.

_____. "Growth and Changing Structure of China's Twentieth-Century Economy." In *China's Modern Economy in Historical Perspective,* pp. 115–65. Edited by Dwight H. Perkins. Stanford, Calif.: Stanford University Press, 1975.

_____. "Introduction: The Persistence of the Past." In *China's Modern Economy in Historical Perspective,* pp. 1–18. Edited by Dwight H. Perkins. Stanford, Calif.: Stanford University Press, 1975.

_____. "Issues in the Estimation of China's National Product." In *Quantitative Measures of China's Economic Output.* Edited by Alexander Eckstein. Ann Arbor: University of Michigan Press, forthcoming.

_____. *Market Control and Planning in Communist China.* Cambridge, Mass.: Harvard University Press, 1966.

_____, and others. *Rural Small-Scale Industry in the People's Republic of China.* Berkeley: University of California Press, 1977.

Plant Studies in the People's Republic of China. Washington, D.C.: National Academy of Sciences, 1975.

Rawski, Evelyn Sakakida. *Education and Popular Literacy in Ch'ing China.* Ann Arbor: University of Michigan Press, 1979.

Rawski, Thomas G. "China's Industrial Performance, 1949–1973." In *Quantitative Measures of China's Economic Output.* Edited by Alexander Eckstein. Ann Arbor: University of Michigan Press, forthcoming.

_____. *China's Transition to Industrialism: Producer Goods and Economic Development in the Twentieth Century.* Ann Arbor: University of Michigan Press, forthcoming.

_____. "Chinese Industrial Production, 1952–1971. *Review of Economics and Statistics,* vol. 55, no. 2 (1973), pp. 169–81.

_____. "Choice of Technology and Technological Innovation in China's Economic Development." In *The Relevance of China's Experience for the Other Developing Countries*. Edited by Robert F. Dernberger. Forthcoming.

_____. "The Growth of Producer Industries, 1900–1971." In *China's Modern Economy in Historical Perspective*, pp. 203–34. Edited by Dwight H. Perkins. Stanford, Calif.: Stanford University Press, 1975.

_____. "Regional Distribution of Industrial Production." Toronto: University of Toronto, processed, 1971.

_____. "On the Reliability of Chinese Economic Data." *Journal of Development Studies*, vol. 12, no. 4 (1976), pp. 438–41.

_____. "The Role of China in the World Energy Situation." Unpublished, 1973.

Rawski Trip Notes. Author's notes as a member of the Rural Small-Scale Industries Delegation sponsored by the Committee on Scholarly Communication with the People's Republic of China. This group visited China for four weeks during June and July 1975.

Report of the Canadian Electrical Power Mission to the People's Republic of China, August 29 to September 18, 1973. Ottawa: Ministry of Industry, Trade and Commerce, 1973.

"Report of SMMT Trade Mission to the People's Republic of China, 2–17 November 1973." Unpublished report by the Society of Motor Manufacturers and Traders Limited. London, 1974.

Reynolds, Harold. "Chinese Insect Control Integrates Old and New." *Chemical and Engineering News*, March 15, 1976, pp. 30–32.

Richman, Barry M. *Industrial Society in Communist China*. New York: Random House, 1969.

Riskin, Carl. "Small Industry and the Chinese Model of Development." *China Quarterly*, no. 46 (1971), pp. 245–73.

Scalapino, Robert. "Trip Notes." Berkeley: University of California, processed, 1972.

Schran, Peter. *The Development of Chinese Agriculture, 1950–1959*. Urbana: University of Illinois Press, 1969.

_____. "Farm Labor and Living in China." Champaign: University of Illinois, 1976. Processed.

_____. "Handicrafts in Communist China." *China Quarterly*, no. 21 (1964), pp. 151–73.

Scott, David. "China Opens Doors for Rare View of Auto Production." *Automotive Engineering*, vol. 82, no. 8 (1974), pp. 30–33.

"Several Points About Mechanized Irrigation in Kiangsu." *Chung-kuo shui-li* [Chinese Water Control], no. 1 (1957), pp. 49–52.

Seybolt, Peter J., ed. *The Rustication of Urban Youth in China*. White Plains, N.Y.: M. E. Sharpe, 1975.

Shin Chūgoku no kikai kōgyō [New China's Machinery Industry]. Tokyo: Tōa keizai kenkyūkai, 1960.

Shue, Vivienne. "Reorganizing Rural Trade." *Modern China*, vol. 2, no. 1, (1976), pp. 104–34.

Sigurdson, Jon. "Rural Industrialization in China." In U.S. Congress, Joint Economic Committee, *China: A Reassessment of the Economy*, pp. 411–35. Washington, D.C.: U.S. Government Printing Office, 1975.

———. *Rural Industrialization in China*. Cambridge, Mass.: Harvard University Press, 1977.

"Some Problems in Speeding Up Industrial Development." Translated in *Issues and Studies*, vol. 13, no. 7 (1977), pp. 90–113.

Sprague, G. F. "Agriculture in China." *Science*, vol. 188, no. 4 (May 9, 1975), pp. 549–55.

Stavis, Benedict, *Making Green Revolution*. Rural Development Monograph no. 1. Ithaca, N.Y.: Cornell University Rural Development Program, 1974.

———. *The Politics of Agricultural Mechanization in China*. Ithaca, N.Y.: Cornell University Press, 1978.

Stepanek, James B. "Planning of Urban Small-Scale Industry in China." Paper presented at a conference sponsored by the Subcommittee on Research on the Chinese Economy, Social Science Research Council, on "Regionalism and Economic Development in China: Historical and South Asian Comparative Perspectives," Philadelphia, January 20–21, 1978.

"Strengthen Scientific Research on the Farm Economy." *Kuang-ming jih-pao* [Kuang-ming Daily], December 7, 1978.

Swamy, Subraminian. "Economic Growth in India and China, 1952–1970: A Comparative Appraisal." *Economic Development and Cultural Change*, vol. 21, no. 4, pt. 2, pp. 1–83.

Ta-chung jih-pao [Mass Daily]. Chinan.

Ta-kung pao [Impartial Daily]. Hong Kong.

Tang, Anthony M. "Input-Output Relations in the Agriculture of Communist China, 1952–1965." In *Agrarian Policies and Problems in Communist and Non-Communist Countries*, pp. 280–301. Edited by W. A. Douglas Jackson. Seattle: University of Washington Press, 1971.

Ten Great Years. English translation of *Wei-ta ti shih-nien* (Peking, 1959). Occasional paper no. 5. Bellingham: Western Washington State College Program in East Asian Studies, 1974.

Terrill, Ross. *Flowers on an Iron Tree.* Boston: Atlantic–Little, Brown, 1975.

Thorborg, Marina. "Chinese Employment Policy 1949–78 With Special Emphasis on Women in Rural Production." In U.S. Congress, Joint Economic Committee, *Chinese Economy Post-Mao*, pp. 535–604. Washington, D.C.: U.S. Government Printing Office, 1978.

Tien, H. Yuan. *China's Population Struggle.* Columbus: Ohio State University Press, 1973.

Tsu-kuo hsin-kuang ch'eng-shih [Newly Brilliant Cities of the Fatherland]. Shanghai: Shang-hai jen-min ch'u-pan she, 1974.

Tsuchiya, Keizo. "Economics of Mechanization in Small-Scale Agriculture." In *Agriculture and Economic Growth: Japan's Experience*, pp. 155–72. Edited by Kazushi Ohkawa, Bruce F. Johnston, and Hiromitsu Kaneda. Princeton, N.J.: Princeton University Press, 1969.

Ullman, Morris B. *Cities of Mainland China: 1953 and 1958.* International Population Reports, Series P-95, no. 59. Washington, D.C.: U.S. Department of Commerce, 1961.

U.S. Central Intelligence Agency. *China: Agricultural Performance in 1975.* Research Aid ER 76-10149. Washington, D.C., 1976.

———. *China: Role of Small Plants in Economic Development.* Research Aid A(ER)74-60. Washington, D.C., 1974.

———. *People's Republic of China: Handbook of Economic Indicators.* Research Aid ER 76-10540. Washington, D.C., 1976.

U.S. Consulate General, Hong Kong. *Extracts from China Mainland Magazines.*

———. *Survey of the China Mainland Press.*

U.S. Foreign Broadcast Information Service (FBIS). *Daily Report, People's Republic of China.*

U.S. Joint Publications Research Service (JPRS), Washington, D.C.

U.S. National Foreign Assessment Center. *China: Economic Indicators.* Reference Aid ER77-10508. Washington, D.C., 1977.

———. *China: Economic Indicators.* Research Aid ER78-10750. Washington, D.C., 1978.

———. *China: In Pursuit of Economic Modernization.* Research Paper ER78-10680. Washington, D.C., 1978.

Wang Hu-sheng. "Several Problems of Classifying Heavy and Light Industry." *Ching-chi yen-chiu* [Economic Research], no. 4 (1963), pp. 22–25.

Wang Kuang-wei. "How to Organize Agricultural Labor Power." *Chi-hua ching-chi* [Planned Economy], no. 8 (1957). Translated in ECMM, no. 100 (1958), pp. 11–15.

Wang Te-yüan. "Perceive the Conditions of Steel Supply, Dig Up Latent Sources of Domestic Supply." *Chi-hsieh kung-yeh* [Machinery Industry], no. 9 (1957), pp. 29 and 13.

Wen-hui pao [Wen-hui News]. Hong Kong.

Whyte, Martin King. "Inequality and Stratification in China." *China Quarterly*, no. 64 (1975), pp. 684–711.

Wiens, Thomas B. "Agricultural Statistics in the People's Republic of China." In *Quantitative Measures of China's Economic Output.* Edited by Alexander Eckstein. Ann Arbor: University of Michigan Press, forthcoming.

Wilkinson, Endymion P. "Studies in Chinese Price History." Ph.D. dissertation, Princeton University, 1971.

World Bank. *Rural Enterprise and Non-farm Employment.* A World Bank Sector Policy Paper. Washington, D.C., 1978.

Wu Yung-hsiang. "Appraisal of the Economic Effect of Dryland Cotton Cultivation in Wu-kung County." *Ching-chi yen-chiu* [Economic Research], no. 10 (1963), pp. 27–36.

Yamamoto Hideo. *Chūgoku nōgyō gijutsu taikei no tenkai* [Development of China's System of Agricultural Technology]. Tokyo: Ajia keizai kenkyūjo, 1965.

Yen Jui-chen. "Several Questions on Increasing the Economic Benefits of Fertilizers." *Ching-chi yen-chiu* [Economic Research], no. 6 (1964). Translated in ECMM, no. 429 (1964), pp. 13–25.

Yü Ch'iu-li. "Summation Report on Agricultural Mechanization." Translated in FBIS, January 31, 1978, pp. E6-25.

Yung Ta-chai ching-shen kao nung-yeh chi-hsieh-hua [Use the Ta-chai Spirit to Raise Farm Mechanization]. T'aiyuan: Shan-hsi jen-min ch'u-pan she, 1974.

Index

Academy of Social Sciences, 23
Administrative system, rural, 142–43, 167–68
Age structure, 22–23, 132
Agricultural employment, 8–9, 38–40, 123–32; projections for, 133–35
Agriculture: Chinese system of, 73–74, 141–46; collectivization and, 75–79; crop management in, 97–102; cropping cycle in, 102–06; cropping practices in, 91–102; as defined in this study, 71; diminishing returns in, 138–39; factor productivity of, 118–22; increase of labor use in, 106–09; industrial inputs to, 82–91; intercropping system of, 105–06; inventory data on, 82–83; labor absorption in, 71–122; labor supply-demand balance in, 113–18; land improvement for, 109–13; land preparation for, 91–96; management of, 139–41; marginal labor productivity in, 129–30; mechanization of, 82–91; multiple cropping system of, 102–05; output growth of, 106–09, 135–41; planting and transplanting in, 96–97; productivity trends in, 118–22; research on, 137–38; water conservancy for, 109–13; and winter works campaigns, 109–13
Aird, John S., 19n, 20–24, 25n, 35, 40n, 117, 118n, 123, 132
American Wheat Studies Delegation, 10, 32, 97, 112, 116, 117, 130
Annual workdays in agriculture, 115, 117–18, 127
Armed forces, 169

Banister, Judith, 20n
Banking, 165
Barnett, A. Doak, 20n
Beemer, Halsey L., Jr., 10n, 33n, 91n, 97n, 98n, 103n, 105n, 112n, 116n
Bernstein, Thomas P., 13n, 127

Biological control agents, 101
Brown, David M., 29n
Buck, John L., 74n, 85n, 97–103, 106, 110
Burki, Shahid Javed, 31, 32, 78n
Burns, John P., 141n

Capital deepening, 44, 45, 47–48
Capital intensity, 46–50, 55
Cement manufacture, 80–82, 170–71
Census of 1953, 20, 22
Chang Ch'un-ch'iao, 62n, 160
Chao I-wen, 174n
Chao, Kang, 95n
Chekiang, 165
Chemical fertilizers. See Fertilizers
Ch'en Chih-ho, 37n, 161n, 169n
Chen, Nai-ruenn, 68n, 92n, 94n, 102n, 151n, 165n, 167n, 168n, 172n
Chen, Pi-chao, 26n
Ch'eng Chin-chieh, 96n, 104n, 105n
Chi I-chai, 108n
Chi Ti, 164n
China: economic growth in, 3–6; economic statistics on, 14–16, 147–54; farming system of, 73–74; as model for other developing countries, 141–46; population of, 19–29; socioeconomic system of, 141–46
Chou Chin, 169n
Chou En-lai, 17, 45, 109
Chu Li, 84n, 96n
Chuan, Han-sheng, 148n
Clark, Colin, 22
Coal industry, 50, 172–73
Collectivization: of farming, 7–9, 75–79; of industry, 38, 61–64, 161–62; and rural labor absorption, 75–79. See also Communes
Communes: administration of, 142; farming by, 76–79; fringe benefits to members of, 67–68; industrial employment in, 161–62; labor force of,